MEDIA, FEMINISM, CULTURAL STUDIES

The Sacred Cinema of Andrei Tarkovsky
by Jeremy Mark Robinson

Liv Tyler
by Thomas A. Christie

The Cinema of Hayao Miyazaki
Jeremy Mark Robinson

Stepping Forward: Essays, Lectures and Interviews
by Wolfgang Iser

Wild Zones: Pornography, Art and Feminism
by Kelly Ives

'Cosmo Woman': The World of Women's Magazines
by Oliver Whitehorne

The Cinema of Richard Linklater
by Thomas A. Christie

Andrea Dworkin
by Jeremy Mark Robinson

Cixous, Irigaray, Kristeva: The Jouissance of French Feminism
by Kelly Ives

*The Erotic Object: Sexuality in Sculpture
From Prehistory to the Present Day*
by Susan Quinnell

Women in Pop Music
by Helen Challis

Sex in Art: Pornography and Pleasure in Painting and Sculpture
by Cassidy Hughes

Erotic Art
by Cassidy Hughes

Jean-Luc Godard: The Passion of Cinema / Le Passion de Cinéma
by Jeremy Mark Robinson

Genius and Loving It! Mel Brooks
by Thomas Christie

The Comic Art of Mel Brooks
by Maurice Yacowar

Marvelous Names
by P. Adams Sitney

The Art of Katsuhiro Otomo
by Jeremy Mark Robinson

Akira: The Movie and the Manga
by Jeremy Mark Robinson

The Art of Masamune Shirow (3 vols)
by Jeremy Mark Robinson

Detonation Britain: Nuclear War in the UK
by Jeremy Mark Robinson

Julia Kristeva: Art, Love, Melancholy, Philosophy, Semiotics
by Kelly Ives

Luce Irigaray: Lips, Kissing, and the Politics of Sexual Difference
by Kelly Ives

Helene Cixous I Love You: The Jouissance *of Writing*
by Kelly Ives

FORTHCOMING BOOKS

Legend of the Overfiend
Death Note
Naruto
Bleach
Hellsing
Vampire Knight
Mushishi
One Piece
Nausicaä of the Valley of the Wind
The Twilight Saga
Harry Potter

ONCE UPON A TIME IN CHINA

TSUI HARK

A CRITICAL STUDY

Once Upon a Time In China
Tsui Hark

A Critical Study
Jeremy Mark Robinson

Crescent Moon

Crescent Moon Publishing
P.O. Box 1312
Maidstone, Kent
ME14 5XU, Great Britain
www.crmoon.com

First published 2024.
© Jeremy Mark Robinson 2024.

Set in Helvetica 9 on 12pt.
Designed by Radiance Graphics.

The right of Jeremy Mark Robinson to be identified as the author of this book has been asserted generally in accordance with sections 77 and 78 of the Copyright, Designs and Patents Act 1988.

All rights reserved. No part of this book may be reprinted or reproduced, stored in a retrieval system, or transmitted, in any form or by any means, electronic, mechanical, photocopying, recording or otherwise, without permission from the publisher.

British Library Cataloguing in Publication data available for this title.

I.S.B.N.-13 9781861719171

CONTENTS

Acknowledgements ❖ 9
Picture Credits ❖ 9
Abbreviations ❖ 9

**PART ONE
TSUI HARK
BIOGRAPHY**

1 Tsui Hark: Biography ❖ 14
2 Tsui Hark: Aspects of His Cinema ❖ 35

**PART TWO
ONCE UPON A TIME IN CHINA**

1 The *Once Upon a Time in China* Series ❖ 85
2 *Once Upon a Time in China* ❖ 104
3 *Once Upon a Time in China 2* ❖ 124
4 *Once Upon a Time in China 3* ❖ 135
5 *Once Upon a Time in China 4* ❖ 144
6 *Once Upon a Time in China 5* ❖ 160
7 *Once Upon a Time in China and America* ❖ 167

Appendix ❖ 184
Filmography ❖ 190
Recommended Books and Websites ❖ 193
Bibliography ❖ 194

ACKNOWLEDGEMENTS

To the authors and publishers quoted.
To the copyright holders of the illustrations.

ABBREVIATIONS

LM *The Cinema of Tsui Hark* by Lisa Morton

PICTURE CREDITS

Golden Harvest. Shaw Brothers. Paragon. Cinema City. Film Workshop. China Entertainment. Paka Hill. Eastern Production. Win's Entertainment. Star East. Jing Productions. Media Asia. Beijing Polyabana Publishing. United Filmmakers Organization. China Film Co-Production. Big Pictures. China Juli Entertainment Media. Distribution Workshop. Different Digital Design. Huxia Film Distribution. New Classics Pictures.

NOTE

Parts of this book appeared in my full-length study of Tsui Hark: *Tsui Hark: Dragon Master of Chinese Cinema* (2023), published by Crescent Moon.

PART ONE
TSUI HARK
BIOGRAPHY

1
TSUI HARK: BIOGRAPHY

INTRODUCTON

Tsui Hark is the dragon master of Chinese cinema (Stephen Teo calls Tsui a 'lion dancer among film directors' [173]). Yes – a master, a lion dancer, a *sifu*, a wizard, a dragon.

Tsui Hark is a one-man film industry – as a glance as his list of credits will show, along with setting up his own film company in 1983, Film Workshop.

Tsui Hark directs movies like a force of nature. The *energy* coming off the screen is stupendous! He is a fearless filmmaker, willing to try *anything* to get a good shot. And I do mean *anything*! That feeling of fearlessness, and wildness, coupled with imagination and technical brilliance, makes Tsui an incredibly *formidable* filmmaker. There are very few filmmakers on the scene today with those qualities in such abundance.

When you come back to a Tsui Hark picture after looking at other movies for a while, you realize, wow, this guy is *so* passionate about cinema, *so* willing to try anything, to experiment, to push the boundaries of what cinema can do, of what cinema can *be*. I've never felt, for example, that Tsui is a 'director for hire', unengaged with the material, or that he is merely punching through the shots as if he's on a factory floor.

No, this man is *on fire*.

BIOGRAPHY

Tsui Hark was born on January 2, 1951 (or February 15; some sources say 1950), in French Cochin China (Saigon, Vietnam). His name was originally Tsui Man-kong (he has also been known as Mark Yu). In Cantonese, his name is Chui Hak; in Mandarin, it's Xu Ke (Xu2 Ke4). He had sixteen siblings (from three marriages). His father was a pharmacist. Tsui changed his name from 'Tsui Man-kong' to 'Tsui Hark' because he thought it was too soft, and for his 'King Kong' nickname (1997, 136). It's pronounced 'Choy Hawk'. Tsui grew up in Saigon until the family moved to Hong Kong in 1966 (Tsui said he migrated around the age of 13, which makes it 1964; Lisa Morton says he was 14).[1]

Tsui Hark is a truly international filmmaker, as well as being a thoroughly Chinese/ Vietnamese one. After going to Hong Kong, he studied filmmaking in the U.S.A., at Southern Methodist University, Dallas in 1969 (for a year) before transferring to the University of Texas in Austin (Austin is a minor filmmaking centre in North America, with its own film culture, where filmmakers such as Richard Linklater are based). He also travelled around the U.S.A.

Tsui Hark graduated in 1975 (he studied for 2 years in Austin, where he was known as 'King Kong'). Tsui later worked in New York City: his first jobs were in television, not cinema: he gravitated from TV to film, as so many filmmakers have done (and as his fellow Hong Kong New Wave filmmakers did). His first jobs in Gotham were as a reporter for a Chinese TV cable station; he was a Chinese newspaper editor; worked with a community theatre group (New Art Drama Group); and helped to make a documentary about Chinatown (as a DP) called *From Spikes To Spindles* (Christine Choy, 1976). Tsui moved back to Hong Kong in 1976 (when he was 25).

Tsui Hark's film career got off to a roaring start with three outstanding pictures. Tsui's first theatrical movie as a director was *The Butterfly Murders* (1979), which combined martial arts, horror, sci-fi, comedy and romance. This was followed swiftly by *We're Going To Eat You* (1980) and *Dangerous Encounter of the 1st Kind* (1980) – both released in 1980.[2]

Directors often work in contrasts – if they've just done a comedy, they might fancy a drama next. Tsui Hark wanted to do something silly after his first three movies, which were 'very serious and very depressing' (LM, 47). Hence *All the Wrong Clues,* which was his first commercial hit (in 1981). And since then, Tsui had rarely let a year pass without releasing a movie as a director or producer (sometimes two! Sometimes three!). By 2014, Tsui had directed around 43 feature films.

As a producer, Tsui Hark has been responsible for masterpieces including: the *A Better Tomorrow* series, the *Chinese Ghost Story* series, the *Swordsman* series, *New Dragon Gate Inn* and *The Killer,* plus a host of

---
[1] Some accounts have Tsui coming to Hong Kong at the age of thirteen; others at fifteen (Tsui's year of birth is usually given as 1950 or 1951). It was in 1966 that Tsui's family moved to Canton.
[2] After *We're Going To Eat You*, Tsui Hark became 'very disappointed in myself', and considered giving up filmmaking.

hugely enjoyable films, such as: *Once Upon a Time in China 4, Once Upon a Time In China 6, Vampire Hunters, The Climbers* and *Black Mask*.

Tsui Hark is much more than a film director. Many directors do the job and go home afterwards. That's it. Some offer to produce other people's projects. Some form their own companies to develop and produce items they might direct themselves, or they might bring in colleagues they know. But only a few opt to take on numerous producing jobs, to the point where their career as a producer is as significant as their directing work. Tsui thus is not only a film director, *and* a film producer, he is also a movie mogul. (To do that amount of work, you have to *really* be committed).

In the press interviews for *Detective Dee and the Mystery of the Phantom Flame*, Tsui Hark was described by the cast and crew as brilliant, stern, tough, sweet, a free spirit, a teacher, boundlessly imaginative, and someone who lives in a different world from the rest of us.

Like many film directors, Tsui Hark has also filmed TV commercials (tho' not as many as some directors). They include *China Motion* (1998), for a telecommunications company on the Mainland (which was likened to the 1984 Apple ad); and *Singapore National Day* (1998).

Change and transformation are key elements in survival in the Hong Kong film industry, Tsui Hark asserted: if you don't change rapidly, you won't survive (LM, 22).

> For me, being commercial is very basic because you need the box office record in order to keep the investor surviving in this industry. But then, you need to be different. You need to be outstanding in terms of film. (2011)

Over the course of his film career, Tsui Hark has worked with practically every big star[3] in the Chinese film industry, as well as every action choreographer,[4] every DP and every major player in film production. (The Hong Kong film industry is small – everybody knows everybody else).

Tsui Hark's energy is legendary. Does he ever sleep? Can he survive on two or three hours sleep a night when he's shooting? (according to rumour). It does seem like that (it seems as if the last time that Tsui slept was in 1978). Tsui is one of those filmmakers who doesn't sit down on set, and is running at a high level of intensity as he's filming.

For instance, in more recent times, Tsui Hark has directed an enormous film production each year! *Detective Dee and the Mystery of the Phantom Flame* (2010), *The Flying Swords of Dragon Gate* (2011), *Young Detective Dee: Rise of the Sea Dragon* (2013) and *Taking Tiger Mountain*

---

[3] As a producer, Tsui Hark has been influential on the careers of Brigitte Lin, John Woo, Chow Yun-fat, Jet Li, Tony Ching Siu-tung, and many others. Jenny Kwok Wah-Lau noted that 'in Hong Kong, most people realize that it is Tsui Hark, the *producer* of *A Better Tomorrow*, who almost single-handedly revised and modernized the action genre and thus directly or indirectly launched the Hollywood careers of John Woo and superstars Chow Yun-Fat (through the same film) and Jet Li (through *Once Upon a Time In China*, which Tsui directed).' (in J. Geiger, 739).

[4] Tsui Hark has worked with practically every celebrated action choreographer in the Hong Kong film business: Sammo Hung, Jackie Chan, Yuen Bun, Yuen Woo-ping, Tony Ching Siu-tung, Yuen Wah, Lau Kar-leung, Xiong Xin-xin, etc.

(2014). Plus directing other movies, such as *Catching Monkey 3-D.*

There are times in the writing of this book (starting in 2013-14), that I couldn't believe just how much Tsui Hark has achieved. Even compared to other workaholic film directors and producers, Tsui stands out. He really is a one-off. (Sometimes I wonder if 'Tsui Hark' is really a conglomerate of writers, producers, directors and visual effects mavens which uses the person we know and love, Tsui Hark, as their spokesman).

Tsui Hark's films have earned numerous awards. 1992 was one of Tsui's best years for awards – 21 nominations at the Hong Kong Film Awards – for *Once Upon a Time In China 2*, *New Dragon Gate Inn*, *The Swordsman 2* and *King of Chess.*

It's usually the same movies from Tsui Hark that feature in top ten lists – *Zu: Warriors From the Magic Mountain*, *Once Upon a Time In China*, *A Better Tomorrow*, *The Killer*, and occasionally the early, angry films: *We're Going To Eat You* and *Dangerous Encounters of the First Kind*. Tsui Hark has 7 films in the Top 100 Hong Kong Films in *Time Out.*

Some observers reckoned that Tsui Hark's film career stalled somewhat in the late 1990s and early 2000s, and that his movies didn't seem to find an audience during that time. Tsui said, yes, he had been trying different things; but he had also been doing the same thing he always did – make movies. It's all relative, tho', and box office success doesn't always match up with critical praise, or what a filmmaker regards as his best work. We all know filmmakers who produced much better movies than the ones that made the most $$$$$. However, commercial success *is* important if you want to produce movies on an ambitious scale (which Tsui often does).

A filmmaker of Tsui Hark's astounding abilities might be expected to go to Hollywood, as some of his Chinese contemporaries have done (notably John Woo, Tony Ching Siu-tung, Jet Li and Yuen Woo-ping). Tsui could've worked in Europe or Hollywood for all of his career following the big success of *Aces Go Places*. But Tsui's career in the U.S.A. has been patchy and somewhat disappointing. For example, instead of being hired by a film studio to helm a historical epic or a contemporary fantasy blockbuster (*Memoirs of a Geisha*, *X-Men*, *The Avengers* or *Pirates of the Caribbean*, say – Tsui would be perfect for *Pirates!*),[5] Tsui was hired to direct two Jean-Claude van Damme actioners. While John Woo directed *Mission: Impossible* and *Face-Off*, and Ringo Lam Ling-tung and Ronnie Yu made *Maximum Risk* and *Replicant* (Lam) and *51st State* and *Freddy vs. Jason* (Yu), high budget action movies, Tsui helmed a couple of van Damme movies which nobody has seen (altho' Woo also directed a Muscles From Brussels picture, *Hard Target*, 1993, as did Ringo Lam – *Maximum Risk*. Everyone in Hong Kong, it seemed, worked with van Damme at one time or another).[6]

Altho' the three Hollywood pictures helmed by Tsui Hark – *Knockoff*, *DoubleTeam* and *Time and Tide* – were fascinating (and *Time and Tide* was

---
[5] And he delivered his own version in the *Detective Dee* series.
[6] The deal seemed to be: you can make an American production, but only if van Damme is the star.

as good an action thriller as has ever been made), the first two were still below the potential and talents of a director like Tsui. (All three were pointedly *not* filmed in the United States of America, however, but in Europa and Asia).

The anti-American politics in some of Tsui Hark's movies may have contributed towards his lack of success in the U.S.A (LM, 14), even tho' his movies are steeped in Hollywood/ Western cinema.

Following his uneven spree in Tinseltown, Tsui Hark has remained devoted to *Chinese* subjects – nearly *all* of his movies as director and producer have had Chinese settings, Chinese stories, Chinese themes and Chinese characters.

❂

Tsui Hark has gained a reputation for arguing with his collaborators, for taking over from other directors, or for directing when he should be producing. Or for being 'difficult'. Tsui doesn't understand it himself, but there are too many stories for there to be nothing in it! (Yet when actors meet him, expecting a difficult or irritable guy, they find someone very different).

When Tsui Hark is involved in a production, whether as producer, director, writer or backer, you know it's going to be interpreted as 'a Tsui Hark movie' (the same thing happens with filmmakers such as Steven Spielberg or George Lucas – they are such big, influential names in the movie business). Tsui is like that – he's the gorilla in the room that nobody talks about.

But one look at Tsui Hark's filmography, and you see an *enormous* amount of work, containing quite a few classics, plenty of ambitious works, and also several landmark movies in Chinese film history. Any history of recent cinema will have to include an entry on Tsui.

Tsui Hark is not a martial artist, and doesn't practise martial arts. He is not, as are Steven Spielberg, John Milius, Masamune Shirow and Mamoru Oshii, a gun nut.[7] For him, martial arts and guns are part of creating a fantasy.

Stephen Teo likens Tsui Hark's role in Hong Kong cinema to the Taoist priest in *A Chinese Ghost Story*: 'although he's not the hero, the Doaist plays the role of a *deus ex machina* in putting things right and making sure that the natural order is not disturbed' (1997, 228).

That Tsui Hark is a workaholic goes without saying. Tsui could've retired ages ago, or found a much easier way of making a buck than producing movies. Everybody who works with Tsui attests to his boundless energy. On the set, Tsui seems to wear everyone out with his relentless determination to get what he's after.[8] Tsui may come over in interviews as a slim and affable Asian guy who's happy to discuss any topic, but on the set[9] he must be a tough task-master at times.

---

[7] Tsui Hark doesn't know much about guns, or martial arts, and relies on other people for that. Instead, Tsui says that he's a fantasist, he imagines things that're the opposite of his real life.
[8] According to rumours, actors would bring their toothbrushes and pyjamas to the studio, because sometimes filming wended on for 48 or 72 hours.
[9] According to onlookers, the mood on a Tsui Hark set is pretty serious; not much goofing around, but getting on with the job.

When it comes to work, Tsui Hark's philosophy is simple: *if you see an opportunity, take it!* It sums up Tsui's incredible drive and ambition: this is a filmmaker with a truly extraordinary level of energy.

Hong Kong filmmakers are not known for their integrity: they have to survive, so, as Tsui Hark noted, 'they will do anything' (LM, 27). So it's the worst, because the filmmakers don't have integrity, but it's also the best because they are always looking for the next thing, for change.

Tsui Hark is happy to be interviewed and there are many interviews available of Tsui. Among the pieces on video and television about Tsui (apart from the usual 'making of' pieces on home releases), I would recommend *Action et Vérité* (2006), about the production of *The Blade*, a short but illuminating interview on *The Butterfly Murders*, *The Incredibly Strange Film Show* (1988-89), and *Yang ± Yin*, a documentary on gender in Chinese cinema directed by Stanley Kwan (1997).

Among Western movies, Tsui Hark has cited Orson Welles (*Citizen Kane*), Francis Coppola, John Ford, Roman Polanski (*Macbeth*), and Frederick Wiseman. The Marx Brothers have certainly influenced Tsui's comical style – not the speedy quips of Groucho, but the surreal bickering, and the silent comedy of Harpo.

You can see Tsui Hark's influence in many places: in movies like *The Stormriders* (Andrew Lau Wai-keung, 1999), *Initial D, He's a Woman, She's a Man, Ashes of Time*, and in filmmakers such as Wong Kar-wai, John Woo, Daniel Lee, Tony Ching, Peter Chan, Andrew Lau, Ang Lee, and Wong Jing. And the many Hong Kong movies which have emulated the Tsui Hark approach are easy to spot.

The *Once Upon a Time In China* series, as Jeff Yang put it, 'single-handedly revived the *kung fu* genre,[10] re-energized the Hong Kong film industry, and launched Mainland *wushu* master Jet Li's career into superstardom throughout Asia, and eventually, the world' (2003, 97). Tsui Hark called Jet Li a 'very special person'.

To make so many movies, as producer and director, means that Tsui Hark must *really* ♥ movies and filmmaking. Hooked on it, perhaps. Obsessive, even. Tsui is simply a natural filmmaker, like Jean-Luc Godard, Ingmar Bergman and Akira Kurosawa, filmmakers who seem to be live and breathe cinema. Tsui seems happiest when he's deep into production on a wild adventure in the archaic *jiangzhu*, or exploring a little-known corner of Chinese history.

Some have dubbed Tsui Hark the 'Asian Steven Spielberg', while others have noted that Spielberg should be so lucky.[11] Because Tsui goes beyond Spielberg in some respects. But they share numerous affinities: they are film buffs, they enshrine cinema of the past, they remake and update old classics,[12] they have taken on a wide variety of genres, they prefer storytelling with music and images above all, they are workaholics,

---

10 Certainly *Once Upon a Time In China* was a key movie in reviving the *kung fu* and martial arts genre – to the level of an artform.
11 Tsui has remarked: 'I don't know – it's unfair to him, I think. It's unfair to me too: he's so rich' (1997, 136).
12 Altho' Tsui Hark has gone back and remade the movies he enjoyed as a kid, he also knows that sometimes those movies one enshrined turn out to be silly and disappointing (LM, 23).

they work very fast on set, they make 'movie-movies', they are both moguls with their own companies, they have worked as film producers extensively, they adore visual effects and the artificiality of cinema, and they are master showmen.

Tsui Hark is also a movie and television generation filmmaker, like the 'movie brats' of the 'New Hollywood' era, such as Steven Spielberg, Brian de Palma, George Lucas and Jonathan Kaplan. There's no doubt that, like his N. American counterparts, Tsui is also remaking and updating many of the movies and TV shows he enjoyed as a youth. There is certainly a strong baby boomer aspect to Tsui's cinema, and a postmodern reworking of earlier forms and genres.

Stephen Teo calls Tsui Hark 'Hong Kong cinema's one genuine prodigy', a filmmaker who's 'primitive, even brutish', whose movies are too fast and too cluttered for some and remain indigestible. Teo reckons that the super-fast Tsui doesn't really have a counterpart in the West.

Stephen Teo:

> Tsui Hark has what Hong Kong critics call a "devil's talent" (*gui cai*), a talent so broad and brilliant that it does not seem human. He is one of the prime movers in the industry and an original New Wave director who pushes his commercial instincts to the limit. (1998, 157)

Lisa Morton summed up Tsui Hark in her 2001 study:

> Tsui Hark is unique in world cinema, a prolific filmmaker (Tsui has directed, written, produced and/ or acted in more than 60 feature films since 1979) who is also a master stylist; a political auteur and a populist; an artist with an obsessive private vision who is also commercially successful; and a filmmaker who seems to revel in deconstructing genres even while celebrating their tropes. (6)

Jeff Yang described Tsui Hark as 'one of the most reliable box office breadwinners of the eighties', a conceiver of new trends, a developer of new technologies and new cinematic techniques, a filmmaker who 'has generally beaten a path for the rest of the industry to follow' (2003, 95).

THE FILM CREDITS OF TSUI HARK

MOVIES AS DIRECTOR

The Butterfly Murders, 1979
We're Going To Eat You, 1980
Dangerous Encounters of the First Kind, 1980
All the Wrong Clues, 1981

Zu: Warriors From the Magic Mountain, 1983
Search For the Gods, 1983
Aces Go Places 3, 1984
Shanghai Blues, 1984
Working Class, 1985
Peking Opera Blues, 1986
Spirit Chaser Aisha, 1986
The Master, 1989
A Better Tomorrow 3, 1989
The Swordsman, 1990
Once Upon a Time in China, 1991
The Banquet, 1991
The Raid, 1991
Once Upon a Time in China 2, 1992
Twin Dragons, 1992
Once Upon a Time in China 3, 1993
Green Snake, 1993
Once Upon a Time in China 5, 1994
The Lovers, 1994
The Chinese Feast, 1995
Love In the Time of Twilight, 1995
The Blade, 1995
Tristar, 1996
Double Team, 1997
Knock Off, 1998
Time and Tide, 2000
The Legend of Zu, 2001
Black Mask 2: City of Masks, 2002
In the Blue, 2005
Seven Swords, 2005
Triangle, 2007
Missing, 2008
All About Women, 2008
Detective Dee and the Mystery of the Phantom Flame, 2010
The Flying Swords of Dragon Gate, 2011
Young Detective Dee: Rise of the Sea Dragon, 2013
Catching Monkey 3-D, 2013
The Taking of Tiger Mountain, 2014
Journey To the West: Conquering the Demons, 2017
Detective Dee and the Four Heavenly Kings, 2018
The Battle At Lake Changjin, 2021
The Battle At Lake Changjin: Water Gate Bridge, 2022

MOVIES AS PRODUCER

All the Wrong Spies, 1983
A Better Tomorrow, 1986
The Laser Man, 1986
A Chinese Ghost Story, 1987
A Better Tomorrow 2, 1987
The Big Heat, 1988
Gunmen, 1988
Diary of a Big Man, 1988
The King of Chess, 1988/ 1992
The Master, 1989
A Better Tomorrow 3, 1989
The Killer, 1989
Just Heroes, 1989
The Terracotta Warrior, 1989
The Swordsman, 1990
A Chinese Ghost Story 2, 1990
A Chinese Ghost Story 3, 1991
Once Upon a Time in China, 1991
New Dragon Gate Inn, 1992
The Swordsman 2, 1992
The Wicked City, 1992
Once Upon a Time in China 2, 1992
Once Upon a Time in China 3, 1993
Green Snake, 1993
The Swordsman 3: The East Is Red, 1993
Once Upon a Time in China 4, 1993
Once Upon a Time in China 5, 1994
The Lovers, 1994
Burning Paradise, 1994
The Chinese Feast, 1995
The Blade, 1995
Shanghai Grand, 1996
A Chinese Ghost Story: The Tsui Hark Animation, 1997
Once Upon a Time in China and America, 1997
Time and Tide, 2000
The Legend of Zu, 2001
Old Master Q, 2001
Tsui Hark's Vampire Hunters, 2002
Black Mask 2: City of Masks, 2002
Xanda, 2004
Seven Swords, 2005
The Warrior, 2006
Triangle, 2007
Missing, 2008
All About Women, 2008

Detective Dee and the Mystery of the Phantom Flame, 2010
The Flying Swords of Dragon Gate, 2011
Young Detective Dee: Rise of the Sea Dragon, 2013
Christmas Rose, 2013
The Taking of Tiger Mountain, 2014
Sword Master, 2016
The Thousand Faces of Dunjia, 2017
Journey To the West: Conquering the Demons, 2017
Detective Dee and the Four Heavenly Kings, 2018
The Climbers, 2019
The Battle At Lake Changjin, 2021
The Battle At Lake Changjin 2, 2022

By any standards, that list of film credits is completely remarkable! And it's a selective list, which doesn't include everything that Tsui has done.[13] You have to add writing credits to that list, and entries in anthology films, plus several TV series, as well as plenty of acting and cameos. And design work, editing and visual effects.

Up to 2013, Tsui Hark had writing credits on 36-42 movies,[14] story credits for 10 films, director credits for 43-45 movies, producer credits for 58-62 productions, and actor credits for 26 films.

Tsui Hark has writing credits on most of the movies he's directed, and he has producer credits on most of them, too. Which means that Tsui can properly be regarded as an *auteur*. The key production credit in many respects, in relation to the cinema of Tsui (and most cinema), is *producer*, more even than director or writer. (But Tsui is also more than a producer, director and writer, he is also a movie mogul with his own production company and visual effects company).

Among the movies directed by Tsui Hark, the following are masterpieces: *Once Upon a Time In China 1*, *Once Upon a Time In China 2*, *Once Upon a Time In China 3*, *Seven Swords*, *Detective Dee and the Mystery of the Phantom Flame*, *Young Detective Dee*, *Zu: Warriors From the Magic Mountain*, *The Flying Swords of Dragon Gate*, *The Taking of Tiger Mountain*, *Shanghai Blues*, *Peking Opera Blues* and *The Swordsman*. Many other movies directed by Tsui are fantastically enjoyable cinema: *Green Snake, The Blade, The Master, Detective Dee and the Four Heavenly Kings, The Legend of Zu* and *Time and Tide*. Only one or two movies with Tsui at the helm are disappointing: *Triangle* (co-directed with To and Lam), and *All About Women*.

One striking aspect of Tsui Hark's output is that fully half or more of his movies as director and producer have been historical pictures, a much greater ratio than most other filmmakers. Tsui is a specialist in costume films, and most of his masterpieces have also been historical movies. Notice, too, that in the more recent part of his career, the 2000s and 2010s, Tsui has been focussing on history – going back to the mid-20th

---

13 *The Legend of Famen Temple* (*Fa Men Si Mi Ma*), another historical fantasy, was rumoured in 2016-2017, based on a novel by Huang Shang Jin-yu, and starring Kenny Lin, Chen Kun, Zitao Huang and Xun Shou.
14 44 films to 2016, at Internet Movie Database.

century in the war pictures (*Tiger Mountain, Lake Changjin*) or Ancient China (*Detective Dee*). The last feature films set in the contemporary era was in 2008 (*All About Women* and *Missing*).

The production roles are important, because we know that Tsui Hark is a very hands-on producer. The role of a producer varies widely, from someone way back in a project's history who oversaw one of the numerous script rewrites to a producer who oversees every aspect of the production.

Well, we know that Tsui Hark has performed second unit direction on some movies he's produced, and also co-directed some of them. And when Tsui insists that he *didn't* direct some of the movies (such as those directed by Tony Ching Siu-tung), his influence as writer or co-writer and of course as producer can felt everywhere in those movies.

TSUI HARK AS FILM PRODUCER

The movies that were produced by Tsui Hark can be regarded as part of his *œuvre* to a greater degree than many films which other directors have acted as a producer on – because Tsui is a hands-on producer.

But what is a film producer? Critics don't really know, yet the Western/ Hollywood film industry is a producer-led, producer-based business, and in the Hong Kong industry, too, producers lead the way. Among the many functions a good film producer does is: (1) buying and developing material; (2) hiring writers; (3) putting together deals; (4) approaching investors, and finding backing/ money/ resources; (5) hiring directors and other personnel; (6) over-seeing the all-important pre-production, which includes 100s of elements; (7) casting; (8) over-seeing shooting; (9) over-seeing post-production (again, this involves 100s of ingredients); (10) music, selecting composers; and (11) publicity, marketing, advertizing.

Tsui Hark has performed all of those tasks many times, and there's no doubt that as a film producer he is right in there, selecting and developing projects, and shepherding them to pre-production (that's when a movie is really made). If he's sometimes a dictator, well, he replies, the creative process needs that.[15]

Among Tsui Hark's numerous production credits, apart from acting as the producer on the movies he's directed, are (Tsui also has writing credits on most of these movies):

• *All the Wrong Spies* (Teddy Robin, 1983), a sequel to *All the Wrong Clues* (dir. by Tsui Hark). Written by Raymond Wong Pak-min, it starred George Lam, Teddy Robin, Paul Chun Pui, Brigitte Lin, Shing Fui-on, Joe Junior, Tsui Hark and Anders Nelsson. Tsui and his wife Nansun Shi Nan-sheng are credited as production designers.

---

[15] Is he a dictator? Yes, he admits, 'But the creative process needs that'.

- The two *A Better Tomorrow* movies[16] (1986 and 1987).
- *The Laser Man* (1986), was executive produced by Tsui Hark and Sophie Lo, written, directed and co-produced by Peter Wang, and starred Marc Hiyashi, Peter Wang, Tony Leung and Sally Yeh.
- *Gunmen* (Kirk Wong, 1988),[17] starring Tony Leung, Adam Cheng, Elvis Tsui, Waise Lee and Carrie Ng.
- *The Big Heat* (Johnny To & Andrew Kam, 1988), written by Gordon Chan, starring Waise Lee, Philip Kwok, Paul Chu-kong, Stuart Ong Sai Kit, Michael Chow Man Kin, Ken Boyle and Joey Wong. Tsui Hark appears in some credits as the co-director in this very troubled production.
- *Diary of a Big Man* (1988) was produced by Tsui Hark, directed by Chor Yuen, and starred Chow Yun-fat, Joey Wong, Sally Yeh, Waise Lee and Kent Cheng.
- *A Chinese Ghost Story* (Tony Ching Siu-tung, 1987), starring Leslie Cheung, Joey Wong and Wu Ma.
- *A Chinese Ghost Story 2* (Tony Ching Siu-tung, 1990) starring Leslie Cheung, Joey Wong, Michelle Reiss, Jacky Cheung and Waise Lee.
- *A Chinese Ghost Story 3* (Tony Ching Siu-tung, 1991), starring Tony Leung Chiu-wai, Joey Wong, Jacky Cheung and Nina Le Chi.
- *I Love Maria* (a.k.a. *Roboforce*, 1988), was a Hong Kong version of *RoboCop* (1987), co-produced by Tsui Hark with John Sham, directed by David Chung Chi-man,[18] starring Sally Yeh, Tsui Hark, John Sham and Tony Leung.
- *The Killer* (John Woo, 1989), starring Chow Yun-fat, Danny Lee, Shing Fui-on and Sally Yeh.
- *Deception* (a.k.a. *Web of Deception*, David Chiang, 1989), starring Brigitte Lin, Joey Wong and Pauline Wong.
- *The Terracotta Warrior* (Tony Ching Siu-tung, 1989), starring Zhang Yimou, Gong Li and Yu Rongguang.
- *Just Heroes* (a.k.a. *Tragic Heroes*, 1989) was a benefit movie for the Hong Kong directors' union. It starred a host of names, including David Chiang, Danny Lee, Chen Kuan-tai, Stephen Chow, Lo Lieh, Ti Lung, Cally Kwong, Wu Ma, Shing Fui-on, James Wong Jim, Bill Tung, Zhao Lei and Tien Niu.
- *Spy Games* (David Wu Tai-wai, 1990) was a spy movie spoof directed by Wu, who's edited many of Tsui's movies. It was written by Ng Man-fai, Philip Cheng, Lam Kee-to and Lau Tai-mok, and starred Joey Wong, Kenny Bee, Noriko Izumoto, Waise Lee and Shut Yam.
- *The Raid* (Tony Ching Siu-tung and Tsui Hark, 1991) was a 1930s adventure comedy co-written by Tsui Hark and Yuen Kai-chi, and starring Jacky Cheung, Dean Shek, Tony Leung, Paul Chu, Fennie Yuen and Joyce Godenzi.
- *The Swordsman* (King Hu et al, 1990), starring Sam Hui, Cecilia Yip, Yuen Wah, Jacky Cheung and Cheung Man.

---

16 The *Better Tomorrow* movies inevitably inspired cash-ins – such as *Return To Better Tomorrow* (Wong Jing, 1994).
17 Critics have discerned the influence of Tsui Hark in *Gunmen* (which he produced), in the romantic atmosphere, and in the action.
18 Tony Ching Siu-tung was 2nd unit director.

- *The Swordsman 2* (Tony Ching Siu-tung, 1991), starring Jet Li, Brigitte Lin, Rosamund Kwan, Michelle Reiss and Fennie Yuen.
- *The Swordsman 3: The East Is Red* (Tony Ching Siu-tung & Raymond Lee, 1993), starring Brigitte Lin, Yu Rongguang, Joey Wong and Eddie Ko.
- *Dragon Inn* (a.k.a. *New Dragon Gate Inn*, Raymond Lee, 1992), starring Tony Leung, Brigitte Lin, Maggie Cheung and Donnie Yen.
- *The Wicked City* (*Yiu Sau Do Si*, dir. Peter Mak Tai-kit, 1992), a live-action version of the Japanese *animé* (1987), staring Leon Lai Ming, Jacky Cheung Hak-yow, Michelle Reiss and Tatsuya Nakadai.
- *Iron Monkey* (Yuen Woo-ping, 1993), co-written by Tsui Hark with Tang Pik-yin and Lau Tai-mok, and starring Donnie Yen, Yu Rongguang and Jean Wong.
- *The Magic Crane* (Benny Chan, 1993), co-written by Tsui Hark (with Jobic Chui Daat-Choh), and starring Anita Mui, Tony Leung Chiu-wai, Rosamund Kwan and Damian Lau.
- *Burning Paradise*, a.k.a. *Red Lotus Temple* (Ringo Lam Ling-tung, 1994), starring Willie Chi, Wong Kam-long and Carman Lee.
- *Once Upon a Time In China 4* (Yuen Bun, 1993), co-written by Tsui and Tang Pik-yin, was released only four months after the third *Once Upon a Time In China* movie, and starred Vincent Zhao, Jean Wong, Xiong Xin-xin, Max Mok and Lau Shun.
- *Shanghai Grand* (Poon Man-kit, 1996), was a period gangster tale co-written by Sandy Shaw, Matthew Chow Hoi-kwong and Poon Man-kit. It starred Andy Lau Tak-wah, Leslie Cheung and Lau Shun.
- *Black Mask* (Daniel Lee Yan-kong, 1996) was a wild superhero adventure co-written by Koan Hui-on, Teddy Chan Tak-sum and Joe Ma Wai-ho, and starring Jet Li, Karen Mok, Lau Ching-wan, Francoise Yip, Moses Chan and Anthony Wong.
- *Once Upon a Time in China and America* (Sammo Hung Kam-bo, 1997), was co-written by Roy Szeto Cheuk-hon, Shut Mei-yee, Sharon Hui Sa-long, Philip Kwok and So Man-Sing, and starred Jet Li, Rosamund Kwan, Xiong Xin-xin, Chan Kwok Pong, Richard Ng and Jeff Wolfe.
- *Old Master Q* (2001) was co-written by Tsui Hark with Roy Szeto Cheuk-hon, Herman Yau and Man Choi-lee, exec-prod. by Charles Heung and Tsui Hark, and dir. by Herman Yau.
- *Tsui Hark's Vampire Hunters* (2002) was produced and written by Tsui Hark, and dir. by Wellson Chin Sing-wai.
- *Xanda* (*Sanda*, 2004) was wr. by Kai-Cheung Chung, Derick Lau, Ask Lee, Xiao-Long Lin and Tsui Hark, exec-prod. by Satoru Iseki, Nansun Shi Nan-sheng and Le Qun Song, prod. by Tsui Hark, and directed by Marco Mak Chi-sin.
- *The Warrior* (literal title: *Wong Fei-hung: Brave Into the World*, 2006) was a Wong Fei-hung movie as an animation, directed by Tiger Fu Yin and Chen Yue-Hu and produced by Yang Yong.
- *Sword Master* (Derek Yee, 2016) was a 3-D *wuxia pian* produced by Tsui Hark and co-written by Tsui with Derek Yee and Chun Tin-nam.

Another aspect is immediately obvious: there were years when Tsui

Hark was directing not one but two movies! And in some years, even more! In 1995: *The Chinese Feast, Love in the Time of Twilight* and *The Blade!* (In the North American film industry, it's typical for a film director to direct every three years).

TSUI HARK AS WRITER

Among Tsui Hark's writing for cinema credits are: *Di yu wu men, Dangerous Encounters of the First Kind, All the Wrong Clues, A Better Tomorrow 2*,[19] *Tit gaap mou dik maa lei aa, The Master, A Better Tomorrow 3: Love and Death in Saigon, A Chinese Ghost Story, A Chinese Ghost Story 3, Once Upon a Time in China, The Banquet, Twin Dragons, The Swordsman, Once Upon a Time in China 2, New Dragon Gate Inn, Once Upon a Time in China 3, The Swordsman 3: The East Is Red, Once Upon a Time in China 4, Iron Monkey, Ching Se, Yiu sau dou si, The Magic Crane, Once Upon a Time in China 5, The Chinese Feast, Love In the Time of Twilight, The Lovers, The Blade, Da san yuan, Black Mask,* the animated *Chinese Ghost Story, Time and Tide, Old Master Q, The Legend of Zu, Black Mask 2: City of Masks, The Era of Vampires, Xanda, Seven Swords, Missing, All About Women, Flying Swords of Dragon Gate, Young Detective Dee: Rise of the Sea Dragon, Sword Master, Detective Dee and the Four Heavenly Kings, The Thousand Faces of Dunjia* and the two *Battle of Lake Changjin* movies.

Tsui Hark has also worked uncredited as a writer, sometimes helping out pictures that are in trouble. For ex, Tsui contributed (along with Gordon Chan) to *Dr Wai* (Tony Ching Siu-tung, 1996), a Jet Li actioner.

Lisa Morton noted that Tsui Hark has only made one proper sci-fi movie – *I Love Maria* (a.k.a. *Roboforce*). Actually, the two *Black Mask* movies are science fiction. But Tsui has acknowledged that he hasn't done much in sci-fi – he prefers Ancient Chinese fantasy and mythology.

However, Tsui Hark has certainly directed movies which portray savage realms that come across like post-apocalyptic worlds: the brutish martial arts world (*jiangzhu*) of *The Blade*[20] and *Seven Swords* come to mind.

---

19 *A Better Tomorrow 2* (1987) was written and directed by John Woo, produced by Tsui Hark, with action direction by Tony Ching Siu-tung, and starred Chow Yun-fat, Dean Shek, Ti Lung, Leslie Cheung and Emily Chu.
20 Paul Fonoroff reckoned that 'if movies were judged on visuals alone, *The Blade* would certainly rank as one of the decade's most stunning motion pictures' (527).

THE HONG KONG NEW WAVE

Like other filmmakers of the Chinese New Wave cinema, Tsui Hark is a film school graduate: Ann Hui and Yim Ho studied in London; Tsui in Austin, Texas; and Ringo Lam Ling-tung in Toronto (York University). They studied in the West, or in Western-style institutions in Hong Kong. They could speak English with critics, which no doubt helped, because they'd spent time in the West. And they were familiar with the art film traditions of Europe and the U.S.A.

Following film school, they went to work in television. (Hui, Ho and Tsui were part of the first wave of the New Wave, along with Allan Fong, Patrick Tam, Kirk Wong, and Tony Ching Siu-tung); the second wave included Stanley Kwan, Alex Law, Clara Law, Jacob Cheung, Wong Kar-wai, Cheung Yuen-ting, and Eddie Fong.[21]

The Hong Kong New Wave did not have a unified style or an approach: it took on aspects of youth: 'school, sex, drugs and other travails of growing up in a materialistic society, misunderstood by parents and adults in authority', according to Stephen Teo (1997, 156).

Tsui Hark said that the Hong Kong New Wave wasn't really a *nouvelle vague*, like the French New Wave, and didn't have a philosophy behind it. For some critics, the New Wave of 1979 ended with the crude commercialism of comedies such as *All the Wrong Clues* (1981), directed by Tsui.

It was no surprise that many of the first films of the Hong Kong New Wave were thrillers or crime stories (including Tsui Hark's films) – because they are a staple of Hong Kong cinema, and of cinemas the world over, because they tend to be cheap to make, because the genre was versatile, and because a huge proportion of source material was in the crime or thriller genre.

For Stephen Teo, the two strands of the Hong Kong New Wave cinema – realism and genre conventions – developed towards the latter: the New Wavers started out tackling realism but leant towards genre filmmaking (1997, 149). The forms and conventions of genre were updated for modern audiences in the 1980s. (The first official, Hong Kong New Wave film was *The Extras* (1978), but the unofficial film that launched it, according to Cheuk Pak-tong, was *Jumping Ash* (1976). In 1979, some of the first New Wave films included *The Secrets* (dir. Ann Hui), *The Butterfly Murders* (dir. Tsui Hark), *The System* (dir. Peter Yung) and *Cops and Robbers* (dir. Alex Cheung)).

At the height of the 1990s New Wave, actors and crew were commonly rushing from one movie set to another. Andy Lau Tak-wah slept in his car while filming a movie a month in 1991, and according to rumour making four movies in four locations at the same time. (Chinese filmmakers became geniuses at stretching footage of actors who could only give them a day or so, by using doubles, re-arranging scripts, focussing on reaction shots, etc).

---

21 According to Jenny Kwok Wah-Lau, 30-40 directors made their debut films in 1979-80 (in J. Jeiger, 740).

You'll see the same actors and directors in the New Wave of Hong Kong and Chinese cinema, continuing up to the present day. The actors include: Jet Li, Jackie Chan, Brigitte Lin, Tony Leung, Leslie Cheung, Michelle Yeoh, Zhao Wei, Donnie Yen, Maggie Cheung, Jacky Cheung, Zhang Ziyi, Yuen Biao, Chow Yun-fat, Josephine Siao, Stephen Chow, Gong Li, Rosamund Kwan, Zhao Wenzhou, Kent Cheng, and Xiong Xin-xin.

And directors such as Tsui Hark, Ronny Yu, Ringo Lam Ling-tung, King Hu, Sammo Hung Kam-bo, Zhang Yimou, Ann Hui, Wong Jing, Yuen Woo-ping, Wong Kar-wai, Peter Chan, Stanley Tong, Tony Ching Siu-tung and John Woo.

TSUI HARK AND TELEVISION

Television nurtured the New Wave filmmakers in Hong Kong – becoming something like a Shaolin Temple for *cinéastes*, as critic Law Kar put it. They worked at stations such as C.T.V. (Commercial Television), R.T.H.K. (Radio Television Hong Kong) and T.V.B.[22] (Hong Kong Television Broadcast, Ltd.). Selina Chow, a TV executive, was instrumental in hiring the 'New Wave' filmmakers in television (LM, 221). They were also a film school generation: the New Wave directors studied at film schools abroad partly because they didn't really exist in Asia (the Chinese State film school, Beijing Film Academy, didn't re-open until 1978). Tsui Hark:

> I went to film school simply because I like to express my feelings on certain issues through film, which was a pretty popular medium during the 1960s. We spent a lot of time in movie theaters. At that time I was already thinking how to make Chinese cinema more interesting.

Tsui Hark first worked in television in the late 1970s; his first TV shows were *Golden Dagger Romance* (1978), made for C.T.V., adapted from a novel by Gu Long (during Tsui's 6 months there) and *Aries, Scorpio, Aquarius* (T.V.B., 1978). Tsui was also one of five directors (Ringo Lam Ling-tung was another) of *The Family* (1978, at T.V.B.), a 104-episode soap opera ('people die, get rich, get divorced', as Tsui summed it up [1997, 133]). Tsui came back to television several times – for the *Wong Fei-hung* and *Seven Swordsmen* TV series, for example.

For Stephen Teo, Tsui Hark's cinema is a vivid embodiment of the maturation of the New Wave, and the postmodernism of commercial cinema:

> Using Tsui as a yardstick, the postmodern phenomena grew from a ragbag of causes and effects: new wave æsthetics mixed with Cinema City-style slapstick, anxiety over 1997 and the China

---
[22] T.V.B. was the television arm of Shaws.

syndrome, the assertion of Hong Kong's own identity as different from China, and a new sexual awakening arising from an increasing awareness of women's human rights and the decriminalisation of homosexuality. (1997, 246)

CINEMA CITY

Tsui Hark was part of the group of filmmakers at Cinema City (from 1981). A new studio, Cinema City wasn't independent – it was owned by Golden Princess. It had been founded by Raymond Wong Pak-min, Karl Maka (b. 1944) and Dean Shek in 1979 (as the Fun Dao Film Company). The so-called 'Gang of Seven' at Cinema City were Tsui, Maka, Wong, Shek, Teddy Robin Kwan, Eric Tsang and Tsui's wife Nansun Shi Nan-sheng. As Tsui recalled, they would consider everything, go thru scripts at length and discuss them.

All the Wrong Clues… For the Right Solution (1981) was Tsui Hark's first Cinema City production: it was produced by Karl Maka and Dean Shek, written by Roy Szeto Cheuk-hon (a regular collaborator with Tsui) and Raymond Wong Pak-min, and starred George Lam, Teddy Robin Kwan, Maka and Wong Tso-sze (for some critics, this movie announced the end of the Hong Kong New Wave).

Aces Go Places 3 (a.k.a. *Mad Mission 3,* 1984) was another installment in the successful *Aces Go Places* franchise from Cinema City (the earlier films were released in 1982 and 1983. The movies were the top films of each year (the first *Aces Go Places* grossed HK $26 million[23] when ticket prices were HK $15 (= U.S. $1.95).) It was produced and written by Raymond Wong Pak-min, and starred Sam Hui, Karl Maka and Sylvia Chang. According to Stephen Teo, 'Tsui's own dynamic style of filmmaking initiated a level of structural experimentation which was to be highly influential' (153).

The 'Cinema City style' emphasized comedy above all, stunts, visual effects, big budgets, and movies constructed by a creative team. For a period in the 1980s, Cinema City cornered the market for theatrical comedies. About 17% of films were comedies between 1985 and 1997 in Hong Kong.

---

[23] There are typically 7.75 Hong Kong dollars to the U.S.A. dollar. (So when a movie makes HK $30 million in theatrical release in Hong Kong, that equals US $3.87 million).

FILM WORKSHOP

In 1984 Tsui Hark founded Film Workshop with his wife, Nansun Shi Nan-sheng (he had decided to create a company during post-production of *Zu: Warriors From the Magic Mountain*; it was partly because Cinema City were only interested in making comedies). Film Workshop is based in Kowloon Bay.

Terence Chang[24] worked as general manager at Film Workshop in the 1980s (at Nansun Shi Nan-sheng's invitation). Following Tsui Hark's dispute with John Woo over *The Killer* and *A Better Tomorrow 3*,[25] Chang left with Woo. Chang described his time at Film Workshop thus:

> The first year was really exciting. The company was new, vibrant, and a lot of great films came from that time. Tsui Hark was very idealistic. He wanted to round up the best directors in Hong Kong and put them under one roof. He wanted to create an environment where all the directors, under his leadership, could be given the opportunity and nourishment to make artistic, yet commercial pictures.

The productions of Film Workshop include: *Shanghai Blues* (1984), *The Master* (1989), *King of Chess* (1992), *The Swordsman 2* (1992), *Wicked City* (1992), *New Dragon Gate Inn* (1992), *Once Upon a Time in China 2* (1992), *The East Is Red* (1993), *The Magic Crane* (1993), *Iron Monkey* (1993), *Once Upon a Time in China 3* (1993), *Once Upon a Time in China 4* (1993), *Green Snake* (1993), *A Chinese Ghost Story: The Tsui Hark Animation* (1997), *Knockoff* (1998), *Time and Tide* (2000), *The Era of Vampires* (2002), *Xanda* (2004), *Seven Swords* (2005), *Triangle* (2007), *All About Women* (2008) and the *Detective Dee* movies.

Tsui Hark has worked with Golden Harvest for much of his career; they have enjoyed many successes. However, they have also fallen out – over the release of *Zu: Warriors From the Magic Mountain*, for instance. And in the late 1990s, Golden Harvest sued Tsui for over-runs on 8 films (and Tsui's lawyers responded with a counter-suit for revenue from the *Once Upon a Time In China* pictures).

---

[24] John Woo's regular producer, Terence Chang (b. 1949), had studied in New York and Oregon before working at Golden Harvest and in TV before joining Film Workshop. Chang also worked at D. & B.
[25] He rushed his own sequel to *A Better Tomorrow* into theatres, for instance (which he had co-produced), to beat John Woo's sequel (altho' Woo doesn't like doing sequels).

SOME GREAT MOMENTS IN TSUI HARK'S WORK

- Avoiding the cannibals in *We're Going To Eat You*
- The finale of *Zu*
- Meeting under the bridge in *Shanghai Blues*
- Backstage in *Peking Opera Blues*
- Chow Yun-fat versus the tank in *A Better Tomorrow 3*
- Maggie Cheung in *New Dragon Gate Inn*
- The first act of *Once Upon a Time In China*
- The ladders duel in *Once Upon a Time In China*
- Leslie Cheung in the haunted inn in *A Chinese Ghost Story*
- Wu Ma's Taoist dance in *A Chinese Ghost Story*
- Jet Li versus Donnie Yen in *Once Upon a Time In China 2*
- The Lion Dance competition in *Once Upon a Time In China 3*
- Jet Li in a clinch with Brigitte Lin in *The Swordsman 2*
- The watery finale of *Green Snake*
- The musical/romantic montage in *The Lovers*
- The final duel in *The Blade*
- The motorcycle chase in *Black Mask*
- The market chase in *Knock-Off*
- The apartment fire-fight in *Time and Tide*
- The arrival of the warriors in *Seven Swords*
- Jet Li vs. Gordon Liu in *Flying Swords of Dragon Gate*
- Andy Lau and Jinger in *Detective Dee*
- The sea monster in *Young Detective Dee*
- The snow tiger scene in *The Taking of Tiger Mountain*
- The Battle of the Buddhas in *Journey To the West*
- The monster battle in *Detective Dee 3*

Tsui Hark on the sets of the Detective Dee films.

On the set of Flying Swords of Dragon Gate (above).

2

TSUI HARK: ASPECTS OF HIS CINEMA

FAST FILMS.
This man is *fast*!

Not only does Tsui Hark produce and direct more movies than five filmmakers put together, his movies zip along at a cracking pace. 'Tsui's films move with such breakneck speed that one is hard put to find a Western equivalent,' noted Stephen Teo (153). He can't slow down.[1]

Tsui Hark should offer a competition to movie fans: a $10,000 prize to anyone who can come up with a camera angle [2] he hasn't used in a movie.

One of the great pleasures of Tsui Hark's cinema is the length of his movies. So many filmmakers are tempted into out-staying their welcome, into lingering over scenes, often because they actually don't have much of a story to tell, or their stories simply aren't that compelling in the end.

The typical Tsui Hark movie comes in at 80-90 minutes, a perfect and satisfying length for a picture (filmmakers such as Jean-Luc Godard, Woody Allen and Ingmar Bergman also thankfully keep to that sort of running time). Why carry on into 110, 120 or 140 minutes, when you've said everything you want to say, done everything you want to do, and told the story you want to tell?

A master showman, the two most entertaining segments of a Tsui Hark movie tend to be the opening act and the final act.[3] The first acts tend to be incredibly busy, as the filmmakers cram in everything they can think of – not only to set-up the rest of the movie, but to evoke a huge world (and to dare the audience to be bored). The first acts seem to acknowledge that the audience, if it's watching this movie in a theatre, has just walked in off the streets of Hong Kong which, as we know, can be crazy, busy and loud.

And the final acts are among the greatest finales in movies of recent

---

1 Grady Hendrix noted in 2013: 'All of his collaborators over the years feel that his movies would be better if he focused on fully expressing one idea rather than several, but Tsui doesn't have the time. He's saving China from extinction and if he has a thousand ideas in the three months when he's making a movie, then that movie will contain a thousand ideas.'
2 Tho' Tsui Hark is fond of high angle shots, but he doesn't film them himself – he has a fear of heights.
3 George Lucas often spoke of the importance of a good beginning and ending.

times. Make the opening and the ending special, they say, and the cinema of Tsui Hark certainly does that. At least half of the final act is filled with action, usually comprising several action sequences which run together. And Tsui Hark's movies also know that their audiences are busy people, and they haven't got time to hang about after the plots have been resolved. Thus, the *dénouements* are mercilessly (and quite correctly) short.

SCRIPTS AND ACTS.

As to the issue of who originates the idea for the movies he produces and directs, Tsui Hark is a little ambiguous: he says that most of the ideas come from him first, then he starts to gather the people together to produce the movie (which is what a film producer does). But just who writes the script, and who is originating most of the ideas is a bit vague (LM, 27). However, rewriting scripts is pretty much mandatory: you 'rewrite it and rewrite it and rewrite it' (ibid.). Finding a script that's ready to shoot without requiring rewriting hasn't happened yet for Tsui.[4] Of his relationship with writers, Tsui remarked: 'My common experience is to fight with [writers] all the time. As a result some people think I'm very demanding'.

In 2011, Tsui Hark said (in *Twitch*):

The best thing actually to do is write according to what you feel. If you feel your heart would take you to the point where you would want to express something to do with the story or the film. Sometimes it's not the story; sometimes it's the way you tell the story. Sometimes it's the attitude you have with the story. The attitude is something you build and you accumulate for a long time for no reason and no logic, it's there. When you write that way, you might want to make it that way.

For Jean-Luc Godard, having a good script and a good subject were not the same thing. Having a *subject*, 'a meaning, a belief in something' was more important than having a good script or story. 'A pretty woman is not a subject', Godard asserted (1998, 177). North American cinema tended to have 'no subject, only a story'. For Godard, it's a 'good script when you know the subject and try to [explore] it' (ibid.). And a beginning, middle and an end, as Godard famously observed once (to Claude Lelouch in 1965), 'but not necessarily in that order'.

In her excellent study of Tsui Hark's cinema, Lisa Morton asserts that Tsui doesn't use conventional structures (of acts, or three-act models) for his movies. Actually, yes, he does. Right down the line. In fact, not only Tsui's movies, but almost all Hong Kong movies employ conventional narrative structures. (However, the way that Tsui tells stories is quirky, and it's that which makes his pictures look as if they avoid narrative conventions).

Instead of the three-act model, a better way of thinking of acts in film scripts, however, is to see them as 25-30 minutes narrative units

---

[4] As to storyboarding, Tsui Hark said that he uses animatics now, and used to storyboard a lot for a while, until it became restricting.

(following Kristin Thompson in *Storytelling In the New Hollywood*). Thus, a two-hour movie will have *four*, not *three* acts. However, in Hong Kong, the industry usually releases films of 85-90 minutes, so that, yes, they are three-act movies. (And thus, for the action movies of Hong Kong, the *second act* is the big challenge – because any decent action movie can deliver a couple of great action scenes in the first act, and a Big Finale for the third act. But coming up with something in the middle which keeps the movie (and the audience) afloat is trickier).

For Tsui Hark, it's not necessarily the era or other elements that attracts him to a project, it's the characters (LM, 24). This is certainly true of movies such as the *Swordsman* series, the *Detective Dee* films, and of course the *Wong Fei-hung* series.

Grady Hendrix noted in 2013:

Tsui's characters are neither here nor there, subject to sudden, traumatic changes in status and identity. Demons become human, men become women, swordsmen become monks, criminals become heroes, and heroes become villains. Shape-shifting aliens become bangable pinball machines, robots turn into sexy sirens, human bodies are pulled apart, hung from hooks, deflated, de-faced, skinned alive, castrated, amputated, and exploded. Twins and endlessly replicating time travelers proliferate exponentially.

Tsui Hark has taken up Chinese folktales and fables and classic stories many times as sources for his films, with movies such as *Zu: Warriors From the Magic Mountain, Seven Swords, Green Snake, A Chinese Ghost Story, The Swordsman, Detective Dee* and the *Once Upon a Time In China* series. In fact, Tsui is extremely fond of exploiting ancient and mediæval fables and tales (and not simply, as with the Walt Disney corporation, because they are well out of copyright!). The ancient and Middle Ages tales offer Tsui a framework that are well-known and familiar to audiences, which're also loose enough for him to do whatever he likes with them.

These folk, mythic and historical stories don't only appear in Tsui Hark's movies – they are the subject of many versions, and every famous Chinese tale will have not one but several television series produced from it. For example, the butterfly lovers theme has been remade many times, including on TV; the *Detective Dee* movies are not Tsui's invention – there are C.C.T.V. series (in the early 2000s), and many writers (such as Robert Van Gulik) have explored Judge Dee as a character; the mythic martial arts movies of Tsui's like *Zu* and *Green Snake* are regular topics on Chinese TV; and of course Wong Fei-hung is a central figure in literally 100s of movies and TV shows.

TSUI HARK THE MEDDLER.

Tsui Hark has been known to muscle in other film directors' projects (which seems to be more common in Hong Kong cinema than in the West).5 Tsui admits that when he produces movies, 'I get too involved in the project, and there is not enough room for some directors to breathe'.

David Chung claimed that Tsui Hark 'took things over completely' during *I Love Maria* (a.k.a. *Roboforce*, 1988), which Tsui was producing and Chung was directing; Peter Wang complained that Tsui 'interferred' with his movie *The Laser Man* (1986); John Woo maintained that Tsui 'wrested away control of the sequel to my greatest masterpiece [*A Better Tomorrow*], and when I left to make the movie I wanted to make, rushed his version out just to make sure that it was a flop'. Rumours of Tsui's influence have also been suggested for *A Chinese Ghost Story* and *The Swordsman*.

However, there are a number of assumptions about this tendency of Tsui Hark's to hijack movies that he wasn't directing and their directors. One is that Tsui has the time to do that. Another is that he even *wants* to. Another crucial point is the assumption that the film directors that Tsui co-opts are weedy people with no defences. Many film directors are actually tough cookies who're over-seeing a large group of creative people. (Another factor is that the roles of director, producer and manager can be more vaguely demarcated than in the Western film industry, which's thoroughly unionized).

But there's no doubt that Tsui Hark is a force of nature, an immensely talented, ambitious and driven personality with seemingly boundless energy who's dedicated a substantial part of his life to movies and television. And apart from directors such as Wong Jing, few talents in Hong Kong cinema or Chinese cinema have been so productive. (Also, the accusations that Tsui has stepped into a director's territory have occurred too many times for there not to be some truth in it).

TSUI HARK THE ACTOR.

As an actor, Tsui Hark has done brief cameos, longer cameos, and full roles. As well as cameos in his own movies, Tsui has worked for other directors (such as *Yes, Madam!*, Corey Yuen Kwai, 1985, and *Final Victory*, Patrick Tam, 1987). His finest turn was as 'Big Bo' in *Final Victory*, according to Stephen Teo (1997, 157).

Tsui Hark also appears in *It Takes Two* (1982), *The Winter of 1905* (1982), *Twinkle Twinkle Little Star* (1983), *All the Wrong Spies* (1983), *Run, Tiger, Run* (1985), *Kung Hei Fat Choy* (1985), *Happy Ghost 3* (1986), *I Love Maria* (1988), and *The Big Heat* (1988).

Here's a fuller list: Tsui Hark has appeared in the following movies:

• *It Takes Two* (Karl Maka, 1982), with Tsui as a priest who poses as a gangster.

• The first two *Aces Go Places* movies: *Aces Go Places* (Eric Tsang, 1982), as a ballet stage manager, and *Aces Go Places 2* (Eric Tsang,

---
5 This has also occurred with Jackie Chan – during *Crime Story*, for instance, where Chan apparently took over from Kirk Wong.

1983), with Tsui as a madman.
 • *All the Wrong Spies* (Teddy Robin Kwan, 1983), a spy spoof sequel to *All the Wrong Clues* (which Tsui helmed), with Tsui as 'Hiroshima Tora'.
 • *Run, Tiger, Run* (John Woo, 1985), a reworking of *The Prince and the Pauper*, which was made in Taiwan and had Tsui as a grandfather figure.
 • *Yes, Madam* (Corey Yuen Kwai, 1985), known as the break-out movie for Michelle Yeoh, featured Tsui as one of three con men (John Sham and Mang Hoi were the others);
 • *Happy Ghost 3* (1986) was part of Cinema City's comedy franchise; Tsui was the 'Godfather' who matches up spirits with their homes.
 • *Final Victory* (Patrick Tam, 1987), playing a nasty gangster ('Big Bo') in a white suit.

TSUI HARK AND CHINA.

Tsui Hark is heavily invested in the theme of nationality, and China, and Chinese nationality, and Chinese identity, and Chinese history. It is a central theme in his cinema. Even in the fantasy martial arts movies, issues such as Chinese history are also being explored. It's not only the *Once Upon a Time In China* series that tackles the question of China's relationship with the rest of the world. Some of Tsui's movies are *very* Chinese, and *very* dense with Chinese tradition – so that Western audiences confess to confusion. 'Tsui has always been the most traditionally Chinese of Hong Kong directors' (Lisa Morton, 98).

In fact, one aspect of Tsui Hark's cinema, both as producer and director, is that it is entirely grounded in Chinese characters, Chinese stories, and Chinese issues. Nearly all of Tsui's films feature Chinese characters as the main characters, for instance. Thus, it might not be a coincidence that the two movies regarded as disappointments, the two 'American' films, *Knockoff* and *Double Team*, had a white European as the main protagonist.

Tsui Hark has tended to focus on making films in China – in Hong Kong and the New Territories, mainly, but also in Mainland China and Taiwan (his first movie, *The Butterfly Murders*, was filmed in Taiwan, and he was filming on the Mainland from early in his career). Why? Because Tsui is concerned with Chinese history and culture: most of his films feature Chinese characters in the main roles, for instance. Not Americans in China, not Europeans in China, but Chinese in China (or Chinese abroad).

Of course, an international filmmaker such as Tsui Hark has also filmed in locations such as South France, Italy, Paris and Los Angeles. And for film festivals and awards and the career that goes with being a film director, Tsui is everywhere.

Tsui Hark has raided Ancient Chinese legends several times – *The Four Great Tales of China*, for instance, are *The Tale of the White Snake* (used in *Green Snake*), *The Story of a Tragic Love* (adapted in *The Lovers*), *The Cowherd and the Weaving Maid* and *Seeking Her Husband At the Great Wall*. Tsui remarked he wanted to make movies with Hollywood's production values but with a Chinese sensibility.

Tsui Hark said he has always wanted to make a movie featuring the Monkey King,[6] a famous mythological figure in Chinese culture. In the end, it was Jet Li who appeared as the Monkey King instead, in *Forbidden Kingdom* (2008). But there have been many appearances of the Monkey King in recent movies and television shows – the *Journey To the West* story has been told many times in the Chinese media. Indeed, one of Tsui's biggest hits economically as a director was the *Journey To the West* sequel of 2017, which finally featured the Monkey King.

Altho' we think of Tsui Hark as a supremely Chinese filmmaker, he was in fact born in Saigon in Vietnam, and only moved to Hong Kong when he was thirteen or fourteen (so he is really a Vietnamese/ Chinese filmmaker). Tsui has become devoted to notions of Chineseness and the history of China in his cinema. Stephen Teo relates Tsui's deep fascination with Chinese history and culture to his background as a Vietnamese/ Chinese citizen, to being an overseas Chinese, not born on the Mainland or in Hong Kong.

Tsui Hark has been criticized for his nationalistic politics, and the denunciations of foreign cultures in his movies. But you can probably find issues of nationalism in most major film directors, and certainly most film cultures around the world use nationalism of some kind in most of their movies. In the West, we almost can't see it, because it's everywhere. But if you watch a lot of Asian movies then come back to a North American movie, it's striking just how strong the nationalism is. (However, some nations neighbouring China have an ambiguous attitude towards the country, and they certainly don't admire it as passionately as Tsui does).

And after a while, you get sick to hell of watching North American movies which crow about the U.S.A.'s dumb family values, its vacuous but all-pervasive capitalism, and, most disturbing of all, North America's war-mongering, its insistence on maintaining, at colossal expense ($798 billion a year in 2021), the military-industrial machine, its pro-military politics, and its insistence on the right to bear weapons: this is what I call 'Amerika Über Alles'.

That Tsui Hark is keenly interested in Chinese history and modern politics is easy to spot: it forms the background of some of his most celebrated works, from *Once Upon a Time In China* to *Seven Swords*. But Tsui doesn't employ historical events to stage spectacle cinema (in the manner of David Lean or Steven Spielberg); there is more to it than that (not least is Tsui's unabashed nationalism, his devotion to the idea of China). Tsui says: 'China has such deep cultural resources – it's just that we haven't utilised them yet'.

Stephen Teo, one of the better critics on Chinese cinema, pointed out that Tsui Hark's movies employ some of the icons and clichés of Chinese culture (such as acupuncture, martial arts, Peking Opera) in order to help make the movies appealing to outsiders. Yes – but as Tsui himself has noted, in the New Wave of Hong Kong cinema, the filmmakers were producing movies for the *local market*, *not* for the global market (that came

---

6 And a monkey-man does appear in *Iron Monkey*.

later). But there's no doubt that Tsui in the movies he directs likes to evoke traditional, Chinese culture and practices – but you could see that as a way of presenting the clichés and icons back to the home audience (just as every American Western flick contains numerous iconic elements which sell the cowboy and frontier lifestyle back to the American audience).

Stephen Teo also talks of 'cultural nationalism', more an emotional desire among Chinese people living abroad for Chinese culture. Chinese nationalism, Teo asserts, is found everywhere in Chinese cinema, from *kung fu* flicks to New Wave films, from Mandarin historical epics to Cantonese melodramas (1997, 110-1). In the *kung fu* movies of the 1970s, Teo identified an abstract nationalism in which *kung fu* heroes were using traditions (often from Shaolin) to fight foreign Manchus to restore the Chinese race (1997, 113).

As more of the Hong Kong film industry angled its products at Mainland China, Tsui Hark was conscious of the limitations that it put upon filmmakers: 'In the last 10 years Hong Kong movies have been gradually moving to the market in China', Tsui said in *Hyphen* magazine in 2011. 'And in that market, there is some degree of restriction on the subjects of the films we can make. We are very much constrained by the kind of rules and taboos of the censorship bureau'.

IDENTITY.

French philosopher Julia Kristeva (b. 1941) has developed a fascinating conception notion of the 'outsider'. Being exiled from Bulgaria helped Kristeva see both her own country and her adopted country (France) more clearly. Her experience of displacement was an ingredient in her idea of the 'cosmopolitan' individual, the 'intellectual dissident'. As Kristeva knows, strangeness or otherness (being a foreigner) is fundamental to being human: as Kristeva put it, *étrangers à nous-mêmes* (we are strangers to ourselves). In *Strangers To Ourselves* Kristeva describes the foreigner as the 'cold orphan', motherless, a 'devotee of solitude', a 'fanatic of absence', alone even in a crowd, arrogant, rejected, yet oddly happy (1991, 4-5). The stranger is always in motion, doesn't belong anywhere, to 'any time, any love' (ib., 7).

Julia Kristeva's notion of strangeness or otherness relates directly to the poet Arthur Rimbaud's 'Je est un autre ('I is an other')', Rimbaud's sense of exile and otherness. Living with a foreigner, then, in Kristeva's view, means not just accepting them but being them:

> Rimbaud's *Je est un autre* was not only the acknowledgement of the psychotic ghost that haunts poetry. The word foreshadowed the exile, the possibility or necessity to be foreign and to live in a foreign country, thus heralding the art of living of a modern era, the cosmopolitanism of those who have been flayed. (1991, 13)

This throws light on Tsui Hark's cultural identity as an overseas

Chinese man, always dreaming of China, the homeland.

TSUI HARK'S COLLABORATORS.

Tsui Hark has worked with pretty much everybody in the Hong Kong film industry (and more recently on the Mainland). This is a partial list: the following actors have been important in the development of Tsui Hark's career:[7] Sylvia Chang, Brigitte Lin, Jet Li, Eric Tsang,[8] Leslie Cheung, Karl Maka, Chow Yun-fat, Jacky Cheung, Maggie Cheung, Waise Lee, Lau Shun, Sammo Hung Kam-bo, Rosamund Kwan, Anita Mui, Tony Leung Ka-fai, Joey Wang, Teddy Robin,[9] John Sham, Sally Yeh, Raymond Wong Pak-min, and Vincent Zhao.

Other regular actors in Tsui Hark's cinema include: Kenny Bee, Yuen Biao, Cheriie Cheung, David Chiang, Paul Chun, Paul Chu, Norman Chu, Kent Cheng, Adam Cheng, Andy Lau, Lau Ching-wan, Lau Siu-ming, Carman Lee, Loletta Lee, Leon Lai, Sam Hui, Dean Shek, George Lam, Michelle Reiss, Max (Benny) Mok, Carrie Ng, Tony Leung Chiu-wai, Wu Ma, Anthony Wong, Kenneth Tsang, Elvis Tsui, Donnie Yen, Ti Lung, Fennie Yuen, Charlie Yeung, Yan Yee-kwan, Nicky Wu, Jean Wong, Yu Rong-guang, Anita Yuen, Kenny Lin, Zhou Xun, Stephen Chow and Yuen Wah.

Producers Raymond Chow, Nansun Shi Nan-sheng, Leonard Ho, Terence Chang, Karl Maka, Chen Kuo-fu, Huang Jianxin and Ng See-yuen. (Tsui clearly learned plenty from producers such as Chow and Ho, and rapidly became a major player himself – founding Film Workshop five years or so after directing his first feature film). Writers such as Roy Szeto Chak-hon, Charcoal Cheung Tan, Ng Man-fai, Koan Hui, and Sharon Hui Sa-long.

An important collaborator with Tsui Hark was writer Sze-To Cheuk-Hon (a.k.a. Roy Szeto or Szeto Chak-Hon, b. 1954), the author of *All the Wrong Clues, Dangerous Encounter, Zu: Warriors From the Magic Mountain, Shanghai Blues* and *Once Upon a Time In China and America.* Szeto also wrote the *Lucky Stars* movies, the *Mr Vampire* movies, *The Emperor and the White Snake,* and Jackie Chan movies such as *Armor of God* and *Dragons Forever.*

Composers James Wong Jim, Joseph Koo, Lowell Lo, Mark Lui Chang-dak, David Wu, Romeo Diaz, William Hu, Teddy Robin Kwan, Kenji Kawai, and Woo Wai-laap. (This stable of composers is not to be underestimated: music is a very big deal in Tsui's cinema).

Composer James Wong Jim has delivered more pieces of music (and songs) for Tsui Hark than anyone else; the incredible Wong, one of those composers who can turn his hand to anything (*very* useful to have on any production), has also appeared as an actor many times. Joseph Koo is another oft-used composer (beginning with *The Butterfly Murders* and the *Better Tomorrow* films).

---

[7] The same actors crop up in movies of the 1980s and 1990s which Tsui Hark either directed, produced, co-wrote or acted in: Sally Yeh, Sylvia Chang, John Sham, Joey Wong, Eric Tsang, Teddy Robin, Karl Maka, Chow Yun-fat, Tony Leung, Leslie Cheung, Kenny Bee, Jet Li, Carrie Ng, Waise Lee, Brigitte Lin, Sammo Hung, etc.

[8] Eric Tsang is another Tsui collaborator – a Cinema City honcho, a director/ writer/ producer with numerous credits, he has worked many times with Tsui.

[9] Teddy Robin Kwan is one of the key figures in Hong Kong cinema of this period – he provided the score for *Black Mask*, directed the *All the Wrong Clues* sequel, and acted in *Working Class, All the Wrong Clues, Twin Dragons* and *It Takes Two*.

For some of the foreign prints of the movies of Tsui Hark (and John Woo), Western rock music was added – Peter Gabriel, the Alan Parsons Project, Jeff Beck, etc (presumably by distributors or companies or producers who thought that rock/ pop music would appeal to Western audiences). But it isn't a good fit – either cinematically or culturally. Altho' we can enjoy the pop music on its own, the original scores would be much preferred, for numerous reasons.

Editors Marco Mak Chi-sin, Gam Ma, Angie Lam On-yee, Poon Hung, Peter Cheung and David Wu Tai-wai (also composer). The significance of editors hardly needs to be mentioned in connection with the films directed, produced and written by Tsui.

DPs such as Arthur Wong (who's probably worked with Tsui Hark more than any DP), David Chung, Peter Pau (*Crouching Tiger, Hidden Dragon*), Lau Moon-tong (Tom Lau), [10] Hermann Yau Lai-to, Andrew Lau Wai-keung (not the singer/ actor – later a director of very Tsui-ian movies like *The Stormriders*), Poon Hang-sang, and Wong Wing-hang. Johnny Choi Sung-fai became Tsui's regular DP from *Seven Swords* onwards.

For such a visually sophisticated and inventive director as Tsui Hark, the on-set relationship with the cinematographer is absolutely vital.

Sometimes five or more DPs are credited on some productions. Why? Because Tsui Hark goes thru DPs like no one else – some only last a day before they're fired. Keeping up with Tsui is very challenging. As Arthur Wong explained:

> Tsui is very creative, but he changes his mind every minute. So sometimes, even though you've done a lot and a lot of preparation, suddenly he comes up with an idea and changes everything! And, he won't even give you enough time! That's the problem! He keeps pushing you, pushing you, pushing, squeezing you, and hurrying you. (D. Vivier)

Production designers William Cheung,[11] Bill Lui and Ma Poon-chiu. (Tsui has done production design himself, as has his ex-wife, Nansun Shi Nan-sheng).

And action directors Tony Ching Siu-tung, Yuen Woo-ping, Yuen Bun, Xiong Xin-xin, Cheung Yiu-sing, Wong Shu Tong, Ma Yuk-shing, Stephen Tung and Corey Yuen Kwai.

Action directors such as Yuen Bun, Yuen Woo-ping, Tony Ching Siu-tung and Xiong Xin-xin are vital in the cinema of Tsui Hark: they are the people, with their tough, hard-working stunt teams, who co-ordinate the action sequences (often appearing in them, too, as actors). Bun, for instance, has credits on a large number of Tsui movies.

MORE ON TSUI HARK'S COLLABORATORS.
NG SEE-YUEN.

A key influence on Tsui Hark's career, and in the *Once Upon a Time In*

---
10 DP for *The Magic Crane, Once Upon a Time In China 5, The Swordsman 2* and *3, A Chinese Ghost Story 1* and *3*, etc.
11 Cheung has credits on many of Tsui Hark's movies, and most of Wong Kar-wai's films.

China movies, was the producer, Ng See-yuen (known as 'N.G.'), who had backed Tsui Hark's first movie, *The Butterfly Murders* (Ng also co-produced *New Dragon Gate Inn* with Tsui, plus *We're Going To Eat You, Twin Dragons* and others). Ng (b. 1944, Shanghai) was a major force in Cantonese cinema, starting out (like so many others) at Shaw Brothers (in 1967), and forming his own production company, Seasonal Films, in 1975 (some say 1973). N.G. was one of the first to recognize the importance of Bruce Lee, and tried to convince Run Run Shaw to sign Lee to Shaws.

N.G. has directing credits, writing credits, acting credits and producer credits. He is an industry advisor on many boards and festivals. N.G. is also the founder of Ultimate Movie Experience International Cineplex, a chain of cinemas in China (including an IMAX theatre in Beijing).

Ng See-yuen's movies included the *Secret Rituals* films, *Anti-Corruption* (1975), *Bruce Lee: The Man, the Myth, The Invincible Armour* (1977), *Dance of the Drunk Mantis* and *Drunken Master 2*. N.G. saw the potential of Jackie Chan, and put him in the two important early Chan movies *Snake In Eagle's Shadow* and *Drunken Master* (both 1978, and both directed by Yuen Woo-ping), which made Chan a superstar. ('It was a partnership that was as good as any I've had in my life', Chan said: 'in every way that mattered, this was the first *real* Jackie Chan picture').

Ng See-yuen also introduced Jean-Claude van Damme to the world (in *No Retreat, No Surrender*) – van Damme would later star in two of Tsui Hark's movies, *Knockoff* and *Double Team*. Other credits of N.G.'s include: *Game of Death II, Ninja in the Dragon's Den, The Unwritten Law, The King of the Kickboxers, Superfights, The Soong Sisters, Legendary Assassin, Bloodmoon, Evening of Roses, Kung Fu Wing Chun,* and *The Grandmaster*.

THE FILM EDITORS.

Marco Mak Chi-sin (b. Nov 6, 1951) is Tsui Hark's regular editor (along with David Wu Tai-wai and Angie Lam On-yee). He has edited not only a high proportion of Tsui's movies as director but also Tsui's producer movies (such as the *Swordsman* and *Chinese Ghost Story* series, plus *The Magic Crane, The Era of Vampires* and *Iron Monkey*). Other credits include *The Stormriders,* the *Conmen* films, and *The Duel* (and several for Wong Jing). Mak is thus a vital collaborator in the world of Tsui's cinema, which puts such a high premium on editing. (Mak has been editing since 1977, and has also directed fifteen movies, including *Xanda, Dancing Lion, Set To Kill, The Wall* and *Haunted Office*).

David Wu Tai-wai (b. 1952) is another of many unsung contributors to the Tsui Hark empire – a regular editor and composer, Wu has directed as well as appeared in Tsui's movies. Wu also edited most of the celebrated John Woo movies. As Bey Logan pointed out, Wu is a key influence on the editing of action cinema, not only in Hong Kong (purely for his work with Woo – add Tsui and Ronny Yu, and you have a very formidable editor of action movies). Wu said he didn't have to talk with Tsui or Woo – they were in sync, and knew what they were doing.

Angie Lam On-yee (b. 1965) is another superstar cutter in Hong Kong. She is particularly brilliant with cutting action sequences. Her C.V. includes *Hero, House of Flying Daggers, Tai-Chi Master, Fong Sai-yuk 2, The Bodyguard From Beijing, C.J. 7, Kung Fu Hustle, The Warlords,* and numerous movies for Tony Ching, John Woo and Tsui Hark (beginning with *Once Upon a Time In China 2* in 1992).

What must it be like being Tsui Hark's editor?! Does the director visit the editing suite and ask of Angie Lam, Marco Mak or David Wu, 'can we make it go even faster?'!

Sometimes it seems as if editors Mak, Lam and Wu are like the crazy cannibals in *We're Going To Eat You*: when Mak, Lam and Wu get going on the celluloid pouring through the cutting rooms each and every day during production, they are chop-chop-chopping like mad axemen who haven't been fed for days. *Slash!* – there goes a gag they liked for about the first 22 times they saw it; *chop!* – there goes a bit where Jet Li turns to grin at Rosamund Kwan (we don't need that, it's covered elsewhere); and *wheee!* – there goes an entire action sequence which took the stunt team weeks to film. Why was it cut out?

Because it's not fast enough!

JET LI.

Jet Li was born on April 26, 1963 in Hebel, China. (In Cantonese, Li's name is Lei Lin Git; in Mandarin, it's Li Lanjie). Li is short (5' 6"), but can take on anyone in movies. Li won the first national *wushu* competition in China since the Cultural Revolution (aged 9); he was the Chinese Men's All-round National Wushu Champion at the age of twelve. (*Wushu* is a form of martial arts as performance, combining Peking Opera, gymnastics, and colourful costumes, developed during the Cultural Revolution). Li moved to San Francisco with a Chinese actress (Huang Qiuyan) in 1988; they married (1987-90) and had two daughters. In the U.S.A., Li received his Green Card. Li later married actress Nina Li Chi (they have two daughters).

Jet Li appeared in several martial arts movies[12] right after the first *Once Upon a Time In China* film, including *Tai Chi Master, New Legend of Shaolin* (about Hung Gar), the *Fong Say-yuk* films, *Last Hero In China*, and *Kung Fu Cult Master* (a.k.a. *Evil Cult*).

Tsui Hark didn't want Jet Li to play villains, and always cast him as the hero. Tsui wasn't convinced by Hollywood's use of Li as a villain (in movies such as *Lethal Weapon 4*); it didn't work, and Li didn't look right, Tsui said. Tsui wanted Li to play the hero, the character who tries to do the right thing. 'When he stars in my movies, he must be a heroic figure'.

One should also note here Tsui Hark's genius with casting. Rarely commented upon by critics (tho' discussed endlessly by fans), casting is enormously important in a movie. And it's not an easy job. Tsui certainly has a knack for finding new talent, for getting the right people for the roles (he has also created roles specially for certain actors), and also for filling in the secondary roles and the character roles with suitable people.

---

12 Jet Li didn't make much money from his Shaolin pictures (he was paid a State subsidy).

BRIGITTE LIN.

Brigitte Lin is... Brigitte Lin. Lin was born in Sanchong, Taiwan on Nov 3, 1954.[13] (she is Lam Ching Hsia in Cantonese, and Lin Qinhxia in Mandarin; she is also known as Venus Lin). Lin was in many Taiwanese films (beginning in 1973) before appearing in Hong Kong films such as *Zu, All the Wrong Spies, Police Story, Peking Opera Blues*, the *Bride With White Hair* films, the *Royal Tramp* films, *New Dragon Gate Inn,* Wong Kar-wai movies such as *Chungking Express* and *Ashes of Time,* and the *Swordsman* series.

Brigitte Lin is one of the most remarkable of all recent Asian stars. She 'must certainly be one of the most fearless performers in the world' (Lisa Morton, 101). Lin, tho' straight, is known for playing lesbian and crossdressing women in films such as *All the Wrong Spies* (a lesbian disguising herself as a guy), *Fantasy Mission Force* (she shoots the clothes off a tied-up woman), *The Swordsman 3* (she's a lesbian transsexual superhero), *New Dragon Gate Inn* (steals another woman's clothes for herself), *Peking Opera Blues* (she wears men's military uniforms), *Boys Are Easy* (she's a lesbian cop), *Ashes of Time* (she plays both a brother and a sister), *Eagle Shooting Heroes* (she's a butch princess), and *Fire Dragon* (she's a masked male warrior).

Brigitte Lin's crossdressing or transgender character in the *Swordsman* movies (as Dongfang Bubai = Asia the Invincible) draws on the Peking Opera tradition (where actors can be both warriors and princesses. Indeed, the Tsui Hark movie *Peking Opera Blues* explores issues of gender[14] at length).

Brigitte Lin, according to Bey Logan, was one of the few bankable female stars in Asia: 'basically, all the ageless Ms Lin has to do is wave her arms and smile enigmatically and local audiences will pay to watch' (166).

Tsui Hark has tried to entice Brigitte Lin back to acting – for the remake of *Zu: Warriors From the Magic Mountain* in 2001, for instance, and to play the Empress Wu in *Detective Dee and the Mystery of the Phantom Flame*. Lin retired from acting in 1994, when she married businessman Michael Ying and had children.

❂

OTHER ACTORS.

Lau Shun is one of Tsui Hark's favourite character actors, and he's appeared in probably more Tsui movies than anyone else. Lau can do anything – from bumbling, comical servants to imperious government officials to insane sorcerers and deities. (Tsui had originally brought Lau in to advise on Peking Opera culture in *Peking Opera Blues*).

Charlie Yeung Choi-nei (b. 1974) is one of Tsui Hark's favourite actresses: following her winning turn in *The Lovers*, she appeared in *Love In the Time of Twilight, Catching Monkey 3-D* and was the lead in *Seven Swords* (among others, such as *Ashes of Time, Fallen Angels* and *Dr Wai*).

---
13 Some sources say 1957.
14 Peking Opera had a huge impact on the young Tsui Hark – including the play with gender.

Yeung is the classic Tsui Hark Girl – small and slightly-built, tomboyish yet feminine, soft but also tough, and with classical, Chinese features. Yeung retired in 1997, at the height of her fame, but returned to movies in 2004 (with *New Police Story*, and she appeared in *Seven Swords* in 2005).

Xiong Xin-xin (b. 1965), has numerous credits as a stunt co-ordinator and actor. He's one of those faces that you see in many Chinese movies of the 1990s and 2000s, including many of Tsui Hark's films. Xiong has been Jet Li's stunt double since 1986 (on *Shaolin Temple 3*).

❂

One should note again that actors – and crew too – are attracted to great filmmakers like Tsui Hark (or Ken Russell or Orson Welles or Akira Kurosawa) because they get to do things that few others ask them to do. The canvas, the world, the stories that the great film directors move in are huge.

Jean-Luc Godard said that it was natural for him to say to his actors and crew: 'give me more. Let's do what has not been done'.[15] One gets the impression that it's the same with Tsui Hark.

Altho' Tsui Hark has a reputation of being a little demanding on set at times, I would imagine that many actors and crew are happy to work with him. For the simple reason that they know that their work will be seen by millions of people. Which's what it's all about. They also know that Tsui is one of the great, celebrated talents in Asian cinema, and that working on a Tsui movie raises their own profile considerably.

Another reason that actors and crew want to work with Tsui Hark is that he is a powerful presence in the Chinese film business – his movies will get released, a lot of people will see them, they won't be re-cut by studios or backers (or censored – usually), the marketing and promotion will be good, they will be reviewed, and they will have an after-life on TV, cable, DVD, etc.[16]

CASTING POP STARS.

In casting many performers from the world of pop music, Tsui Hark said he and his production teams did that partly because they were seeking acting styles that were different from the stylizations of the old Shaw Brothers movies (which they grew up on), and different from the stylizations of television acting. And, besides, it didn't hurt that pop icons already had a built-in audience and fan base (include teens). Also, pop stars were used to performing and expressing themselves: as Tsui explained:

> I like to use singers in my films because they are already experienced in communicating their feelings to an audience.[17]

Cantopop stars include Alan Tam, Andy Lau, Karen Mok, Aaron Kwok,

---
15 Quoted in A. Sarris, 1968.
16 All actors, East or West, have been in or know about projects that were sat on for years, or never got released, or were distributed poorly, or were hacked about by distributors or studios.
17 Quoted in B. Logan, 181.

Jacky Cheung, Leslie Cheung, Anita Mui, Ekin Cheng and Leon Lai (most of whom have appeared in Tsui Hark's movies).

The 'Four Golden Kings' – singers Leslie Cheung, Andy Lau, Jackie Cheung and Leon Lai – were hugely popular in the 1980s and 1990s. And, as Bey Logan noted, and as we know well, the 'Four Golden Kings' have appeared in numerous Hong Kong movies. In the West, Logan reckoned that it would be like the Osmonds and the Jackson Five uniting for a remake of *The Wild Bunch* (179).

In Asian cinema, casting pop stars has worked so many times. There isn't the stigma attached to using pop musicians as there is in the West (even so, Western cinema has cast from the world of pop and rock numerous times, with some incredible results: Prince in *Purple Rain,* Mick Jagger in *Performance*, Kris Kristofferson in *Pat Garrett and Billy the Kid* and *Heaven's Gate,* and David Bowie in *The Man Who Fell To Earth*).

COMICS.

Tsui Hark is a big fan of Japanese *manga* and *anime*[18] (who isn't?!), and also Asian types of comicbooks, such as *manhwa* (Korean *manga*), and *manwua* (Chinese *manga*).[19] As his wife Nansun Shi puts it, comics are 'Tsui's one big vice' (LM, 224). 'I wanted to be a comic artist', Tsui remembered of his youth (LM, 19).[20] He reads lots of *manga* and other comics: 'because those things are very interesting to me' (ibid.). Tsui draws a lot, including when he's shooting, and he also paints. For Tsui, drawing is a great way of expressing visual ideas.

Manga have moved into many Asian territories, such as Taiwan, Hong Kong, Thailand and South Korea (Thailand is a major market for Japanese *manga*, and all of the main Japanese boys' and some girls' magazines are published there). And Korea has developed an animation industry increasingly in the past few decades (so it's now the third largest producer of animation after Japan and the U.S.A.).

Conversely, one of the biggest markets for Chinese action movies, and Hong Kong action cinema in particular, is Japan. You only have to look at any *manga* or *anime* to see the influence of Chinese action movies (and in particular anything starring Jackie Chan).

And the influence of comicbook style and visuals on the cinema of Tsui Hark is obvious everywhere. Tsui has deployed the comics approach many, many times – even the epic sweep of the history of China evoked in the *Once Upon a Time In China* series is cartoony. And comics pacing and storytelling – which, in Japanese *manga*, is *incredibly* fast, and yet has time for 'pillow moments' and interludes, for character-based scenes (the real impact of Japanese *manga* is in the areas of characters and storytelling). By contrast, Tsui finds N. American comics over-rich (their colours) and too slow (LM, 19).

And Tsui Hark has had a go at making artwork for comics – such as

---

18 'I like Miyazaki a lot' (LM, 31).
19 One reason that *manga* proved popular in Korea, Taiwan and Hong Kong was because the reading system was the same: from right-to-left and from top to bottom. Which meant that publishers didn't need to flip and re-format the pages..
20 He drew a lot as a kid partly because he was inspired by animated films (LM, 31).

Ma Wing-shong's *Red Snow* (1999). Using Photoshop software, Tsui has created images for comicbooks (he says it takes 4 hours to produce an image). Tsui appreciates how cheap drawing is for trying out ideas:

> with drawing you can just start over and do it again. You put it down and look at it and you see the right reaction without really costing a lot of money or causing a lot of commotion because of something going wrong. (LM, 19)

There are numerous *manga* that one could cite in connection with Tsui Hark's cinema: samurai epics are obvious choices (*Lone Wolf and Cub, Vagabond, Yongbi, Lady Snowblood, Blade of the Immortal*), historical stories (*Buddha, Hero Tales),* fantasy and horror comics (*Akira, Ogre Slayer, Urotsukidoji, Hellsing, Mushishi*), alien babes and goofy guys and harem stories (*Urusei Yatsura, Love Hina, Oh! My Goddess*), gangster/ thriller adventures (*Lupin III, Gunsmith Cats*), hi-tech cyber yarns (*Ghost In the Shell, Appleseed*), and of course the giant franchises of *manga* like *One Piece, Bleach* and *Naruto*.

Indeed, some *manga* come across as Tsui Hark movies: deadly female assassins in *Lady Snowblood* and *Ghost In the Shell*; wispy, wistful other-worldly women and goddesses in *Oh! My Goddess*; epic re-interpretations of ancient history in Osamu Tezuka's incredible *Buddha;* action-adventure in *Lupin III*; and ninja hurtling thru the treetops in *Basilisk* and *Naruto*.

The first animated movie that Tsui Hark saw was *Bambi* (1942) – and it's the same for many filmmakers: many saw a Disney movie as their first movie of any kind (Steven Spielberg, Woody Allen, Hayao Miyazaki, etc). Tsui recalled that his mom wouldn't let him see *Snow White and the Seven Dwarfs* (1937) because there was kissing (!), and because the heroine wore a low-cut dress. But *Bambi* – all animals – was OK. When Tsui later saw *Snow White*, he called it 'my most favorite movie', with a level of artistry and intricacy that's almost impossible to reproduce today.

VISUAL EFFECTS AND TECHNIQUE.

Tsui Hark is a filmmaker who foregrounds the tricks and visual effects of cinema, often in a self-conscious, stagey manner. Western filmmakers who also take this approach include: Orson Welles, Jean Cocteau, Walerian Borowczyk, Sergei Paradjanov, Tim Burton, Vincente Minnelli, Terry Gilliam, Powell & Pressburger, Ken Russell, and Francis Coppola.

Visual effects are one of Tsui Hark's chief concerns in cinema: from *Zu: Warriors From the Magic Mountain* onwards,[21] Tsui has attempted to develop a sophisticated and technically accomplished visual effects resource in China. This has involved nurturing visual effects teams and technical back-up and the infra-structure to make it all possible from scratch. Critics find this aspect of Tsui's cinema very difficult to analyze.

It's the same with crucial elements such as editing and cinemato-

---

21 As well as the optical and comping visual effects, there is animation, stopmotion, miniatures, and special make-up.

graphy. Critics have no idea how movies are edited, and how vital the process is. Film critics will mention that Tsui Hark's movies are ✂✂✂ rapidly, but that's as far as they go. They have little knowledge of the editorial process.

Tsui Hark says that special effects are there to help the story – but they're not the *raison d'être* of the film, nor the reason why the film is good or bad.

WOMEN AND FEMINISM.

Unlike many of his contemporaries, the films directed/ produced/ written by Tsui Hark offer many great roles for women. Not only are there juicy dramatic roles, but plenty of comical ones, too. Tsui's movies celebrate *active* women, proactive women, busy women, women who drive the plot with their desires, their hopes and dreams.[22] While ancient, mediæval and modern Chinese society might be patriarchal through and through, Tsui fills his films with strong and resourceful women, who are three-dimensional characters. Tsui remarked:

> I think I'm trying to do something where the women are less predictable and a stronger character.

The turning-point for Tsui Hark in terms of the roles of women in his cinema was 1984:

> So, I think 1984 was a very critical moment when I decided to write about women and simply ignore the men's characters for one project that was called *Shanghai Blues*. I know so many friends that were actresses like Brigitte Lin and they felt very frustrated for having no scripts written about women. That's why after all these experiences with these people; I decided to start making movies with these people being the priority character of the story.

The crossdressing and gender-bending in Tsui Hark's cinema focusses on women – women dressing up as men. No one can fail to notice that the women tend to be tomboyish (the Tsui Hark Girl is short, slim and a tomboy), hinting at the homoeroticism of the romances with men, as well as father complex women (in common with most women in adventure and fantasy fiction). Another recurring motif is a gorgeous woman who turns out to be either an ugly woman underneath, or a guy.[23]

In the historical pictures, the Tsui Hark Girl is typically a proud warrior, a tomboy great at fighting assailants (and with a few moves of her own). She's stubborn, even difficult, but has a soft, feminine side underneath (which she only reveals reluctantly, and only to the hero). Sometimes the Tsui Hark Girl is a punky, aggressive personality, with suitable accessories like tattoos and jewellery. Another Tsui-ian female type is the Kook. She's batty, scatter-brained, clumsy and adorable. She dresses

---
22 A woman who defies tradition is 'something that's very dramatic' for Tsui Hark (LM, 21).
23 Maybe Tsui had a terrible experience with a woman who was actually a man or transvestite, because this scenario pops up so many times in his cinema!

funny, and wears big, Eighties glasses (i.e., she's a female version of Tsui himself).

Far fewer critics tackle the issues of feminism and the role of women in Tsui Hark's cinema.[24] It's not one of Tsui's primary themes, for sure (altho' some critics claim it is),[25] but in the subplots of his pictures (and not only in the romantic subplots), issues revolving around women are explored. 'Tsui Hark's women triumph by remaining or becoming feminine', reckoned Lisa Morton (LM, 13). On the one hand, there is certainly a proto-feminism at work in Tsui's cinema, tho' I'm sure many feminists could find plenty of material to back up their argument that women are portrayed in negative, demeaning and exploitative lights in Tsui's movies (the lesbian lovers in *Time and Tide,* for instance).

The cinema of Tsui Hark features strong, independent women, yes, but some Hong Kong movies have gone further in depicting wild women who can wield guns and kick ass – the *Naked Killer* movies, for instance, or the films of Wong Jing.

SEQUELS AND FRANCHISES.

Many of Tsui Hark's movies as producer and director have been remakes and sequels. But Tsui does something very different with the existing material every time: there is never a feeling that Tsui is rehashing a story, or warming up a corpse. (Compared to Western sequels and remakes, those of Tsui are in a wholly different realm). Tsui has even remade earlier movies he's directed (*Zu: Warriors From the Magic Mountain* and *Flying Swords of Dragon Gate*), as have filmmakers like Alfred Hitchcock and Tim Burton.

Among the franchises and series that Tsui Hark has contributed to as producer and director are: *Black Mask, Once Upon a Time In China, The Swordsman, Detective Dee, Aces Go Places, All the Wrong Clues, A Better Tomorrow* and *A Chinese Ghost Story.* Very significantly, Tsui has been the originator of many of those movie franchises and series, including *Once Upon a Time In China, The Swordsman, Detective Dee* and *A Chinese Ghost Story.*

As with most filmmakers, the majority of the movies directed/produced by Tsui Hark are adaptations of existing material. Among the movies and stories that Tsui has originated himself are *The Master, Detective Dee, Shanghai Blues, Peking Opera Blues* and *Dangerous Encounters of the First Kind.* (Tsui is not a filmmaker who works predominantly from scripts which are completely original ideas, like Ingmar Bergman and Woody Allen).

REMAKES AND UPDATES.

A very important element of Tsui Hark's cinema is updating and remaking previous movies. Tsui is clearly enamoured of cinema from previous generations, and intent on updating it for a contemporary

---

[24] 'He may also be the world's greatest feminist director', reckoned Lisa Morton (6).
[25] For Lisa Morton, 'the single most defining theme in the œuvre of Tsui Hark, beginning with his very first film', is the deconstruction of male and female roles (LM, 68).

audience. Even though Tsui has occasionally insisted that he is not remaking old movies, because it's disrespectful (*pace Flying Swords* of 2011), some of his most well-known and celebrate movies are remakes and updates: *The Blade* reworks *The One-Armed Swordsman,* the *Once Upon a Time In China* series delivers the familiar *Wong Fei-hung* legend to new audiences, *A Better Tomorrow* is a remake of *True Colors of a Hero, The Taking of Tiger Mountain* is a remake of the famous 1970 production, and *Flying Swords of Dragon Gate* updates both the King Hu-helmed movie of 1967 and Tsui's own *New Dragon Gate Inn* of 1992.

Maggie Lee Man-yuk calls Tsui Hark 'the king of remakes, or, rather, reinvention, drawing on diverse sources and blending genres, tones, and technique with the most imaginative abandon' (2021).

'Not only has he produced or directed films in nearly every conceivable category, he's consistently recreated, resurrected and revitalized dying or stagnant genres', noted Lisa Morton (10). In discussing why he keeps reviving old genres and movies, Tsui Hark said:

> I feel that much of it has to do with my childhood memories, my childhood impressions and my childhood preferences. When I look back at those movies, because of their dated approaches… it's impossible to share these special feelings with the audience today. That's why we're shooting those [old] stories with a contemporary approach.

The adherence to previous genres, forms and movies in Tsui Hark's cinema isn't mere recycling or mindless exploitation (tho' it is that, too). There is more to it than that. At one level, yes, business-wise, it makes sense for all the obvious reasons to update stories and movies that're familiar to audiences (which Hong Kong cinema has always done). But Tsui is doing much more than that. I think he is a true visionary filmmaker, going beyond what many forms of commercial cinema do.

In thriving film cultures, like France, Japan, Korea or the U.S.A., it is completely expected and normal to remake movies and stories all the time. *New actors in old stories* is one of the definitions of the Hollywood movie machine in the glory days of the 1930s thru 1960s, but the phrase still sums up a large proportion of the output of any flourishing filmmaking centre. Often, the remakes and updates are simply old stories dressed up in new clothes, with some new gimmicks to help sell them (such as 3-D,[26] or visual effects, or a postmodern spin on an old chestnut).

But the remakes and updates of Tsui Hark are in a different class, coming from a different place, and operating in a different arena. While Tsui clearly has an *incredibly* keen eye for commercialism and showmanship (you could hire Tsui to over-see any of the big spectacles in the modern era like the Oscars, the Golden Globes, or the opening of the

---

[26] Tsui Hark was interested in 3-D filmmaking immediately it became a possibility again in the 2000s. It would help cinema to compete with TV, the internet and all the other forms of entertainment that audiences could enjoy: 'I think also because movies are sharing audiences' time with TV and the Internet, even with a bigger screen, movies still have to be different from other mediums. Thus when the possibility for 3D came up, it was right away an attraction to me as a filmmaker'.

Olympic Games, whatever, and you'd be guaranteed a real treat), he is also doing much more as a filmmaker.

Hong Kong audiences are used to movies from Canton being different. They know, said Tsui Hark, that a Hong Kong movie won't be normal, will experiment, might not even be understandable or easy, but it will be different (LM, 28).

TSUI HARK'S FLOPS.

Among the movies of Tsui Hark regularly derided by fans and critics are: *The Magic Crane, Twin Dragons, The Master,* both *Black Masks,* with *Double Team* receiving the fiercest venom. *Green Snake* and *Knockoff* divide admirers. (Some also add *Once Upon a Time in China 4*).

I don't agree: *all* of the above movies have their enjoyable aspects, and even *The Master* and *DoubleTeam* aren't as woeful as fans and critics make out. But I care little for *Triangle, Missing* and *All About Women* (movies of 2007 and 2008). And, you'd have to admit, that some of Tsui's choices in the latter part of his career have been a little wayward: *Black Mask 2, Double Team, Triangle, All About Women, Missing* and maybe even *The Legend of Zu* (and yet *Black Mask 2, Double Team* and *The Legend of Zu* contain plenty of entertaining sequences, and some outstanding ones). Of all his attempts at remakes and updates, *The Legend of Zu* was probably a mis-use of his energy and resources. But Tsui roared back to masterpiece form with *Seven Swords*, with the *Detective Dee* movies, and with *Flying Swords of Dragon Gate.*

EDITING.

Tsui Hark's cinema seems to come from someone who never sleeps, who is never bored, who finds every aspect of living in the contemporary world fascinating, and who can operate at a higher level of energy and fever than the rest of us. Lazy, work-shy, boring and restrained are not characteristics you can hurl at Tsui! His stamina and energy are legendary.

Tsui Hark's movies are being edited as he shoots: Tsui likes to see what he's got as he films it. With digital editing workflows, Tsui and his editors can put together scenes quickly (using temporary visual effects, timing and colour grading). Versions of the film, before it's complete, can be sent to producers, distributors, visual effects houses, etc.

Baiyang Yu, Tsui Hark's editorial consultant, commented:

> We had a very good workflow going for several pictures using Final Cut Pro 7. Tsui likes to see things assembled while we shoot, and typically that involves a lot of temporary visual effects compositing, color grading, and retiming. But that meant a lot of time waiting for things to render, and Tsui doesn't like to wait.

And like many filmmakers (such as Stanley Kubrick, George Lucas and Francis Coppola), Tsui Hark likes to work on his productions right up to the very last moment. As Tsui's editor Baiyang Yu noted:

> On *Flying Swords of Dragon Gate* we went through 15 versions and ultimately had to stop when the distributor reminded us the film was about to be released. It's going to be the same for the [*Detective Dee*] prequel. Our editing will not be complete until the last possible moment. We're changing everything all the time.

Like many Chinese action movies, the movies directed and produced by Tsui Hark often employ slow motion, and also step-motion. Indeed, step-motion (a.k.a. step-printed film) occurs just as much as slow motion. True slow motion is of course filmed on the set, with the camera running at higher speeds (48 frames per second or 96 f.p.s. being typical speeds). But step-motion is created after the fact, in the editing room and by optically treating the celluloid in the processing lab (where you can also select different kinds of step-motion). Sometimes Chinese action movies play whole beats of an action scene in step-motion, but with heightened sound effects (and usually a big music cue).

POST-PRODUCTION.

As noted above, the editor of *Flying Swords of Dragon Gate*, Baiyang Yu, said that the movie went thru fifteen different versions in the editing room before they decided on the final cut. Tsui Hark is a film director who, like many filmmakers, works right up to the premiere or general release date, fine-tuning, altering, cutting, re-cutting, rewriting and re-dubbing the movie.[27] So, well, yes, a Tsui Hark movie isn't really 'finished' – rather, the movie is released in the state it reached before the final, absolutely final, definitely-this-time-is-the-real-true-final date.

If they had their way, filmmakers would probably keep tinkering with their movie for days and weeks, which would drag on to months and then years. Orson Welles, Martin Scorsese, Michael Cimino and Francis Coppola, among numerous other filmmakers, liked to spend a *long* time in post-production. The trouble with that is, backers, financers, producers and film studios start crowing for the movie that *they*, *not* the filmmakers, paid for. Yes: commercial filmmakers *don't* pay for the movies they direct and produce and write! It's the financiers, the investors, and the film studios that actually fork out the dough. Consequently, they want a return for their investment, which can only occur when the darn movie is released!

Furthermore, post-production isn't cheap! If it's just Orson Welles and an editorial assistant and one of the Movieolas that Welles carted around Europe, fine, yes, that's not too expensive. And by that time (1950s thru 1970s), Welles was operating outside of the film studio system, and working on very low budget productions.

But in the commercial film business, post-production can be costly, and can involve quite a few people (if it's a visual effects blockbuster show

---

[27] Tsui Hark described post-production as a 'very sensitive, emotional stage', when you are polishing and shaping, and you are very emotionally attached to the movie (LM, 30).

in the West, we're talking sometimes hundreds of people). For a filmmaker with an established reputation and proven track record, like Tsui Hark, it's much easier to exert the power to exploit resources and man-power on a production.

A minor but significant factor in the post-production of movies from the 1990s to today is digital technology: movies are now often cut using Avid or similar systems (Tsui has employed Final Cut Pro, Apple's editing software). For a director like Tsui, this means that multiple versions of scenes and sequences can be created and organized: Tsui is the kind of director who likes to edit scenes and whole movies in a number of ways. You could still do that with celluloid and Movieolas, of course (filmmakers such as Jean-Luc Godard and Steven Spielberg like to edit using real celluloid), but digital editing systems allow for multiple versions to be saved and viewed and compared very quickly. Also, optical effects can be applied instantly, such as fades, wipes, dissolves, slow motion, speed ramping, etc (in the celluloid days, optical effects had to be sent to the film labs, so you had to wait to see them).

CHANG CHEH AND KING HU.

Two Chinese film directors loom large over Tsui Hark's output: Chang Cheh (Zhang Zhe) and King Hu, the directors who pioneered *wuxia* films. They both hailed from Northern China, spoke Mandarin, and employed the Northern styles of the Peking Opera.

Tsui Hark has re-made movies by both directors (as well as working with King Hu on *The Swordsman*), and has clearly been heavily influenced by them. But then, it's impossible for a Chinese filmmaker working in action cinema *not* to be influenced by Chang Che and King Hu – between they directed many of the classics of *kung fu* and martial arts cinema. (Also, many of the performers and crew in Tsui's movies will have worked with both directors).

King Hu (1931-1997), born in Beijing, was the director of classics such as his 'Inn Trilogy' – *Come Drink With Me* (1965), *Dragon Gate Inn* (1967) and *The Fate of Lee Khan* (1973) – and his 'Buddhist Trilogy': the epic (and, for a martial arts movie, very long) *A Touch of Zen* (1970), *Raining In the Mountain* (1979) and *Legend of the Mountain* (1979). Hu worked at Shaw Brothers.

A Touch of Zen is the movie which's King Hu's crowning achievement for many, and which was a big hit at Cannes. *A Touch of Zen* was based on the same material used for the *Chinese Ghost Story* movies: *Liaozhai Zhiyi* by Pu Songling.

For King Hu, *kung fu* was choreographed like dance: 'I've always taken the action part of my films as dancing rather than fighting', Hu said (many others, including Jackie Chan, have thought the same). For him, the tradition of the Peking Opera was crucial in developing a way of staging action in cinema. For critics, the choreography in Hu's films was movement for movement's sake, rather than exploring themes or ideas or stories: altho' Hu's movies touched on Zen Buddhism, Confucianism, chivalry, history, nationalism and the supernatural, Sek Kei remarked, they were really interested in 'a free and unfettered state'.[28]

As well as influencing how martial arts was depicted in Hong Kong cinema, Hu also emphasized roles for women in his movies (which further endears him to Tsui Hark).

Chang Cheh (b.1923, Zhejiang Province, d. 2002) developed a team of collaborators which included Lau Kar-Leung as action director (along with Tang Jia), Bao Xueii, Wu Ma and John Woo. Chang wrote many of his own scripts (often with Ni Kuang). Chang's directing career was based around *wuxia* movies, and then the *kung fu* genre (they were produced at Shaw Brothers).[29] Chang's famous works include *The One-Armed Swordsman* (1967, updated in 1970), *The Golden Swallow, The Chinese Boxer, The Water Margin, Man of Iron, The Brave Archer* and *The Assassin.* (At one time, Chang produced 70 movies in 5 years at Shaws).

The Blade is a swordplay action movie, a re-make of *The One-Armed Swordsman* (*Dubi Dao,* Chang Cheh, 1967). The Shaw Brothers' *The One-Armed Swordsman* was the first Hong Kong movie to gross U.S. $1 million in Hong Kong. *The One-Armed Swordsman* starred Jimmy Wang Yu in 'a muscular, angst-ridden epic of blood-thirsty masculinity that ushered in an entirely new sensibility for martial arts cinema', according to Jeff Yang (50).

TSUI HARK AND JOHN WOO.

One would've expected Tsui Hark to have been the filmmaker who made it biggest in North America[30] (he 'out-Spielbergs Spielberg', quipped Roy Hoban in the *Village Voice*), but John Woo seems to have made the move into the North American film industry more successfully than Tsui. Both are Chinese filmmakers with a keen sense of what works commercially, both possess a strong style, both like making genre pictures (and remaking old movies), and both deliver movies to the key market of young males. (Timing has played a part, as has the kind of movies that Woo creates – blood and guts amongst guys and cool gangsters in thriller formats, the sort of films which critics exalt, and which are perhaps easier to sell to audiences than some of Tsui's movies). As to Tsui's influence on Woo, critics such as Tony Williams have noted that Woo's films prior to *A Better Tomorrow* are undistinguished (2002, 153).

Critics trot out plenty of guff about the theme of male friendship or brotherhood in the movies directed by John Woo, but there's just as much in the cinema of Tsui Hark. Really? Sure – to cite some titles: *Lake Changjin, Knockoff, Double Team, Time and Tide, Once Upon a Time In China, Blade, Aces Go Places, Seven Swords, The Master, The Flying Swords of Dragon Gate,* and *Black Mask.* Men fighting alongside each other, men looking after each other, men competing with each other – Tsui's cinema is full of those themes (as well as the proto-feminism).

Altho' John Woo's form of slow motion, balletic action is utterly

---
28 S. Kei: "Xingzhe de Guiji", *Film Biweekly*, 13, 1979.
29 They ranged from 'cookie-cutter dreck to creatively innovative masterpieces', as Rovin and Tracy put it (245).
30 Deals such as a co-production with Francis Coppola came to nothing.

compelling, it is *waaay* too slow for Tsui Hark! Tsui's metabolism in cinema runs very, very hot! While Tsui is all for stretching out big dramatic or action-fuelled moments (and much longer than in Western movies), he would never go as far as Woo and editor David Wu Tai-wai in using multiple film speeds to create lengthy, post-Eisensteinian montages of fluttering doves, spattering blood and guttering guns.

TSUI HARK AND AKIRA KUROSAWA.

That Tsui Hark is a huge admirer of the cinema of Akira Kurosawa is obvious (but who isn't?!): the whole look of Tsui's *jiangzhu* and historical pictures derives from Kurosawa's movies (from the meticulously researched costumes and props, to the use of real locations and three-dimensional sets, to the enormous emphasis on environmental elements such as wind, rain, fire and snow). Ever since he saw *Yojimbo* (1961) as a teenager, Kurosawa has been a favourite for Tsui.

For Tsui Hark, Akira Kurosawa managed to produce movies that transcended their cultural origins in Japan. Kurosawa's films are universal, Tsui said, going way beyond the limitations of language and culture (yet you can also argue that Kurosawa's movies remained *very* Japanese).

Tsui Hark has produced his own version of *The Seven Samurai* in *Seven Swords,* and of samurai classics such as *Yojimbo* and *Sanjuro* in *The Blade* and *New Dragon Gate Inn.* The way that Akira Kurosawa filmed royalty, pageants and palaces, the way that he included a huge panorama of human life, from peasants up to kings, the way that he never loses sight of the individual in the epic stories, all have been absorbed by Tsui.

Akira Kurosawa's was a grand cinema that magically crossed international borders, to become one of the great bodies of work in the second half of the 20th century. Kurosawa's cinema is also very big on action, which of course has impressed so many filmmakers as well as Tsui Hark.

Akira Kurosawa's influence has been immense on world cinema. Paul Verhoeven said he put on *Rashomon* or *The Seven Samurai* from time to time to remind himself that films could be art. Terry Gilliam spoke highly of *Rashomon.* Bernardo Bertolucci said Kurosawa (with Federico Fellini) was one of the reasons he wanted to become a film director. And John Woo said he watched the last reel of *The Seven Samurai* before making his films, for inspiration on action. The influence of Kurosawa on Woo is clear to see (a movie such as *Bullet In the Head* is distinctly Kurosawan).

There are Akira Kurosawa moments in Paul Verhoeven (the battles with bugs in *Starship Troopers*); Francis Coppola (the extravagant machine gun death of Sonny Corleone in *The Godfather* recalls Macbeth's demise by arrows in *The Throne of Blood*, or the mythical soldiers in *Apocalypse Now*); George Lucas raided Kurosawa's mediæval *samurai* for the Jedi knights in his *Star Wars* saga; the *samurai* warriors also popped up in *Brazil* (Terry Gilliam); the elaborate gun battles in John Woo's Hong Kong action cinema, and the warrior ethic also appears in John Milius's films; and Bernardo Bertolucci made his own version of a Kurosawa epic in

The Last Emperor. Other filmmakers who've cited Kurosawa as a key influence include Hayao Miyazaki, Wes Craven and Katsuhiro Otomo.

Akira Kurosawa was one of Ingmar Bergman's favourites. Bergman said he had studied *Rashomon* dozens of times (one can detect the influence of Kurosawa on films helmed by the Swedish genius such as *The Virgin Spring* and *The Seventh Seal*). Bergman said he regretted being so heavily influenced by Kurosawa. 'I want to say now that *The Virgin Spring* was a misadventure, a wretched imitation of Kurosawa. It was a period in which I surrendered so completely to the Japanese film that I almost became a bit of a samurai myself' (*Bergman On Bergman*, 120). That seems unnecessarily harsh.

GENRES.

A large proportion of Tsui Hark's movies are action movies. Comedy is key ingredient, as is violence, along with themes such as China, Chinese culture, nationalism, women, feminism, and food.[31] Doing the right thing and how to live in the world, are key moral concerns.

A huge proportion of the movies directed and produced by Tsui Hark have been historical movies: *Detective Dee and the Mystery of the Phantom Flame, The Blade, Green Snake, The Lovers, Peking Opera Blues, Shanghai Blues, New Dragon Gate Inn, Flying Swords of Dragon Gate, The Swordsman, Zu: Warriors of the Magic Mountain, Seven Swords* and the *Once Upon a Time In China* series. (The movies set in the present day tend to be thrillers and action movies). So Tsui and his film teams have spent years and years exploring the past, from the latter part of the 19th century (in the *Wong Fei-hung* series), to the mediæval period of *The Lovers,* and the ancient world of the *Detective Dee* series.

The *jiangzhu*[32] (= martial arts world) and the *wulin* (= martial forest) is where Tsui Hark gravitates towards in history – the wandering world of a China that never really existed (depicted in *The Blade, New Dragon Gate Inn, Flying Swords of Dragon Gate, The Swordsman, Zu: Warriors of the Magic Mountain, Seven Swords, The Butterfly Murders, A Chinese Ghost Story* and *The Lovers*). Indeed, among filmmakers of his generation, no one else has spent so much time imaginatively in the *jiangzhu* as Tsui.

Tsui Hark said he's had a special affinity with *wuxia pian* since childhood: around a quarter of his output as director is martial arts/ *wuxia pian*, and many more as producer.

Wuxia means swordsman/ martial fighter/ knight-errant (*wu* = military or armed; *xia* = hero, chivalrous. Known as *Mo hap* in Cantonese). Thus, *wuxia* movies were swordplay pictures, and they tended to be filmed in Mandarin. *Kung fu*, meaning fist fighting, and were usually made in Cantonese (with the *Wong Fei-hung* movies as the typical product).

Wuxia movies were regarded as more historical and 'authentic' than

---

31 Food? Oh yes – it's a motif in movies such as *We're Going To Eat You, Once Upon a Time In China* (eating Western food), *New Dragon Gate Inn, Iron Monkey* and *The Chinese Feast.*
32 'In *The Blade,* the *jiangzhu* exists in various manifestations that are no longer so abstract. It is country, community, locality; it is the person's character; it is the hero who knows how to develop his talent and achieve victory through the human dimension of speed rather than the superhuman one of flight', commented Stephen Teo (1998, 156).

kung fu movies; their trademarks included fantasy, the supernatural, performers flying, and visual effects. *Kung fu* movies (from Canton) tended to be more 'realistic', emphasizing training and the body.

A significant proportion of Tsui Hark's movies are not only action movies, they are martial arts movies: *The Blade*, the *Detective Dee* series, *Green Snake, Flying Swords of Dragon Gate, The Butterfly Murders, Zu, Seven Swords* and the *Once Upon a Time In China* series. Most of the martial arts movies directed and produced by Tsui are set in the past.

Stephen Teo:

> Tsui Hark's world is inclusive, blending the outrageous with the normal, the paranormal (as in his horror films) with the natural world (as in *The Blade*, with its contortions of mud, sand, and wind), and the supernatural (the notion of flight), with the mundane (the notion of speed). (1998, 154)

ROMANCE.

Love. Hearts and flowers. Romance…

Altho' it's the action movies, the historical movies, the thrillers, and the visual effects extravaganzas that Tsui Hark is usually known for (all masculine genres), and celebrated by film critics (most of whom are men), his cinema is filled with love and romance. Jean-Luc Godard wondered if love between a man and a woman was actually *the* chief subject of cinema; it's true of Godard's cinema, certainly (where romantic and erotic relationships are everywhere), and also true of Tsui's cinema. (Tsui comes from a very large family, which probably influenced the depiction of families in his cinema).

There is just as much romance, love and emotion in Tsui Hark's cinema as action, spectacle, history and visual effects. Some of Tsui's finest achievements have revolved around relationships and families: *Shanghai Blues, The Lovers, Green Snake, A Chinese Ghost Story*, etc. The fantasy and adventure movies, for instance, like *Green Snake* and *A Chinese Ghost Story*, are primarily love stories, and it's the love between a man and a woman that is at the core of the stories (and is what powers the stories along). 'I think we filmmakers often find ourselves trying to fill up the missing something of the audience's emotions and psychological needs', Tsui said.

Love crops up even in the titles of Tsui Hark's movies – *Love In the Time of Twilight, The Lovers, Love and Death In Saigon*, etc. Is Tsui, for all his pioneering achievements, his technical brilliance and action-heavy filmmaking, really a softie? Yes. Even in the harsh world of the *jiangzhu* of *Seven Swords* or *New Dragon Gate Inn*, love and romance are absolutely central (*romantic* is a key term in Tsui Land. Tsui thinks that 'women are more romantic than men'; 'romantic is the most key word in everything' [LM, 22]). Is he romantic? Tsui replied that you'd have to ask his wife.

'Romantic' – the word is uppermost in Tsui Hark's conception of cinema and entertainment – alongside 'emotion'. Cinema, Tsui asserts, must be emotional, there must be an emotional investment from the audience:

> I am looking for ways to make my audience feel. If your audience doesn't have a strong feeling from your story, you fail as a storyteller.

COMEDY.

Too few critical appraisals of the cinema of Tsui Hark emphasize the importance of *comedy* his work. But comedy is everywhere in Tsui's movies: *Peking Opera Blues* is a backstage comedy, as is *Shanghai Blues*; *Aces Go Places* and *All the Wrong Clues* are Cinema City comedies; black comedy is integral to *We're Going To Eat You* and *The Butterfly Murders*; horror comedy appears in the *Chinese Ghost Story* and *Swordsman* movies; the romances contain humour (*The Lovers*, *Green Snake*, *Love In the Time of Twilight*); and comedy is found throughout the *Once Upon a Time In China* series. And Tsui Hark added humour to films he produced, such as *A Better Tomorrow* and *Iron Monkey*.

Tsui Hark is particularly fond of gags using crowds – where mobs act as one. Like the crowd gathered outside the nightclub in *Shanghai Blues* which tilts its head to follow the moving sign of a fan covering the breasts on a billboard of a showgirl; like the villagers who cower in fear behind Leslie Cheung in *A Chinese Ghost Story*; like the guys who hide behind each other when the Chief is ranting in *We're Going To Eat You*.

AVAILABILITY

A *major* problem with approaching the cinema of Tsui Hark (and all Chinese cinema) is availability. You will smack up against the issue of availability as soon as you try to see anything other than the movies released in the Western world. Most of Tsui's films (and TV work) was produced for a Chinese market: the markets of Hong Kong and Mainland China are absolutely crucial. (Hence, Tsui's films are usually released with a Cantonese and a Mandarin soundtrack, which's the norm in Chinese cinema). This doesn't mean, tho', that the movies travel outside of China, either in their original form or in dubbed versions.

The language issue – Cantonese, Mandarin, English, whatever – is a minor one compared to general availability (subtitling is yet another issue). It's true that some of the key works directed and produced by Tsui Hark are easy to obtain in the West – the *Once Upon a Time In China* series, for instance, *Zu: Warriors From the Magic Mountain, Detective Dee and the Mystery of the Phantom Flame,* and of course those produced by or in conjunction with North American distributors (such as Columbia/ TriStar/ Sony), like *Double Team* and *Knock Off.* But many important movies are not easily available in the West: *The Butterfly Murders*, *Peking Opera Blues, Shanghai Blues* and *Dangerous Encounters of the First Kind* (gems of China cinema like *Peking Opera Blues* should be available in supermarket racks like Disney cartoons). It doesn't get better with more recent works, either: *All About Women, In the Blue, The Warrior, Young Detective Dee: Rise of the Sea Dragon* and others of the 2000s and 2010s are hard to source in the West.

Consequently, the following movies, directed by Tsui Hark, have not been explored fully in this study: *Search For the Gods* (1983), *Working Class* (1985), *Spirit Chaser Aisha* (1986), *The Banquet* (1991), *The Chinese Feast* (1995), *Tristar* (1996), *In The Blue* (2005), and *Catching Monkey 3-D* (2013).

The issue of availability affects many celebrated filmmakers – you simply can't find many of their key works. The issue of quality is another consideration: many movies are only available in substandard prints, with bad soundtracks, or in butchered versions (some Hong Kong movies look like they were copied from beat-up release prints that have been kicking around Central for years, then re-copied onto video and back again). Despite new distribution systems like the internet, or streaming, or DVD and Bluray (or older ones like video, or broadcasting on television), it's amazing how many jewels of cinematic art remain in limbo, or are lost, or can only be bought in scrappy versions from dodgy, one-eyed Buddhist monks in the scuzzy end of town for extortionate prices.

Another issue is that the international and Western versions of Hong Kong and Chinese movies sometimes change the following: the music; the dialogue; the scripts (scripts are rewritten during dubbing); add new sound mixes; and whole scenes are dropped.

Thus often the Western/ international cuts of Asian movies are *not* in the form the filmmakers preferred. Tsui Hark has complained many times that distributors have altered his movies for releases overseas.

The practice of dubbing the sound on afterwards in Chinese movies also extends to the stars: it was many years before Chinese movie audiences heard the real voices of Jackie Chan and Jet Li, for instance. Another consequence of dubbing is that the same group of actors tend to be heard in every movie.

For research online, the Hong Kong Movie Database and Hong Kong Cinemagic are excellent (they have photos of the cast and crew, for instance – very helpful when Chinese movies are filled with unusual names (and many alternative names and spellings) in both Mandarin and Cantonese). Love Hong Kong Film has useful reviews.

CRITICAL APPROACHES TO THE CINEMA OF TSUI HARK

The critical reception/ interpretations of Tsui Hark's movies tend to use some of the following approaches:

NATIONALISM AND IDENTITY.

Chinese identity and nationalism – the 'Chineseness' in Tsui Hark's cinema.

What it means to be Chinese, what Chinese history and society is, how Chinese culture relates to the rest of the world – these're some of Tsui Hark's primary concerns, at the thematic level. Chinese identity is a theme that crops up many times in Tsui's movies – in particular how contemporary Chinese identity relates to recent Chinese history.

POLITICAL ALLEGORY.

Politics – ideology – movies as political allegories/ statements.

There are many articles discussing Tsui Hark's cinema as political allegories which explore (1) China's place in the new world order, (2) Hong Kong's political situation *vis-à-vis* Mainland China, (3) Hong Kong as a colony, and, inevitably, (4) Hong Kong during the 1997 hand-over.

Critics often draw attention to the allegorical/ analogical/ metaphorical aspects of Tsui Hark's cinema, how he includes political commentary or side-swipes at authorities, then they castigate the films for not doing more. They forget that movies are *primarily* commercial entertainment – if you want allegory/ metaphor/ political diatribes, look elsewhere. Or, if you've got the guts, make your *own* movie which features hyper-intelligent political satire, pro-socialist/ left-wing propaganda, philosophical essays and metaphysical arguments, while still being highly entertaining, state of the art technically, and cheap to produce.

'Tsui Hark is skillful in channelling the general anxiety of the people in Hong Kong into his films and in manipulating the audiences' responses', noted Leung Ping-kwan (in "Urban Cinema and the Cultural Identity of Hong Kong").[33]

Tsui Hark has not shied away from tackling ideological and political issues head-on: his series about Wong Fei-hung, for instance, *Once Upon a Time In China*, is explicitly political. And the series that sort of follows up *Once Upon a Time In China*, the *Detective Dee* films, also deliver political messages.

For Leung Ping-kwan, Tsui Hark's cinema is explicitly political:

> Among Hong Kong directors, Tsui Hark is the one most obsessed with and skilful in making films into political allegories. In films he produced or directed, in his retelling of old tales as well as in his play with mixed genres, he always weaves in indirect political commentaries as well as references to contemporary issues. (In P. Fu, 242)

A good deal of the political and ideological content of the *Once Upon a*

---
[33] In P. Fu, 242-3.

Time In China movies boils down to simple dramatic oppositions:

West = guns (bad) ··· East = martial arts (good)
West = technology (bad) ··· East = tradition (good)
West = modern medicine (bad) ··· East = Chinese medicine (good)
West = exploitation (bad) ··· East = mercantile capitalism (good)
West = individualism (bad) ··· East = communities (good)

(And you'll find these oppositions throughout Hong Kong cinema).

The *Once Upon a Time In China* series pits the Chinese values of the family, neighbours, communities, tradition and righteousness against Western egotism, selfishness, cynicism, money, science, and negative imperialism.

ACTION, IMAGES, SPECTACLE.

'The imagery is one of the aspects I like about movies. It's like creating a virtual world with a lot of imagery, creating an illusion as well as the storytelling.'

That Tsui Hark's cinema is obsessed with creating spectacular and vivid movies everybody agrees. That Tsui is an image-obsessed filmmaker, a guy who can create extraordinary visuals with apparent ease, is central to his cinema (he has one of the most remarkable eyes for an image in film history). But this is an element of his cinema that critics find challenging to discuss, apart from making obvious statements about the beauty and power of Tsui's imagery.

As to action and choreography, Western critics are hopeless. They don't have the background knowledge of how movies are made. Many of them have probably never been on a soundstage.

And yet altho' issues like political allegory and Chinese identity are important in Tsui Hark's cinema, they are *not* the whole story! In the *Once Upon a Time In China* movies, for example, two minutes might be spent in a scene discussing China's role in the modern era (between Wong Fei-hung and a visiting dignitary, for instance), but seven minutes will be spent on a giant fight scene! And that fight scene will consume *far* more attention from the filmmakers than a little bit of dialogue about China and 20th century politics! (three days to shoot the fight scene, and half-an-hour to shoot the political discussion. Or as Jackie Chan put it, half a day for the talky bit, and four months for the action scene!).

But what will film critics talk about? – the two minutes of blether about Chinese politics! And what do audiences love? – the seven minute action sequence, where Jet Li rolls down the back of Iron Robe, or spins round a pillar twelve feet in the air, or whups the bad guys with an umbrella or a rolled-up shirt!

MORE ON ACTION.

Is Tsui Hark the finest director of action in recent cinema? Anywhere in the world? Even despite fierce competition? You could make a case that, *yes*, he is – even amongst the heavyweights of North America movies like Steven Spielberg, James Cameron, Michael Bay, Gore

Verbinski, Stephen Sommers, Michael Mann and Oliver Stone, or the token Brits (Ridley Scott), or one or two Europeans (Wolfgang Petersen, Renny Harlin, Roland Emmerich, Luc Besson, etc). Plus the stalwarts of the Hong Kong/ Chinese industry, such as John Woo, Tony Ching Siu-tung, Yuen Woo-ping, Johnny To Kei-fung, Ringo Lam Ling-tung and Jackie Chan.

You could cut together two or three full-length documentaries about martial arts and action cinema from Tsui Hark's movies alone. Or just one movie: *Knockoff* or *Time and Tide,* among the more recent contemporary thrillers, or the *Once Upon a Time In China* series, naturally.

And of course, Tsui Hark has worked with some of the great action stars – Sammo Hung Kam-bo, Jackie Chan, Jet Li, Yuen Biao, Michelle Yeoh, Jean-Claude van Damme – and some of the great action choreographers: Yuen Woo-ping, Tony Ching Siu-tung, Jackie Chan, Sammo Hung, Yuen Bun, Yuen Wah and Xiong Xin-xin.

> Action is not just by itself; action always comes with a story, it also comes with a style, it comes with extra information about what the director wants to show to the audience. These sorts of things are always with me. (2011)

MORE ON STYLE.

Tsui Hark is very much of the Akira Kurosawa School of Filmmaking – that is, plenty of natural, elemental material on screen – rain, fire, smoke,[34] wind, torchlight, candlelight, and more fire and more rain.[35] It means filming outdoors in sometimes tough conditions. It means leading the production team up mountains and across rivers. And for the actors it means quite a bit of hardship.

To achieve those Kurosawan effects requires stamina, determination, and, perhaps above all, patience (plus the resources of a fully-equipped studio with its technical staff. You can't stage this kind of production on a shoestring budget). This is perfectionist filmmaking, getting every detail right, composing scenes and frames teeming with incident and gesture.

Tsui Hark has a suitcase full of motifs and symbols which he uses – including tigers, butterflies, rain, water, the sea, funfairs, mothers and babies, goldfish and fish in tanks.

(So many of the motifs of the later historical films directed by Zhang Yimou – *Hero, House of Flying Daggers,* etc – can be found in classics of the Hong Kong New Wave cinema such as *The Terracotta Warrior,* the *Swordsman* series, the *Once Upon a Time In China* series, etc. The floating leaves, the dripping water, the rainfall, the billowing hangings of white and red cloth, the slow motion, etc.)

---

[34] Smoke in Hong Kong cinema is not a pretty effect that drifts in the background of a scene to enhance the lighting – it is used as a setting in itself, a real, physical presence in the scenes. Sometimes smoke provides the whole environment of a scene (and, yes, sometimes that billowing smoke is used to hide things).
[35] On a Hong Kong film set, electric fans are always near the camera – clothes must flap and billow.

STORYTELLING – STORIES AND CHARACTERS.

And yet, amazing as it may seem, one of the chief motivations for many filmmakers is simply storytelling. *Movies are stories*. That's all. Just stories. And *filmmakers are storytellers*. So all of the above elements and issues – the political rants, the anxiety over identity in a global marketplace, the critiques of capitalism and Communism, the exploration of women's issues or visual effects, etcetera – are all *secondary* to the *primary* concern. Which is: to *tell a story*.

Yes: that's what filmmakers do.

They tell stories.

Stories which involve characters and things happening and drama and conflicts and battles and goals and motivations and all the rest. That's one of the things that audiences crave: stories • characters • things happening.

This is the level in Tsui Hark's cinema (or any cinema) that's easiest to discuss, and doesn't require too much expertise. Everybody knows what stories they enjoy (even – *gulp!* – film critics!).

But when I say a movie is 'just a story', that doesn't under-value stories! Or filmmakers as storytellers! We love these stories, we want to hear and see these stories, we construct whole cultures and identities around these stories. (However, too many books about Hong Kong cinema focus solely on the stories and the characters, forgetting everything else. And Hong Kong movies are *supremely* and properly, fully *cinematic*. Ignoring the filmic aspects of the movies misses too much).

FURTHER THEORETICAL APPROACHES.

For those readers/ students who appreciate suggestions for theoretical approaches to subjects, here are some more:

• The relation of identity to art, to being an artist/ filmmaker.

• Approaching the issue of cultural and national identity using postmodern theory is an obvious angle for looking at Tsui Hark's cinema, and Hong Kong cinema.

• Forms of identity: psychological, social, cultural, national, historical, ethnic: for example, one could explore the relation of the Asian/ Chinese cultural identity of Tsui Hark's cinema to the issue of working as a filmmaker.

Some of Tsui Hark's films as director (this page and following).

The Butterfly Murders (1979).

Zu: Warriors of the Magic Mountain (1983).

Shanghai Bues (1984).

Peking Opera Blues (1986).

A Better Tomorrow 3 (1989).

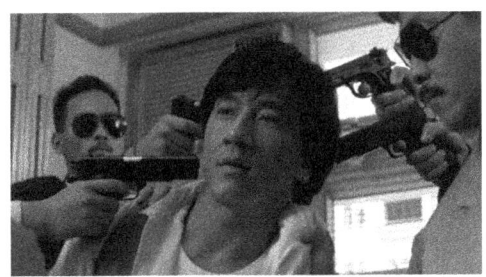

Twin Dragons (1992).

Green Snake (1993).

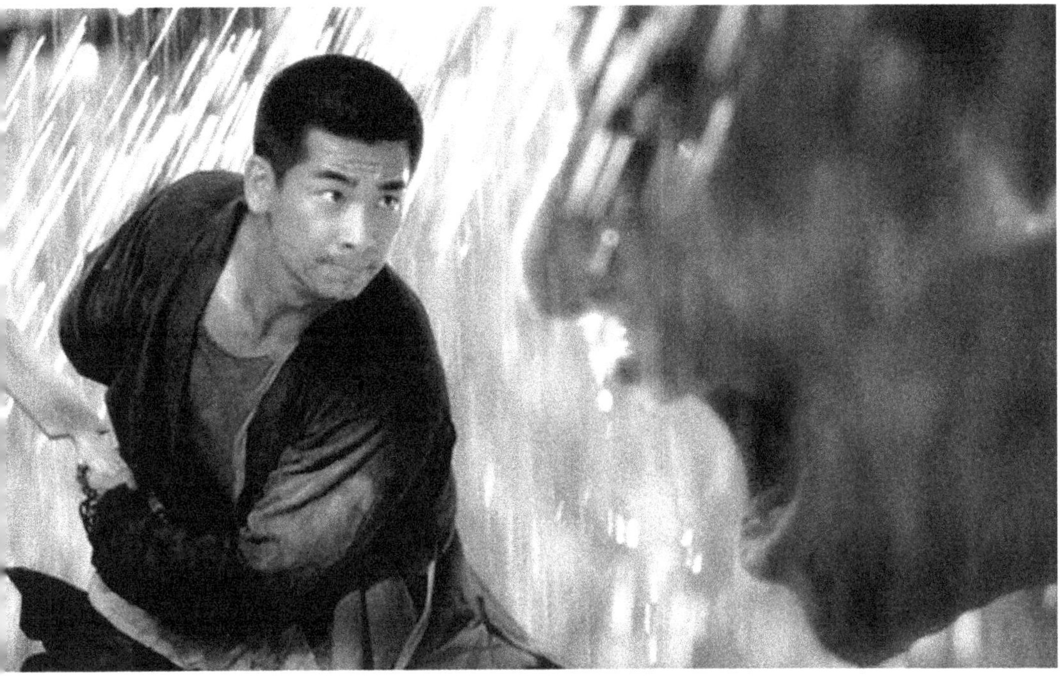

Blade (1995).

「ダブルチーム」ツイ・ハーク監督作品
THE BLADE
ブレード
刀
RAYMOND CHOW
TSUI HARK
TSUI HARK
K2 ENTERTAINMENT

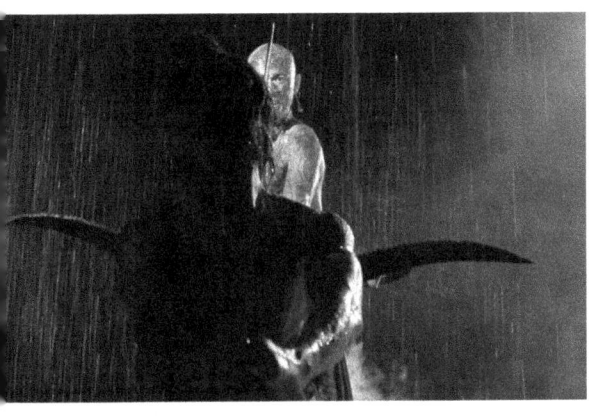

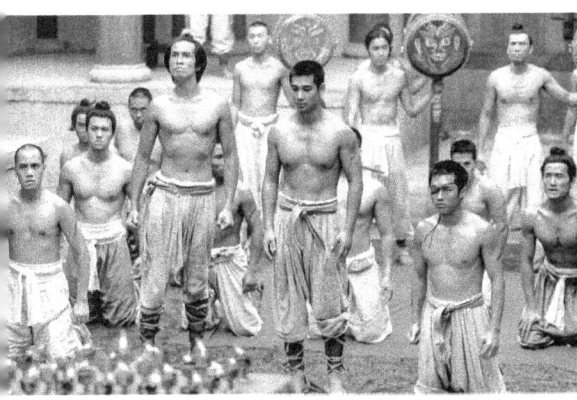

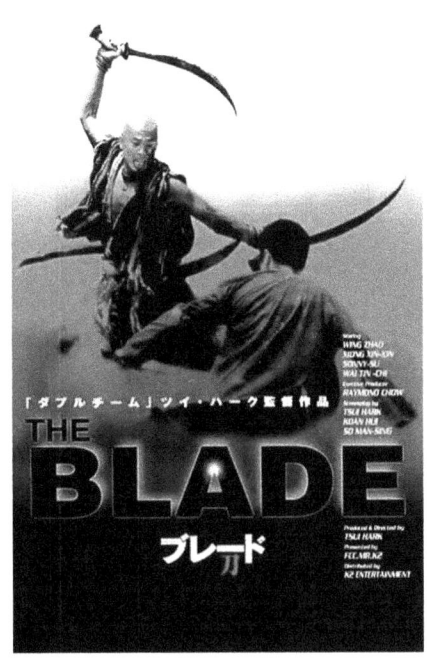

Knock Off (1998).

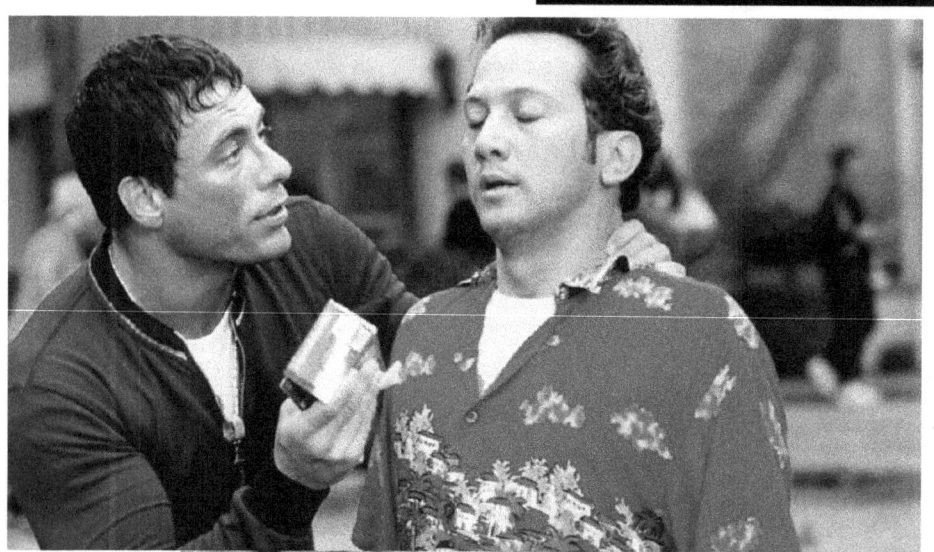

The Legend of Zu (2001).

Black Mask 2 (2002).

Seven Swords (2005).

Detective Dee and the Phantom Flame (2010).

Young Detective Dee (2013).

Making Flying Swords of Dragon Gate

The Taking of Tiger Mountain (2014).

福如東海，壽比南山

Journey To the West 2 (2017).

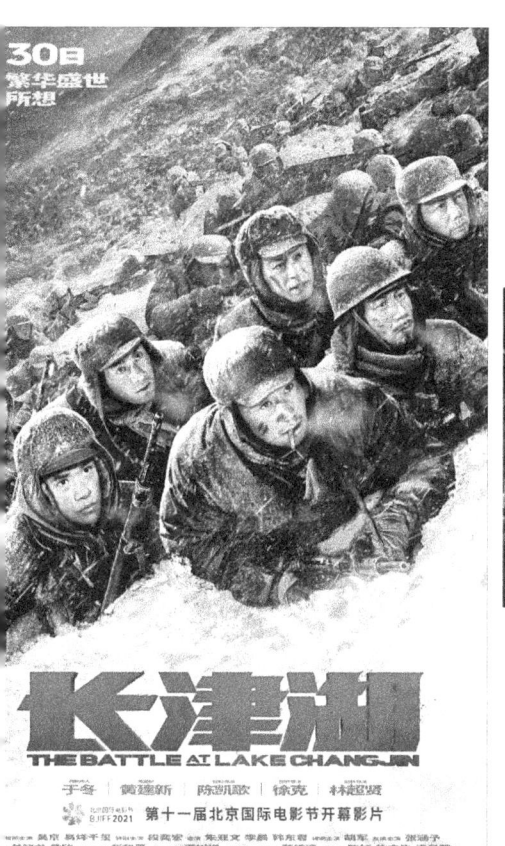

The Battle At Lake Changjin (2021), left and above.

The sequel (2022), below.

PART TWO

ONCE UPON A TIME IN CHINA

1

THE *ONCE UPON A TIME IN CHINA* MOVIE SERIES

The Wong Fei-hung that I created is very different from the Wong Fei-hung that I watched as a kid. There were two reasons to make the films: the first one is to put my favourite subjects on the screen: the hero's personality, his place in the community and his relationships with his protégés. When I watched it during my childhood, I could feel the warmth, and I really revelled in the family-like master-protégé relationships in Po-chi-lam... The second reason is that I gradually realised [the 1940s films] didn't touch on the historical context and the cultural changes in China. These are all topics that I could further develop, which was what I did.

Tsui Hark

INTRODUCTION

The *Once Upon a Time In China* series in movies comprises six features of 1991, 1992, 1993 (films), 1994 and 1997 (four of which were helmed by Tsui Hark – the first three and the fifth one; all were co-produced by Tsui), a TV series,[1] plus other additions – and a host of cash-in movies and parodies.

An animated version of *Once Upon a Time In China* was rumoured in 2005. It might've been along the lines of *A Chinese Ghost Story: The Tsui Hark Animation*, a version in *animé*-style of a live-action movie produced by Tsui Hark. It eventually appeared as *The Warrior* (2006). See below.

Tsui Hark is a master entertainer, who can take his place with the whole roster of master showmen throughout history – including circus showmen, famous impresarios, legendary actors and magicians of all kinds. The movies that Tsui directs and produces are hugely entertaining. There is a beguiling *mix*[2] in the movies of spectacle, melodrama, romance,

---
[1] After the *Once Upon a Time In China* movies, there was also a TV series, produced by Tsui Hark.
[2] The *Once Upon a Time In China* series is a mix of elements and genres, and it happily switches from serious melodrama to comedy to hi-octane martial arts.

action, music, visual effects and morality.

The *Once Upon a Time In China* series, for instance, contains a terrific spread of ingredients. They are also movies that audiences of many ages can enjoy, from the viewers in their 50s and 60s who can remember the *Wong Fei-hung* movies of their youth, to the baby boomers, to teens, and to pre-teens (there is enough music, noise, movement, colour and spectacle in the *Once Upon a Time In China* films to keep young children happy. However, there is plenty of brutality which some might consider unsuitable for younglings).

Tsui Hark used the character of Wong Fei-hung as a way of exploring the formation of modern China. Thru the Wong persona, Tsui aimed to consider many key historical events, including the Boxer Rebellion,[3] President Li-Hong-zhong, Sun Yat-sen (a.k.a. Sun Wen),[4] the Treaty of Nanjing, and the Empress Dowager. The idea, Tsui remarked, was 'to link Wong with every incident in the modern history of China' (it's a common trope of storytelling, of course – there are 100s of characters in world literature who've travelled back in time to Ancient Egypt, say, or the American Civil War).[5]

One thing's for sure, working on a Tsui Hark movie makes everybody look good. Altho' Tsui has a reputation for being a tough and demanding director at times, people flock back to work with him because they know they are going to look amazing, as well as obvious reasons (like, they know they're going to be in a production which will be released and will be seen in theatres by audiences (many movies are made but not released, or only given limited releases); and that it will be distributed around the world (most movies aren't released outside their country of origin); and because they get to do stuff you just don't get to do elsewhere).

Once Upon a Time In China 1 was one of those movies where every element comes together beautifully – the legendary character and story of Wong Fei-hung; a superstar-in-the-making, Jet Li;[6] a terrific supporting cast (including Yuen Biao, Jacky Cheung, Kent Cheng and Rosamund Kwan); outstanding technical aspects from all departments (including historical research); grand political themes; astonishing action choreography (from Yuen Shun-yi, Yuen Cheung-yan and Lau Kar-wing);[7] and of course white-hot direction from Tsui Hark.

Once Upon a Time In China was Tsui Hark's most-awarded movie, with wins for best director, best action choreography, best editing, and best music at the Hong Kong Film Awards (and it was nominated for best photography, best film and best supporting actor, Jacky Cheung).

A key collaborator on *Once Upon a Time In China* was the producer, Ng See Yuen (known as 'N.G.'), who had backed Tsui Hark's first movie, *The Butterfly Murders*, and became a crucial influence in Tsui's film career.

---

[3] The Boxer or Taipeng Rebellion of 1900 was a nationalist movement which had support from the Empress Dowager. The rebels held the ancient beliefs that magic and *kung fu* would make them able to withstand bullets (the rebels were members of the I Ho Chuan Society). Westerners called *kung fu* boxing.
[4] In 1912, Sun Yat-sen founded the Republic of China.
[5] Tsui Hark would later use the figure of Detective Dee for similar ends.
[6] 'When he stars in my movies, he must be a heroic figure', Tsui Hark stated.
[7] Jackie Chan told Tsui Hark to keep his *Wong Fei-hung* movie realistic, without the wires which Chan dislikes. And of course Tsui has his performers flying all over the place!

The *Once Upon a Time In China* movies generated enough money for there to be disputes over earnings: Golden Harvest, for instance, sued Tsui Hark in the late 1990s, including for the *Once Upon a Time In China* films, and Jet Li fell out with Golden Harvest over the arrangement for the later *Once Upon a Time In China* productions.[8]

One version of a Wong Fei-hung movie would've involved (some of) the former 'Seven Little Fortunes': Jackie Chan to play Wong, Sammo Hung to play (guess!) Porky Wing, and Yuen Biao to play Leung Foon. Presumably this would've been contemplated in the late Eighties, when Chan, Hung and Biao had appeared together in several films.

Tsui Hark remarked in 2012:

> For Wong Fei Hung, who was my idol when I was a kid, I wanted to try to bring some of that screen magic I felt so strongly in my childhood to an audience in my adult life. I wanted to know how much difference there was between this gap of 30 years apart. Wong Fei Hung was my expression of childhood fantasy.

For Jeff Yang, writing in his guide to Hong Kong cinema, *Once Upon a Time In China* was cleverly conceived by Tsui Hark as a movie that would appeal to multiple audiences: action fans would have Mainland *wushu* champion Jet Li to ensure that the fights would be impressive; for both genders there was the romantic subplot with the 'Thirteenth Aunt'; for history buffs, there was an emphasis on historical accuracy; for Chinese, there was the legendary figure of Wong Fei-hung; and for a Hong Kong audience, there was the political issue of the clash between Eastern and Western culture, in the lead-up to the 1997 Hand-over. 'Tsui's theme of China [is] a country of lost opportunities' (Stephen Teo, 171).

Maggie Lee enthuses:

> With visual spectacles and dramatic arcs never thought possible in Hong Kong cinema before, the *Once Upon a Time In China* series is fully transporting from start to finish… Having withstood the test of time, the series remains one of the most towering achievements in Hong Kong film history. (2021).

Paul Fonoroff, a film critic who very rarely praised any of the 100s of movies he reviewed for the *South China Morning Post*, was kinder to the *Once Upon a Time In China* movies (maybe because he appeared in *Once Upon a Time In China 2*). Of *Once Upon a Time In China 3*, the Fonster said: 'proves to be more exciting than the dozens of other martial arts epics released since *Part II*' (277).

For Leon Hunt (in *Kung-fu Cult Movies*), *Once Upon a Time In China* was 'a characteristically witty piece of revisionism, synthesizing the Cantonese legend and the 1990s superstar in order to retrospectively create the first kung fu film' (21).

Lisa Morton drew attention to the 'beautifully paced and emotionally

---

[8] Tsui recalled that the issue was also about actors' contracts, and that Jet Li had signed with a company that wasn't part of the *Once Upon a Time In China* productions.

rich script', 'one of the finest casts ever to grace a Hong Kong film', 'a lovely romance', and 'some of the most spectacular kung fu ever caught on film' (77).

Bey Logan (1995) noted that one of the archetypes for the conception of Wong Fei-hung in the *Once Upon a Time In China* series was in the Shaw Brothers' *Martial Club* (Lau Kar-leung, 1980), where Wong is younger [9] and not yet the accomplished *kung fu* fighter he became. *55 Days At Peking* (1963), the giant, Samuel Bronston movie and *Lin Zexu (The Opium War/ Commissioner Lin*, 1959) are influences/ intertexts with *Once Upon a Time In China* for Stephen Teo (1998, 158).

Howard Hampton calls *Once Upon a Time In China* 'equal parts anti-imperialist tract, gleeful exploitation of melodramatic violence, comic folk-tale, and wistful quest for spiritual unity' (1997). *Once Upon a Time In China* is Chow Yun-Fat's nomination for the top Hong Kong movie ever.

Thomas Weisser (in *Asian Cult Cinema*) complained that the *Once Upon a Time In China* series demanded from the audience 'some detailed knowledge of Chinese history', so that parts of the movies don't resonate for Western audiences as they do in Hong Kong (147). Maybe – but these were movies made for a local audience.

Critics have discussed the postmodernism of the *Once Upon a Time In China* series, the issues of 'hysteria' or 'speed' in them, and nationalism [10] and Chinese identity, and they've brought in 1997 and the Hand-over of Hong Kong to the Mainland... Yes, all of that, and many more theoretical concerns, are certainly in there.

But *Once Upon a Time In China* is also a movie series: it's *not* a theoretical analysis of contemporary Chinese society and politics. It's entertainment, it's show-time: for all of the critical and theoretical analyses of Tsui Hark and *Once Upon a Time In China*, let's not forget that in this movie North Americans are depicted as corrupt, rude, aggressive slave-traders! They come to China to trade – but their trade is living humans! They abduct Chinese women – not only to be workers, but to be a particular kinda of worker: hookers! In *Once Upon a Time In China*, Yanks are portrayed as insensitive louts whose drive towards exploitation descends to the lowest levels: slave-trading and prostitution (in *Once Upon a Time In China*, prostitution is used as an emblem of capitalism at its crassest). One of the staple charas in the *Once Upon a Time In China* series is a Chinaman who sells out his countrymen – it's Iron Robe Yim and also the gangster Hung who sells out to the North Americans.

The *Once Upon a Time In China* series made a big impact on filmmaking in Hong Kong: distributors and studios were quick to see the box office revenue the movies generated, and they swiftly ordered up imitations, cash-ins and parodies. So movies were conceived with similar Chinese legendary figures, such as Fong Sai-yuk (in the *Fong Sai-yuk* (a.k.a. *Legend*) pictures of 1993), and some movies sent up the *Once Upon a Time In China* films and the Wong Fei-hung persona (and the way that Jet Li interpreted him), such as *Last Hero In China* (1993). And some

---
9 Lau Kar-leung was the first director to portray Wong Fei-hung as a young man.
10 'One of the greatest films to ever celebrate Chinese nationalism' (Lisa Morton, 77).

studios simply produced their own versions of a Wong Fei-hung adventure (after all, nobody owned the rights to the legend of Wong! And film producers and studios like nothing better'n *not* paying for rights to material!).[11] Imitations included: *Once Upon a Chinese Hero* (Wu Ma, 1993, a.k.a. *Kick Boxer* and *Once Upon A Time In China 6: Kickboxer*), with Yuen Biao as Lau Zhai, *Once Upon a Time a Hero In China* (Lee Lik-Chi, 1992), with Alan Tam, Eric Tsang and Simon Yam, another Alan Tam spoof, *Master Wong vs. Master Wong* (Lee Lik-Chi, 1993), a sequel to *Once Upon a Time a Hero in China*, and *Great Hero from China* (Hwang Jang Lee), with Chin Kar-lok and Lam Ching Ying. In *Flirting Scholar* (1993), Stephen Chow performs the famous Jet Li Wong Fei-hung stance.

THE *WONG FEI-HUNG* TV SERIES

Wong Fei-hung has been the subject of several TV series, apart from the *Once Upon a Time In China* TV series, including: *The Return of Wong Fei Hung* (Television Broadcast, 1984), *The Young Wong Fei Hung* (2002), *Wong Fei Hung – Master of Kung Fu* (T.V.B., 2005), *Five Disciples of Master Wong* (2006), and *The Kung Fu Master Wong Fei Hung* (2008).

The *Wong Fei-hung* TV series aired in 1996 on A.T.V. It was produced by Tsui Hark, directed by Tsui Hark, Daniel Lee, Si Mei-yi, and Mak Dong-kit, scripted by Tsui, Lee, Lam Kei-to, Chung Ngoi-fong, Cheng Pik-yin and Tang Pik-yin, and starred Tsui regulars such as: Vincent Zhao (as Wong Fei-hung), Maggie Shiu, Max Mok, Kent Cheng, Lau Shun, Lau Kar-wing, Yuen Bun, Elvis Tsui, Xiong Xin-xin, Power Chan and Cheung Chun-hung. It was filmed on video, with a TV studio approach (of multiple cameras).

There were five episodes built around Wong Fei-hung: *The Eight Assassins, The Suspicious Temple, The Headless General, The Final Victory* and *The Ideal Century*. Tsui Hark directed two episodes: *The Ideal Century* and *The Final Victory*.

The Final Victory was dir. by Tsui Hark, DP: Gordon Yeung Gwoh-leung, with a cast that included Vincent Zhao, Max Mok, Benny Chan, Kent Cheng, Maggie Siu, Xiong Xin-xin, Cheng Pei-pei, Lau Shun and Jacky Cheung.

The Ideal Century was dir. and prod. by Tsui Hark; Gordon Yeung Gwoh-leung was DP. In the cast were: Vincent Zhao, Max Mok Siu-chung, Kent Cheng Jak-si, Benny Chan Kwok-bong, Maggie Siu Mei-kei and Xiong Xin-xin. 106 mins.

The TV series of *Once Upon a Time In China* takes a different approach to the *Wong Fei-hung* mythos: gone is the out-size spectacle and ravishing photography of the *Once Upon a Time In China* movies, the action is cut down, and, like almost all television – of any kind, in any

---
11 The Disney corporation is the obvious case.

genre – it is very talky. The TV show is more like a stage play of a *Wong Fei-hung* story, but the interaction of the entourage is as enjoyable as in the movies (with veteran performers like Max Mok and Kent Cheng, it's guaranteed a certain verve).

One of the pluses of the *Once Upon a Time In China* TV series is that much of the sound is live, as in many TV shows, and in contrast to all of Hong Kong cinema of this period. So we get to hear the voices of Xiong Xin-xin, Max Mok, Kent Cheng *et al;* this certainly enhances the scenes where there are quickfire conversations, for example. (However, some scenes were dubbed – those with Vincent Zhao, for instance, possibly because he is a Mandarin speaker, and this is a Cantonese TV show).

Most of the ingredients of the *Once Upon a Time In China* movies are present and correct in the TV series, though the scale is cut down: scenes where Wong Fei-hung acts as Wong Fei-hung, imperious and commanding; scenes where rivals pop up to cause trouble; evocations of traditional, Chinese culture and mythology; romantic scenes with the 13th Aunt; goofy scenes for the entourage; and of course food and eating scenes, a Tsui Hark staple.

You can't help noticing, too, that the TV show of *Once Upon a Time In China* gives as much screen time to the coterie around Wong Fei-hung as to the *sifu* himself (this also occurs in the 4th and 5th films, which also starred Vincent Zhao as Wong Fei-hung. It may be due to scheduling).

The Eight Assassins episode (*Huang Fei Hong zhi ba da tian wang,* dir. Daniel Lee, wr. Jason Lam, DP: Gordon Yeung), features the eight assassins of the title (in a blurry, slo-mo, flashback montage of their fighting skills), and scenes of Wong Fei-hung being the doctor and healer; but it's really about life at the Po Chi Lam clinic (which's what Tsui Hark seems to have been most compelled by in the *Once Upon a Time In China* movies). So we have many scenes where Ah Foon, Porky Wing, Clubfoot, Bucktooth So and the others are horsing around at Po Chi Lam; we have scenes where Aunt Yeo introduces more of her Western ways (there's a romantic scene where Wong Fei-hung and Aunt Yeo photograph each other); a scene where one of the entourage Goes Western (Porky Wing – it was Bucktooth So in film one); and comedy scenes (an improbable sequence where the lads pick up Western instruments – violins, an accordion – in order to accompany the 13th Aunt on piano).

The plot of *Eight Assassins* has Prince Cheng (sent by the Empress Dowager) challenging Wong Fei-hung and his Po Chi Lam crew to a series of a *leitai* match. The Po Chi Lam followers fight on when Wong is poisoned, but of course Wong emerges victorious.

THE WARRIOR

The Warrior (a.k.a. *Wong Fei-hung: Brave Into the World,* 2006) was a Wong Fei-hung adventure as a cartoon (a project that likely went back a long way – probably to the mid-1990s, when Tsui Hark was contemplating turning *Green Snake* into animation). The *Wong Fei-hung* cartoon was produced by Yang Yong and directed by Tiger Fu Yin and Chen Yue-Hu. The screenplay is credited to Tiger Fu Yin, Chen Yue-Hu and Yang Yong. The music was by Peter Kam Pau Tat and James Wong Jim. Tsui Hark has credits for art direction, action direction, script as well as 'presented by'. It was released: on July 12, 2006. 88 minutes.

THE POLITICS OF THE *ONCE UPON A TIME IN CHINA* SERIES

One of the concerns of the *Once Upon a Time In China* series is political and ideological: everybody who discusses the series notes the looming date of 1997, when the Hong Kong territories were handed back to the Chinese. Even without that background, there was plenty going on in the 1990s in China and elsewhere for the movies to have all sorts of political and ideological associations.

Many of the political aspects of the *Once Upon a Time In China* series are the same as many movies in the Hong Kong New Wave cinema: the oppositions include: China and the West, China and outsiders, China and capitalism, China old and new, China's older generations and traditions, the younger generation, and so on. There are also the sinister schemes of one of China's age-old enemies and uneasy neighbours, Russia, as some of the visiting Russians plot to assassinate the Governor, Li (in film three).

Also, it should be pointed out that many of the political and ideological issues explored in the *Once Upon a Time In China* series, and in other historical movies in the New Wave of Hong Kong cinema, can be found in cinema everywhere. That the Chinese characters in these movies view Europeans or Russians or North Americans with suspicion is no different from the suspicious attitudes in North American movies about people from anywhere outside the U.S.A. [12]

Altho' the geo-political background of the *Once Upon a Time In China* series involves foreign powers in China, many of the villains and the rivals in the foreground of the stories are actually fellow Chinese. In part two of *Once Upon a Time In China*, it's the White Lotus clan. In part three, it's the rival Tai-pang *kung fu* school.

For Stephen Teo, *Once Upon a Time In China* is
a virtual textbook of Orientalist abstractions that have been passed

---
12 Of course, to humans, everyone is a potential threat, no matter who they are.

down from both Hollywood and Chinese pictures, from Fu Manchu to Charlie Chan, from *The Opium War* (1959) to *55 Days At Peking* (1965), from *The Last Emperor* (1987) to *Tai-Pan* (1986).

The *Once Upon a Time In China* series is absolutely brilliant at depicting the cultural and social differences between the West and the East.[13] Tsui Hark and his teams have an anthropologist's eyes for cultural difference. They conjure numerous obvious differences (such as gadgets like cameras and clocks, or food, or costumes), as well as confusions over language, etiquette and behaviour.

But it's not a one-sided representation of Chinese and Western ways and behaviour. The simplistic view is:

China = good. West = bad.

But the *Once Upon a Time In China* series is much more subtle than that (altho' it does portray many Chinese people who regard anything Western as ugly, stupid, pointless, corrupt, and poisonous). In fact, many of the cultural and social differences between the Orient and the Occident are dealt with comically. Because the politics is so obvious, Tsui Hark and his teams are happy to draw attention to the silliness of arguing over differences (we are all people, right? what does it matter what you wear or what you eat?!).

Western film critics tend to take the *Once Upon a Time In China* series a little too seriously, as if these movies were produced solely as political treatises on cultural and social differences, and to express the anxiety among Cantonese people about their identity caught somewhere between China and the international community. But these are *movies*, they're *not* lectures or essays, and the political and ideological aspects are only *part* of the whole picture.

Besides, all of that material about nationalism and identity and anxiety in the *Once Upon a Time In China* series can be found throughout Western cinema. It's just that audiences in Europe and North America are so used to it, they don't see the ideology and the politics anymore. An Asian audience looking at typical movies from the U.S.A. and Europe would see similarly xenophobic, racist, pro-military, nationalistic and intolerant politics that Western critics keep harping on about in Chinese movies.

Tsui Hark has a wry, sceptical sense of humour.[14] And so his movies often make points about political and social issues in a comical fashion. The scene at the medical lecture, for instance (in film two), contrasts Western and Oriental medicine and science and brings out the cultural and scientific differences between them in a humorous manner which's just as effective as a scene of fire and arrows and people running around yelling (which occurs next).

One of the striking aspects of the *Once Upon a Time In China* series for a Western audience is how the tables are turned so often: now

---

[13] Westerners are introduced in a satirical sequence where a procession of Christians sing 'Hallelujah' (from George Handel's *Messiah*) as they weave thru the town (partly in order to drown out the Chinese musicians).

[14] Humour: the whole *Once Upon a Time In China* series is an action comedy, a martial arts comedy, and a romantic comedy. Far too few Western critics emphasize this.

Westerners are 'foreign devils' (*gweilos*), they are the enemy, the usurpers, the invaders, the imperialists, the destroyers of the Chinese way of life. In a Western movie, a Western audience is always looking *through* the Western characters at everybody else – looking at Native Americans through Western eyes, say, in the cowboy genre. In the *Once Upon a Time In China* series and in Chinese historical movies, the point-of-view is reversed. (I wonder if this simple reversal is why so many Western critics find the *Once Upon a Time In China* series uncomfortable. As Stephen Teo notes in *Hong Kong Cinema*: 'Tsui's work seems to play back, mischievously, the negative Asian stereotypes of Hollywood movies, answering with negative Western stereotypes of his own' [171]).

Yes, but let's not forget that the Holocaust and World War Two was a white, European invention, and that the atomic bomb was developed (and dropped) by North Americans. When it comes to fascism and militarized aggression, modern Europe and North America have few equals in recent history.

One aspect of this East-West cultural reversal that pops out of the *Once Upon a Time In China* series is language: when Western characters speak in English (usually American English). The sound of the English words is foreign, in this context: it reminds us that the English language is not a given, not the default position of cinema (or of humans), and is a cultural construction like everything else.

The Westerners in China are a long way from home: using the White Lotus Cult to dramatize the urge to rid China of foreigners in film two is simply an exaggeration of feelings that're already present (and are still present in China, and every country, today).

RELIGION.

Religion is a striking ingredient in the world of *Once Upon a Time In China*. The impact of the Western powers in China as seen by these movies includes religion – in the form of priests, religious processions, the motifs of Western religion – chiefly Catholicism (crosses, candles, stained glass), and several scenes set in churches. Priests, for instance, act as intermediaries and advisers, and are portrayed in the main in a positive light (the Priest in film one, for instance, throws himself in between Wong Fei-hung and the guns of the Governor's men).

Partly Christianity is depicted as an exotic cult, as often in Asian narratives,[15] and segments of it are fascinating to Chinese eyes (and even ugly – Wong Fei-hung contemplates Christ on the Cross and wonders at this image of suffering). Western religion isn't sent up (too easy), but it's viewed with bemusement by many Chinese locals.

By contrast, Wong Fei-hung and his entourage are not portrayed as religious devotees – there's no need, because they have the vast mythology and customs of China in them, behind them, and all around them. The *Once Upon a Time In China* movies are colourful celebrations of all things Chinese: if there's an opportunity for another street procession

---

15 Especially in Japanese animation and *manga*.

of folk culture, or a demonstration of Chinese medicine, it will be taken up.

And rather than a religious leader, Wong Fei-hung himself is depicted as a man who's decent and right in himself (or 'righteous', as seems to be a popular term today): he's trying to do the right thing, and aims for what is best. He leads by example, you could say, and his philosophy is manifested in his morality and his sayings (he is a teacher, continually admonishing his followers to behave better). However, as Tsui Hark pointed out, Wong is not always correct, and sometimes makes mistakes.

The gloomy, ascetic Buddhist atmosphere of many Chinese fantasy movies (the temples, the statues of Buddha, the incense), is not part of the *Once Upon a Time In China* cosmos, and we don't have dancing, Taoist wizards, either (as in *A Chinese Ghost Story*).

ROMANCE AND COMEDY

Tho' I'm sure some action fans speed thru the romantic scenes when they play the *Once Upon a Time In China* movies on computers, TVs, tablets, phones and other devices, the romance is actually fundamental to the success and the power of the *Once Upon a Time In China* film series. And Tsui Hark makes sure that *a lot* of screen time is given over to the romantic plots – thus, between Wong Fei-hung and Aunt Yeo, there is the wistful yearning from afar, the comical misunderstandings, the gentle ribbing, the affectionate gestures in shadowplay…

Tsui Hark wanted to have a significant female ingredient in his version of the Wong Fei-hung legend: for several reasons: (1) to nod to the proto-feminism of the early modern era; (2) to reflect his own feminist interests; (3) to follow his cinematic instincts (including as a film producer, to play to other segments of the movie audience, such as women); and (4) to have Aunt Lee carry some of the East-West culture clashes.[16]

Aesthetically, the *Once Upon a Time In China* series is completely romanticized and poeticized: this is a dream of China, a fantasy of China, as well as being a history of China and a politics of China. Look at the gorgeous golden light filling the frame, the yellow and red in the costumes, the smoke drifting thru blue-lit night scenes – everything in the *Once Upon a Time In China* movies is romantic (and Tsui Hark's sensibility is deeply, unashamedly romantic).[17]

It's the same with the comedy (probably more palatable for action fans, compared to girlie, romantic scenes). The verbal interplay, the humorous facial expressions, the arguments among Wong Fei-hung's followers – these are also absolutely essential to the *Once Upon a Time In China* series. (Unfortunately, partly because comedy is one of the aspects

---

16 That it's Aunt Lee who carries much of the East versus West subplot, reflects the feminist inflection of Tsui Hark's cinema – suggesting that women are more forward-looking than men in the very patriarchal, very masculinist society of early modern China.
17 Even a moment when Wong calls Aunt Yee by her name (Sin-qun) is a romantic beat.

of movies that doesn't translate so easily, and doesn't always work in subtitles or dubbing, partly because comedy is routinely overlooked, and partly because comedy isn't regarded as worthy of critical attention, critics too often neglect it).

ASPECTS OF THE *ONCE UPON A TIME IN CHINA* SERIES

Acting-wise, the *Once Upon a Time In China* movies are very generous in offering all sorts of things for the secondary charas to do, and in giving them large amounts of screen time (and for including such large casts).[18] Many another movie series doesn't do this (and their minor charas barely make an impression), but the *Wong Fei-hung* films are happy to indulge characters such as Clubfoot or or Ah Foon or Bucktooth So, letting them deliver comical scenes, or *kung fu* action. (The circle surrounding Wong at Po Chi Lam clinic had greatly impressed Tsui Hark as a child, so this *Once Upon a Time In China*, is Tsui's version of the extended family of Wong and his followers. Families, groups and communities are a crucial ingredient in Tsui's cinema).

Thus, altho' the *Once Upon a Time In China* series revolves around the title character, Wong Fei-hung, they really are ensemble shows, and don't split the actors into the Star and Everyone Else. So it's easy to see why so many actors would be keen to appear in these wonderful movies: not only are they directed or produced by one of the superstars of Chinese cinema, and not only do you get to do stuff you seldom get to do in other movies or TV shows, you also have juicy parts and the opportunity to shine. (No matter how tough a Tsui Hark shoot might be, it's all in the service of making a great movie). Also, Jet Li is not a selfish, arrogant star – he is happy to share the limelight with everybody.

There are all sorts of details in the *Once Upon a Time In China* series which you might miss on first viewings. Like the way that Wong Fei-hung flips out a white fan and quivers it impatiently (often when listening to someone else's views that he doesn't agree with). Like the quirks in the ensemble acting – where characters surrounding the main characters are also delivering funny bits of business. Like when Wong has completed a spectacular *kung fu* move, and whips his clothes behind him with his right hand, very rapidly, while standing boldly, like a lion.

Food is another recurring element in the *Wong Fei-hung* films *à la* Tsui Hark, as often in the output of Tsui. Food – not having it, scrabbling around for it, rushing off without paying for it (a recurring gag), trying to eat it on a moving train, not being allowed to eat it until Wong Fei-hung gives permission, and of course attempting to eat Western grub.

The *Once Upon a Time In China* movies are costume movies (by

---

18 Down to details like the old night watchman who wanders the streets with a lantern shouting, 'beware of thieves' and 'beware of fire'.

regular Tsui Hark designer, Bruce Yu Ka-On, and others), and they revel in dressing up the cast in historically-accurate costumes, as well as putting Wong Fei-hung and his cohorts in disguises – Peking Opera costumes, as pirates (in film 5), and crossdressing as Red Lantern Society girls in film 4 (tho' Wong doesn't crossdress).

Tsui Hark is fond of staging scenes in lengthy takes with actors grouped very closely together. Tsui is as inventive at arranging faces and bodies within the frame as, say, Orson Welles (and, like Welles, he often favours low angles, with the camera at or below waist height). So altho' we think of Tsui's cinema as one of extremely rapid cutting, a montage form of cinema, it is also very Wellesian (and Hitchcockian) in allowing actors to run thru whole scenes with single master shots (thus the performers set the pace, in part at least). And Tsui and his editors will hold that master shot, without cutting away from it (which can be distracting). In *Once Upon a Time In China,* Tsui seems more confident in allowing scenes to unfold at a statelier pace, without resorting to gimmickry. Or put it like this: one of the pleasures of Tsui's cinema is that it is extremely well put-together – cinematically as well as technically, dramatically and narratively.

Striking memorable poses is one of the hallmarks of most martial arts movies; in the *Wong Fei-hnug* movies, Jet Li freezes in iconic stances: one arm out in front, the other raised behind the head, legs bent right down to the ground (a position that Li can attain with lightning rapidity). Another famous pose is standing straight and tall, whipping the outer clothing back around the right leg, in preparation for a fight.

The stances, freezes and pauses recall the poses in key animation, where characters strike iconic postures and freeze. In Chinese action movies, the frozen poses also evoke the pauses or 'pillow moments' in Japanese *animé*, where the action suddenly halts for a few seconds. It's about a musical rhythm, a stop-start rhythm, where the halts are as important as the movements.

Sometimes dialogue is delivered (in the prelude to a fight), in the intervals between motion, but often the poses are silent. Samurai duels (in *manga* as well as in movies) are full of interludes and pauses.

The *Once Upon a Time In China* series is clever how it reprises scenes from earlier films and puts them in a new context: a character suffering outside in the rain, for example, is reworked several times; the shadowplay of the romance; the street processions ending in violence, and so on.

As to the humour of the *Once Upon a Time In China* series, it's striking how often Wong Fei-hung is the butt of the jokes, not the perpetrator. It's the polar opposite of a Woody Allen movie, where Allen always delivers the jokes (and even when he's the victim, the coward, the buffoon, he's still carrying the humour). In *Once Upon a Time In China,* no: Jet Li plays the straight man to characters such as Ah Foon and Aunt Lee, who score jokes off him.

WONG FEI-HUING IN CINEMA

Born in 1847, Wong Fei-hung died in 1925. Wong's fighting style included the famous 'shadowless kick', the 'tiger-crane' style, and the 'nine special fists'. His father was Wong Kar Ying, a martial artist of the Ten Tigers of Canton. The elder Wong was a practitioner of Hung's Fist (Hung Kuen). Wong senior refused to teach his son martial arts[19] (tho' Wong junior became an expert at Hung Kuen). Wong was known for combining martial arts with Confucian philosophy, and the healing arts. Bey Logan noted that Wong 'has had a more profound effect on Chinese action cinema than even Bruce Lee' (10).

Wong Fei-hung worked out of the Po Chi Lam clinic, where he founded a martial arts school. He married four times. Wong is both a real, historical figure and a legendary hero: like Robin Hood or King Arthur in the West (or Billy the Kid and Wyatt Earp in North American mythology), it's much more the legendary Wong that's significant, and has more impact for audiences, than the real person.

Wong Fei-hung is an almost impossibly goody-goody character. He is an upright citizen of the people, if ever there was one. He's a local hero, a national hero, a culture hero. He stands for all that is good and right and true. Wong is so goody-goody, he doesn't smoke, gamble, drink, womanize, steal, embezzle, or even lie.[20] He doesn't swear, doesn't shout, and doesn't lose his temper (well, only rarely). He always dresses well, is clean-shaven and neatly turned-out. He is a very traditional, old school Chinaman. He practises an ancient form of medicine. He is suspicious of modern ways and modern technology. He is fairly chauvinist, and upholds patriarchal society and culture. In the *Once Upon a Time In China* movies, Wong embodies all that is best and great in China and Chinese history. (From this description of Wong Fei-hung, you can see why Tsui Hark is so fascinated by him, because onto Wong Tsui can attach many of his own concerns, his themes, his ideals).

The *Once Upon a Time In China* series is also about 'doing the right thing'. It's about doing what you believe in; and it's about righting wrongs. Wong Fei-hung embodies this in his characterization as well as his acts or his words. The goody-goody aspects of Wong can be too much to take for audiences (in the 1950s as well as the 1990s), so Wong's personality, his ethics and morality, are often gently lampooned or undercut by his coterie (tho' always only mildly, and never seriously). Tsui Hark pointed out that Wong wasn't always right (and the films showed that).

For Stephen Teo, Wong Fei-hung embodies the Chinese concept of *ren* (a mix of nobility and benevolence). Wong stands in the middle of the 'foreign devils' trying to obtain a piece of the action in China and the corrupt Chinese officials and administrations: 'Wong Fei-hung is the only person who personifies *ren*; he alone is a man among wolves, one man against the world' (170-1).

---
[19] The elder Wong declined to teach his son martial arts, so the boy learnt from his father's teacher, Luk Ah Choy.
[20] His characterization, in movie terms, is very much like a Buddhist monk.

The first *Wong Fei-hung* movie was directed in 1949 by Wu Pang: Wu and Yong Yao Film Company put together the cast: Kwan Tak Hing (the 'Patriot Entertainer') as Wong Fei-hung, Walter Tso Tat Wah as Leung Foon, Shek Kin as the villain, and Li Lan as the love interest (it wasn't only Kwan who was a household name). The Wong Fei-hung series became one of the longest-running film series in history (25 movies were produced in 1956 at the height of the Wong Fei-hung movies' popularity).

The actor who played Wong Fei-hung the most in the Chinese media – Kwan Tak Hing (1905-1996) – became completely associated with the character, and became something of a legend in his own right. He was a martial artist, who for some embodied the tenets of the martial arts way of life. To the point where Kwan *is* Wong Fei-hung for modern audiences, even tho' many other actors have portrayed him including Jackie Chan, Andy Lau and Jet Li. Kwan became identified so much with the persona of Wong that nobody else could possibly play him, it seemed. Kwan was a Peking Opera performer, and the Peking Opera style informs the series. (Kwan was used to advertize products, particularly those associated with health. He had stores based on Po Chi Lam.)

Kwan Tak Hing has played the same character more times than anyone else in film history. In the heyday of the 1950s and 1960s, there were many Wong movies, with Wong pitted against a multitude of adversaries.

So when Jet Li came to play Wong Fei-hung in the 1990s, this was a character, a story, and a legend that Chinese audiences were very familiar with. Yet the greatness of the *Once Upon a Time In China* movies that they work just fine without all of that history and legend. The situations and the characters are bold enough, and simplified enough, so that a general movie audience anywhere can understand them. You don't need to know about the intricacies of Chinese history, or cinema history, to enjoy these movies immensely.

Indeed, it's almost as if Jet Li was born to play Wong Fei-hung, so elegantly and deeply does his screen persona merge with that of Wong. Li described Wong Fei-hung as 'young and innocent, and daring to do things that are impulsive' (rather like himself, he said). The reception of the *Once Upon a Time In China* movies in China would likely be completely different from that of audiences in the West. But it doesn't matter: movies like this truly are international and global. And action – like sex or horror or very broad comedy – really does translate well. You don't need subtitles or explanations when the hero is battling adversaries in a comical fashion with an umbrella!

Critics said that Jet Li was too young to play Wong Fei-hung (and that he was a *wushu* star, not a true *kung fu* fighter). Yes he was young (he was 28): but by the end of the first movie 1991, the critics must've been silenced. Li *owns* the role, just as Kwan Tak Hing did in 100s of Wong Fei-hung outings.[21] Li seems to have been born to play this character.[22] But this is a Wong for the 1990s, and it's a Wong as conceptualized by one of the great Chinese directors of recent times, Tsui Hark, and a team of fabulously talented filmmakers. Young tho' he is, Li also plays Wong as a commander convincingly. When Li says jump, you can believe that his followers do jump. Li's committment to the role is total on screen, and he is wholly believable. (And let's not forget the many other actors who performed the role of Wong Fei-hung following the famous interpretation by Kwan Tak Hing, including Jackie Chan, Lau Far Fai, etc (see below). And other Wong Fei-hung movies appeared when *Once Upon a Time In China* was seen to be such a success. But it was Jet Li who embodied Wong for a contemporary audience.)

❖

The *Wong Fei-hung* movies ran for 99 productions (tho' 108, an auspicious number, had been planned). Tsui Hark, along with many other Hong Kong filmmakers, has probably seen a good many of them (they were on television in Canton many times). As Bey Logan noted in *Hong Kong Action Cinema*, the *Wong Fei-hung* series 'remains by far the world's longest-running film series, leaving all Western challengers in the dust' (10). The market for these movies was local: Hong Kong and Mainland China. Kwan Tak Hing starred in all of them, usually with Shek Kin (Chin Chi Lok) as his opponent. For Chinese audiences, Kwan *is* Wong Fei-hung. The first Kwan *Wong* movie was *The True Story of Wong Fey Hung* of 1949; the series ran up until 1970,[23] with directors including Hu Peng, Wang Feng and Luo Chi.

Many other actors have played Wong, of course, including Jackie Chan (the young Wong, in *Drunken Master*), Lau Far Fai (in *Martial Club* and *Challenge of the Masters*), Andy Lau (*The Return of Wong Fei Hung*, 1984), Chin Man Chuk (a.k.a. Vincent Zhao, in the later *Once Upon a Time In China* movies), Wong Gok (*Heroes Among Heroes*, a.k.a. *Wong Fei Hung and Beggar So*, 1993), Tse Man (*Iron Monkey*), Wong Kwan (*Fist From Shaolin*), Daniel Lam (*Men Don't Cry*, 2007), Dickey Cheung (*The Kung Fu Master Wong Fei Hung*, 2008), David Chiang (*Grace Under Fire*, 2011), etc. *Kick Boxer* (1993) was a Wu Ma-directed picture about Ghost Foot Seven, played by Yuen Biao (= Clubfoot, played by Xiong Xin-xin in *Once Upon a Time In China*, among others).

Some of the cast and crew in some of the *Wong Fei-hung* movies had studied martial arts with descendants of the students of Wong himself (and also Lam Sai 'Butcher' Wing, Wong's famous follower). Lau Chan, for instance, had studied with Lam Sai and appeared in the series for 10 years. Meanwhile, Lam Sai's son, Lau Kar Leung (a.k.a. Liu Chia-liang), is one of Hong Kong cinema's foremost directors, and also appeared in the *Wong Fei-hung* series, in *Wong Fei-hung Vanquished the Twelve Lions* and

---
[21] It's worth reminding ourselves that it isn't Jet Li we hear as Wong Fei-hung, but a voice artist. This was common in Chinese cinema at the time (where movies were shot wild, without sound). And Jet Li is a Mandarin speaker.
[22] Jet Li injured his ankle during filming the first *Wong Fei-hung* movie, so some of his action scenes were doubled (by Xin-xin Xiong).
[23] The last movie was *Wong Fey hung: Bravely Crushing the Fire Formation*.

Wong Fei-hung Wins the Dragon Boat Race. Lau also appeared in *Seven Swords*, directed by Tsui Hark (and was action director).

THE TYPICAL WONG FEI-HUNG MOVIE

> Take the Wong Fei Hung series as an example. When I was small, I was obsessed with the stories of the Wong Feihung character. The subject matter had become very much outdated, but in my world, it'd never be outdated. That's why I shot the *Once Upon a Time in China*.
>
> Tsui Hark

A movie about Wong Fei-hung contains a number of recurring elements: first, there's Wong, a Robin Hood/ Wyatt Earp figure, a hero,[24] a *kung fu* master, a leader of a group (and a *kung fu* school),[25] a healer and a doctor (Wong is always called 'Wong *sifu*' = Master Wong). Wong is about doing the right thing, about following a righteous path, about clear, noble principles and morals. Sometimes he's too good to be true (so his self-righteous persona is sent up with some light comedy by those around him; but it's never seriously questioned). Wong is also the stern father, the figure who embodies all that is good and right and true in society. Tsui Hark often emphasizes, in interviews, an aspect of Wong Fei-hung that's important for him: Wong as a father figure (maybe that isn't always apparent in the movies because of Jet Li's youthful looks). Wong embodies hard work, too, and dedication to one's calling (whether it be healing or *kung fu*).

Because Wong Fei-hung is such a powerful figure, he is often beset by institutions or groups rather than a single villain. It's too easy for Wong to take down a single individual (no matter how wonderful their fighting skills are). So Wong's opponents tend to be whole Triad gangs, or groups of officials who're in cahoots with the Dowager Empress or visiting foreigners. However, these organizations or gangs will have a leader with whom Wong will do battle one-on-one at the end of the third or fourth act finale.

Wong Fei-hung isn't a killer – he is a doctor, he embodies kind-heartedness, healing, negotiation, and doing the right thing. But he does kill someone in *Once Upon a Time In China* – only one person: Jackson, the leader of the slave-trading Yanks.[26]

There's a host of supporting characters in the Wong Fei-hung legend, including the hapless but well-meaning Leung Foon, the equally hapless

---

24 Bey Logan calls Wong 'a folk hero like the Shadow, the Lone Ranger and Sherlock Holmes all rolled into one' (10).
25 Wong Fei-hung's martial arts was based in Hung Gar, the Southern *kung fu* style descended from the Shaolin Temple.
26 Wong does injure plenty of victims, however.

and even sillier 'Buck Tooth' So (who's studying medicine under Wong), the fat butcher Porky, the '13th Aunt' (a.k.a. Lee or Peony), as the love interest, sometimes Wong's father, Wong Kei-ying, and of course the officials, the Governors, the local militia, militarized/ politicized groups, the foreigners, the students in the martial arts school, the Triad gangs, the villains, and so on. (In the *Once Upon a Time In China* series, some supporting players appear in several roles – sometimes as heavies, sometimes as heroes).

The Po Chi Lam clinic is a key setting for much of a Wong Fei-hung movie. Often it's under attack, or there'll be nighttime raids. There's the big town set. Often a harbour scene.[27] A house or villa for an exile scene. A warehouse. A Buddhist temple. Sometimes a forest (Wong Fei-hung movies are set in Guangdong, not Hong Kong).

Typically the background or action plot will involve Wong Fei-hung and his cohorts battling corrupt officials, or slave traders, or rival *kung fu* schools, or Triad gangs. There's usually some big wrong to be righted, and Wong is the hero who tackles the villain in the end. Structurally, the typical Wong Fei-hung movie follows the formula for all action-adventure movies: a loss or lack or wrong occurs in the first act, which's resolved in the big finale. Between the first action scene and the last action scene, there will be three or four action scenes.

Conflicts're typically depicted (and resolved) with action sequences in Wong Fei-hung flicks – fights in warehouses, fights in the street by day, fights in restaurants, nighttime raids, scenes where the (corrupt) officials burst in to arrest someone, martial arts contests, and martial artists who come to challenge Wong Fei-hung.[28]

ONCE UPON A TIME IN THE WEST

The *Once Upon a Time In China* movies take their name in Western markets from *Once Upon a Time in the West* (Sergio Leone, 1968), a highly regarded movie which continues the themes and tropes of the *Fistful of Dollars* trilogy (also directed by Leone). *Once Upon a Time In America* (1984) is also a reference point (and an influential film on Hong Kong cinema). But Tsui chose the title. It's unfortunate, in a way: it gives the *Once Upon a Time In China* flicks a cinematic title, a title which refers to another movie, making the films 'movie-movies'. *Wong Fei-hung* is a more accurate title – but, of course, that won't carry overseas.[29]

Once Upon a Time in the West contains the familiar elements of the

---

[27] At the time of the *Once Upon a Time In China* movies, Hong Kong was a massive harbour and trade port, with warehousing, shipping, and boat building major industries.
[28] Other recurring scenes in Wong Fei-hung movies include Lion Dances, competitions, festivals, rituals, and torture.
[29] Tsui remarked that the Western title, *Once Upon a Time In China*, was optimistic – it could be 'now, can be the future'. The title *Once Upon a Time In China* influenced the names of subsequent films, such as the *Once Upon a Time In a Triad Society* films (1996).

taciturn gunslinger; an elegiac pace (such as in the opening sequence, a railroad heist); men striking macho poses; moments of sudden violence; and Ennio Morricone's stunning soundtrack. The movie cast against type, with Henry Fonda playing a ruthless villain; Charles Bronson as the laconic, Clint Eastwood character, withdrawn and mysterious, a brilliant shot, who played a harmonica, with Morricone's haunting, echoey riff.

Once Upon a Time in the West paid homage to and parodied the clichés of the American Western movie, with its gun fights, gunmen appearing out of nowhere, and the building of the railroad and frontier towns. It was a pæan to the creation of the Wild West as seen through the history of Western movies, a film about myths and legends of the West.

Once Upon a Time in the West portrays a thoroughly, viciously patriarchal world, a world of male rituals, confrontation, greed, money, violence, torture, dominated by the gun, the saloon, and the railroad. In this all-male sphere, with her thick 1960s kohl, make-up and hairstyle, Claudia Cardinale stands out as the lone woman. The men, meanwhile (Fonda, Bronson, Jason Robards, Jack Elam), are implacably tough and impenetrable. The filmmakers' cinematic approach was baroque and mannered, with sweeping crane shots and long lens close-ups, in widescreen, a style which Bernardo Bertolucci would later emulate (he co-wrote the screenplay with Leone and Dario Argento).

Kwan Tak-hing as Wong fei hung.

2

ONCE UPON A TIME IN CHINA

Wong Fei-hung

INTRO.

*Once Upon a Time In China*1 is called *Wong Fei-hung* in China (*Huang Feihong* in Cantonese) – a better and more accurate title (tho' probably meaningless to a general Western audience, who've never heard of Wong Fei-hung). Western distributors tend to give Chinese movies titles which'll be understood by the target market (the title *Once Upon a Time In China* is misleading, tho', being a movie reference. Also, *Once Upon a Time In China* is far too significant to be reduced to a filmic title, and also to a reference to a 1968 Western called *Once Upon a Time In the West*.2 However, it was Tsui Hark who decided that *Once Upon a Time In China* would be a good title – it suggested for him 'that actually *Once Upon a Time In China* can be now, can be the future' [LM, 82]).

The first two *Once Upon a Time In China* movies were filmed in Hong Kong; Golden Harvest produced (with Raymond Chow as executive producer); Tsui Hark's Film Workshop was the production company (with Paragon Films); the writers were Kai Chi Yuen, Elsa Tang, Yiu Ming Leung, Dang Bik-min and Tsui; Arthur Wong, Bill Wong, David Chung, Angry Lam, Lam Kwok-Wah, Tung Chuen Chan and Paui Kai Chan were the DPs (6 DPs, but the look is consistent);3 Mak Chi Sin (Marco Mak) was editor; Lau Kar-wing,4 Yuen Shun-yee, Yuen Cheung-yan,5 Chia Yung Liu, and Bruce Law were the action choreographers (with Yuen Woo-ping also helping out uncredited); costumes were by Bruce Yu Ka-on; hair by Siu-Mui Chau and Yuk-Mui Wan; make-up by Ka-Pik Lai, Yun-Ling Man and Min-Hua Pan; sound by Chow Shao-lung, Leung Ka-lun and Kwok Wing-kei; and music by

---

1 For more information on the *Once Upon a Time In China* series, see my companion book.
2 Yes, *Once Upon a Time In the West* is regarded as a classic movie, and its title has been used many times. But it demeans *Once Upon a Time In China* by seeming to ride on the coattails of another movie.
3 One of the DPs of the *Once Upon a Time In China* series, Park Yoon Kyo, was also a director (*Bloody Smile*), as is Arthur Wong.
4 Tsui said he and Lau Kar-wing had not gelled in their view of how the action in *Once Upon a Time In China* should be delivered.
5 Yuen Cheung-yan is one of Yuen Woo-ping's many brothers: he is the guy who loses to Wong Fei-hung's rival, and he's the Taoist Priest in *Tai Chi Master* and *Drunken Tai Chi*.

James Wong Jim and Romeo Diaz (George Lam composed the theme song). Many in the team were regulars in the Tsui Hark Movie Circus.

Jet Li and Rosamund Kwan are the top-billed stars (sharing the billing on-screen); others in the cast included Jacky Cheung (Bucktooth So), Kam-Fai Yuen (Kai), Kent Cheng (Pork Wing), Lau Shun (commander of the Black Flag militia), Yan Yee-kwan (Iron Robe Yim), Wong Chi-yeung (Governor), Wu Ma (Grand-Uncle Cheung), Jian-Guo Chiu (Shaho gang leader), Xin-xin Xiong (member of the Shaho gang), Leung Gam-san (the leader of the opera troupe) and Yuen Biao (Leung Foon). Many in the cast crop up in the later installments. Simon Yam and Shih Kien have cameos. Playing the Westerners (boo! hiss!) were: Jonathan James Isgar (Jackson), Steve Tartalia (Tiger), Mark King (General Wickens, a British general), and Colin George (Jesuit Priest). Released August 15, 1991. 134 minutes.

The film is set in Guangdong.[6] *Once Upon a Time In China* cost U.S. $8.4 million.[7] It has four acts (not three). Three acts is usual for Tsui Hark's films, because they generally come in at 80-90 minutes (each act being 25-30 minutes).

That *Once Upon a Time In China* is a masterpiece, pretty much everybody agrees.[8] For Maggie Lee, the *Once Upon a Time In China* movies are 'thrilling action movies. Here, the highest-caliber martial artists and stunt experts were able to reach the peak of their skills' (2021). It's a labour of love – clear to see in every frame. Like *Zu: Warriors From the Magic Mountain*, *Once Upon a Time In China* is a movie that Tsui Hark was born to make.

In it, Tsui Hark and the production team have not only delivered a marvellous updating and reworking of the Wong Fei-hung legend,[9] they also created a terrific action movie, and a satisfying textured and layered historical drama, which also contains a beguiling mix of other elements (such as romance, comedy, nostalgia and political commentary). Tsui won Best Director for *Once Upon a Time In China* at the Hong Kong Film Awards. *Once Upon a Time In China* was his best movie, Tsui thought – until he looked at it again, and saw all the flaws (1997, 136).

In *Once Upon a Time In China*, Tsui Hark throws in a feast of numerous Chinese traditions and cultural forms which fascinate him: Peking Opera performance, Chinese healing and herbalism (and acupuncture), a Lion Dance, fireworks and martial arts *dojos*.

Once Upon a Time In China is a rich movie in its portrayals of the secondary characters – which's one of the marks of a great movie (in many action movies, minor characters are vaguely conceived, often under-written, and usually depicted along stereotypical lines). You can feel the love the film has for its large cast – it's clear throughout *Once Upon a Time In China*: this is definitely a movie made with love.

---
[6] Wong was born in Guangdong, the son of Wong Kai Ying, one of the 'Ten Tigers of Canton', a herbalist and fighter.
[7] Lisa Morton claims it was $12 million, which seems too much (LM, 216).
[8] 'As pure entertainment, it's a hoot from first frame to last' (Lisa Morton, 216).
[9] Tsui Hark: 'When a film genre's [popularity] goes from its peak to its trough to its peak again, it always has to do with new angles, new approaches and new feelings. That's why our movies are always going through cycles.'

Once Upon a Time In China features literally 100s of minor bits of business placed around the edges of the plot and the main characters. You can tell if filmmakers are engaged with their material if they keep coming up with things for the secondary characters to do, where they explore all sorts of details and corners of the sets, where the entourage around the central charas is so vividly evoked.

Thus, *Once Upon a Time In China* is stuffed with Tsui Harkisms, those bits of action and visual gems which Tsui snuffles out and foregrounds.

For example, the fierce, devoted but angry Porky Lang, one of Wong Fei-hung's followers, but someone who's fury at the 'foreign devils' leads him to explode at many points. Porky is not a one-dimensional character, not just the fat, buffoon sidekick: the scene where he stubbornly kneels outside in the rain because the *sifu* hasn't asked him to come inside (after yet another scene where he lost his temper), is moving. And the scenes where Leung Foon makes friends with Iron Robe Yim (Yan Yee-kwan)[10] forms another subplot in *Once Upon a Time In China* which's touching: how Iron Robe, tho' a martial arts master, doesn't even have enough money for food, so he performs in the street, in the rain (much to the scorn of the prostitutes nearby). And how Foon later steals some soup to take to Iron Robe.

We think of *Once Upon a Time In China* as an all-out action and martial arts extravaganza – which it is! – but it also contains numerous intimate scenes, quiet scenes, scenes of characterization and humour. The budding romance of Peony and Wong, the friendship of Leung Foon and Iron Robe, Bucktooth So impersonating the *sifu* – *Once Upon a Time In China* is full of these small-scale scenes which thicken the characters out, making this far more than your average chop socky flick.

Christianity certainly is a grotesque religion to some observing it from the outside. In the chapel inside the British Embassy, for instance, there's a scene where Wong Fei-hung looks up at the large stained glass window of Christ crucified on the cross. How can people worship a god that suffers so much? Yes, it's question that many people have asked (and compared to the smiling Buddha, the crucified Son of God does seem a gruesome icon).

The laserdisc edition of *Once Upon a Time In China* was problematic: as Tsui Hark recalled, the distributors wanted the movie to be reduced from 120 to 90 minutes. Anybody looking at the amount of story packed into *Once Upon a Time In China* can see that it would be a tougher challenge than with many another movie. But Tsui and his editors duly acquiesced, tho' it was frustrating – because the distributors decided to release it as a 120-minute movie anyway, but 'the music and everything was kind of weird', Tsui said (LM, 82). Another release had bad sound when the distributors tried to use a Dolby system.

THE OPENING SCENE.

The opening prologue of *Once Upon a Time In China* is an important

---

10 Yan Yee-kwan is one of Tsui's regular actors – appearing in *The Swordsman 2* and *3*, *Iron Monkey*, and *New Dragon Gate Inn*.

scene which compresses the whole 1991 movie into several minutes. It states many of the key themes (and even uses banners unfurled to make sure the audience gets the messages: 'the people, the land', 'bravery' and 'loyalty'). It also introduces the star, the main character, the period setting, the costumes, and the *very* flamboyant cinematic style that the filmmakers will be employing in the rest of the piece.

It's typical of Tsui Hark that the whole *Once Upon a Time In China* series should open with a model shot – of boats on the ocean (it's a historical movie, but it opens with visual effects).[11] The miniature image is soon intercut with full-size vessels, leading up to the introduction of the star, Jet Li, on a boat, with the commander of the Black Flag militia (played by Tsui regular Lau Shun).

As well as miniatures, *Once Upon a Time In China* makes much use of matte paintings and optical printing to add skies, buildings, etc. You don't think of *Once Upon a Time In China* as a visual effects movie, but actually it is a major vfx picture (for the fire and pyrotechnic effects alone).

The opening shots of ships at sea, tho', announces instantly one of the key themes of the first *Once Upon a Time In China* movie (and of the series as a whole): the arrival of foreign (Western) powers. The boats evoke West meets East; Europe and China; Guangdong as a trading zone; and new, Western technology (guns, boats, firepower) versus older, Asian ways (the gun vs. sword is a recurring motif in Chinese action cinema, as well as Japanese cinema). It wasn't long before the time of *Once Upon a Time In China* that British gun-boats were deployed as superior firepower in the struggle to control trade in China.

The opening scene of *Once Upon a Time In China* has Wong Fei-hung joining the general of the Black Flag Army on board a vessel where a Lion Dance is taking place, led by Hsin Shen (as they do on auspicious occasions. The Lion Dance looks forward to the third *Once Upon a Time In China* movie, and was also a key ingredient in another Wong Fei-hung movie, 1993's *Last Hero In China*. Lion Dances appear in the earlier *Wong Fei-hung* flicks, such as *Dreadnaught*, 1981). It's no surprise that the first scene in *Once Upon a Time In China* is a very traditional, Chinese practice.

The notion that (French?) soldiers on a ship nearby open fire with their rifles when they mistake the fire crackers going off during the Lion Dance for gunfire is over-wrought (and a little unconvincing), but dramatizes one of the central tensions of the *Once Upon a Time In China* series: between foreign powers and the Chinese, between the new, capitalist world then emerging, and the old, traditional, Chinese world (with its Lion Dance customs), between outsiders who come to China to trade, and the Chinese people's ambivalence towards them (the British wanted tea from China; China didn't want anything that the British had to offer; so what did the British government do? It created an opium addiction in China, supplied from India – one of the creepiest things the British rulers have achieved in

---

[11] To show ships on the ocean, I wonder if Tsui Hark saw *Othello* (1952), Orson Welles' version of William Shakespeare which used a scale model of a boat moved by grips offscreen, to suggest a boat on waves.

recent times).

That capitalism and trade is backed up by force, vividly evoked in the opening scene of *Once Upon a Time In China*, is of course a key issue in the late 19th century/ early 20th century period. And it's an issue that remains totally contemporary – it's about the relationship between capitalism and militarism, between the exploitation of capitalism and the individual and the community, which resonates today in issues such as 9/11, or the West's military presence in Afghanistan, or the Western territories' goals of trading into Asia.

These background/ geo-political issues are not why the *Once Upon a Time In China* series is so compelling – who goes to the cinema for a lecture on market forces, global capitalism, and nationalism? But they do give the *Once Upon a Time In China* series a distinctly and overtly political and ideological ambience. There's no doubt that these political issues are uppermost in the *Wong Fei-hung* movies, providing the framework for the stories and the characters, and consciously put there by the filmmakers.

But this is *filmmaking*, this is *storytelling*. If the filmmakers wanted to deliver a lecture, or a PhD thesis, or a Communist or right-wing diatribe, they might've chosen a different arena. The political and ideological elements of the *Once Upon a Time In China* series are only *part* of the mix, yet they have been seized upon by Western critics as one of the main things to discuss about the series. Why? For all the obvious reasons – not least that it's easier for journalists and reviewers to discuss global politics in relation to Chinese filmmaking than *kung fu* or swordplay or action or the characters or the technical aspects of the movies.

However, it is precisely those ingredients – the spectacle, the *kung fu* action, the humour, the romance, the characters and the situations – that draw punters into a theatre (as well as their favourite stars). If an audience wants a lecture or political rant, they can read a newspaper or watch telly (which never miss an opportunity to lecture their audiences). They go to a Chinese action movie for something else!

Some of the gunfire hits the Lion Dance performers, so it's up to Wong Fei-hung to save the day. The opening scene introduces some bravura wirework and nimble rope-straddling footwork from Wong, as he rescues the situation (Wong takes up the lion's head, and dances it up the ropes of the ship). If it's an action movie, you want to see action upfront, right? Yes! And you want to see your star in action too, right? Yes! The scene offers the delight in seeing Jet Li performing aerial stunts.[12] It shows Wong doing the right thing, and the values he embodies (such as upholding traditions, nobility, fighting for Chinese culture, as well as incredible physical agility. Wong is linked to Lion Dances in many *Wong* movies, and he is of course the best Lion Dancer). It pits Wong Fei-hung and his entourage against the foreigners. It shows Wong using martial arts skills against Western firepower.

In short, the scene encapsulates numerous narrative themes which'll

---

[12] Tho' Jet Li is of course doubled throughout the *Once Upon a Time In China* series for more dangerous gags.

play out through the *Once Upon a Time In China* series. Wong Fei-hung repeats this sort of scene many times. The patriarch general advises Wong to train up his Black Flag followers, because they are going to need them in these troubled times. This leads directly into the credits sequence, one of the great set-pieces of the *Once Upon a Time In China* series, the training scene on the beach at sunset involving a hundred or so topless trainees in the Black Flag militia, to the sound of the famous Wong Fei-hung music, 'Under the General's Orders' (reworked as 'A Man Should Better Himself' by James Wong Jim, and sung by George Lam (Cantonese version) and Jackie Chan (Mandarin version)).

Every time that Wong Fei-hung does something noble and heroic, the celebrated music starts up (it has a similar function to the *James Bond* theme music, the twangy guitar, which comes in when Bond performs some incredible stunt). The music has been associated with Wong right back to the 1930s and 1940s.

The opening scene is filmed with Tsui Hark's customary lavish cinematic style: elaborate slow motion, very low camera angles, tilted camera, richly saturated colours, meticulously researched costumes,[13] designs and settings, heightened action, and punchy sound effects.

The prologue introduces the extravagant political conflict (here, white Europeans firing on and wounding Chinese locals), which's a staple of the Tsui Hark approach to movie-making. And the prologue also has Wong Fei-hung and the general unfurling banners which state some of the key themes of *Once Upon a Time In China* (and of Tsui Hark's cinema).

THE STYLE.

Action! *Once Upon a Time In China* is a masterpiece of action cinema, as are the other two movies among the first three *Wong Fei-hung* outings. The first act might've been somewhat leisurely with its set-ups and character introductions (yet is still contains plenty of action compared to most movies). But once this 1991 Hong Kong picture gets going, it doesn't stop! One outstanding action sequence follows another: Iron Robe Yim versus an opponent who dares to take him on by firelight;[14] Iron Robe against Wong Fei-hung in the rain at the medical clinic; Wong beating Hung and the Shaho gang in a restaurant, armed with an umbrella; the attack on the clinic at night; the brawl in the Pearl Restaurant; the tussle with the Governor and his soldiers; the street fight with the Shaho gang; the enormously complex theatre sequence...

This is truly remarkable filmmaking. The feeling of freedom, of movement, of colour, of light, of sound, of music, is just phenomenal. The *sensuality* of *Once Upon a Time In China*, and many Chinese action movies, is *so strong*. You might not see any sex on screen in *Once Upon a Time In China* (the only kiss is when Aunt Lee chastely kisses Wong's shadow! And even that's enough to make him recoil!), but these movies

---
13 Tsui Hark wanted the costume designer to go to England to find the wardrobe for *Once Upon a Time In China*, because he was after authenticity. The costumes for *Project A 2* (1987), a Jackie Chan actioner, were hired from Britain for the same reason.
14 This was choreographed by Lau Kar-wing.

are steaming with beautiful, erotic imagery, movement and sounds.15

Like some horror movies, and like some musicals, with their emphasis on the body, on blood, on dance and movement, the *Once Upon a Time In China* series (and Chinese action movies in general) are hugely *sensual*. They possess the grace and elegance of the finest movie musicals and dance pictures – the choreography alone is fantastically sexy. These movies are *radiant* with bodies, with the body in motion.

And *Once Upon a Time In China* is also a gorgeous movie of *light* – from magic hour photography (the director's favourite time of day, but not the cinematographer's, as it only lasts 10 minutes), through muted, overcast days, to sunsets and dawns, to candlelight, lamplight, firelight and a full-on burning sequence. (Historical movies are dream projects for cinematographers, of course, with their natural light, firelight, candlelight, fireworks, and flaming torches – you'll often find that DPs deliver their most satisfying work on a period picture. And so does everyone else – historical movies raise everyone's game).

The amount of slow motion is striking in *Once Upon a Time In China* – considerably more than in many of Tsui Hark's pix as director. And it's used in places where conventional shots would work just as well.

But *Once Upon a Time In China* didn't please everyone: David West complained in his book on martial arts in movies that the *kung fu* on display in *Once Upon a Time In China* has no relation to Southern Chinese martial arts: 'The film presents a paradox – it is a kung fu movie that contains no kung fu' (182).

THE CHARACTERS.

After the spectacular opening scenes, *Once Upon a Time In China* settles into a much slower, ambling first act. Many characters're introduced, and their relationships: Aunt Lee or Yeo (a.k.a. Cousin Lee, a.k.a. 13th Aunt, a.k.a. Peony),16 played by the delightful Rosamund Kwan (born on Sept 24, 1962, Kwan is one of the iconic faces of the New Wave of Chinese cinema, but she was never better than playing the 13th Aunt in the *Once Upon a Time In China* series). Kwan's speciality is sweet, cute, rather naïve, young women, the older sister or girl next door figure. She has a lovely chemistry with Jet Li. She is consciously not a fighting female, and doesn't go into battle beside the hero (Kwan has refused to do fight scenes). In *Once Upon a Time In China*, she's more the princess who needs to be rescued by the hero. However, in later installments, such as the American jaunt of 1997, she is given more action to do. And in the Peking Opera theatre sequence, she has a pistol and shoots a guy.

Aunt Lee is a woman enamoured of Western ways, including its technology (such as cameras, both still and movie cameras), and its fashions. Wong Fei-hung is asked to look after Lee by an uncle figure (Grand-Uncle Cheung, played by Wu Ma), which begins the romantic subplot in *Wong Fei-hung* (despite her innocence, Peony is more worldly

---
15 The celibate master or teacher is a common type in traditional, Chinese culture – it's all about conserving *chi* and power.
16 Aunt Lee was created as someone who was separate from the family around Wong Fei-hung, who could comment upon him and his life objectively (LM, 82).

than Wong when it comes to modern ways; the *Once Upon a Time In China* series squeezes much humour from the difference in knowledge between the two potential lovers, with Peony often playing the teacher and Wong the pupil).

For Tsui Hark, Wong Fei-hung was a chauvinist, from a chauvinistic society, who is 'being threatened by a very strong woman who knows lots of things about the world that he doesn't know'.[17] The introduction of Aunt Lee early on thus announces that *this* interpretation of the Wong Fei-hung mythology will be overtly proto-feminist, and it will place a woman at the centre of what is usually, in Wong Fei-hung movies, a patriarchal and masculinist world.

Both Aunt Lee and Bucktooth So have recently returned from North America, a plot point which is brought out as soon as they meet Wong Fei-hung (such as in the Western custom of shaking hands, the Western style of clothes,[18] and of course the camera and tripod). Several of the Chinese characters comment despairingly on Aunt Lee speaking or acting like a foreigner. The cultural/ social differences, however, among the Chinese, are often played for comedy; between Chinese and Western characters, they are treated more seriously.

Then there's Porky Wing (Kent Cheng), another staple figure in the Wong Fei-hung legend, one of many Chinese characters in the *Once Upon a Time In China* series who're really angry at the foreign presence in China (Porky cries 'foreign devil!' at the Jesuit Priest, and rushes at him, before Wong tells him to calm down). Porky's an endearing character, but he was dropped from subsequent outings (re-appearing in film 5). And there's Bucktooth So (Jacky Cheung Hok Yau), a rather foolish sidekick with a comical stutter (and another regular character in the Wong Circus); foolish, but So has been to the U.S.A. with Aunt Lee (and, as he points out to Porky, he can read, too). Ling Wan-Kai (Kam-Fai Yuen) is prominent as one of Wong's aides.

Leung Foon, played by the wonderful Yuen Biao (another key face of the Chinese New Wave cinema), is introduced arriving at Po Chi Lam clinic, hoping to learn from Wong Fei-hung (but meeting Bucktooth So instead: the comical scene plays to Biao's strengths as an eager, naïve, acrobatic personality (similar to his character in *Zu: From the Magic Mountains*); the skit is based on a misunderstanding, with So impersonating Wong). The scene is also constructed to introduce another star in Chinese cinema, Jacky Cheung (playing So behind thick glasses).

Ah Foon is shown helping out at a waterside playhouse.[19] In the first act, Foon is given quite a bit of story, including a run-in with the local gang, the Shaho Triads, coming to the theatre for their protection money (the Triad gang's leader Tong is a mean heavy played by Yau Kon-kwok).

As the characters're introduced, the story of *Once Upon a Time In*

---

17 In L. Stokes, 336.
18 Even tho' Aunt Lee is very feminine, she also dresses in (tomboyish) Western clothes, is feisty and assertive, and in some of the later installments she is given key acts in action scenes.
19 He's up on the roof, fixing it, complaining that he's scared of heights – a trait that comes from Tsui Hark.

China gradually emerges – but in leisurely fashion. Meanwhile, the technical aspects of the movie are breathtaking – from the exquisite production design and art direction by Kenneth Lee Chung-man and Ben Lau Man-hung, to the cinematography (of six DPs).

MULTIPLE LEVELS OF VIOLENCE.

Once Upon a Time In China is a very violent movie. Not the martial arts duels, which seem to exist in a cinematic world of their own – a realm of movement, gesture, dance and choreography – but the violence within the story. *Once Upon a Time In China* features scenes of soldiers firing upon civilians and killing them; a very brutal rape; the Shaho gang unloading guns into a victim at point-blank range, etc. (The *Once Upon a Time In China* series are Category II films = 'not suitable for children' but still for general audiences. They are not Category IIB, the equivalent of 'R' rated films, as films such as *The Blade* were).

And *Once Upon a Time In China* contains many other disturbing images: of racism, of slavery, of imprisonment, and one of Wong Fei-hung's patients covered in blood (who expires). This is a romantic-melodramatic epic movie, yes, and it's a re-invention of the Wong Fei-hung legend, yes, and it's filled with outrageously inventive action, yes, but it is also stuffed with very grim material: young women in cells taken as slaves, poverty and hunger, multiple deaths, rape, etc.

The violence on-screen is between individuals – that's what drama does. But unlike many movies, which don't go further than that, *Once Upon a Time In China* is loud and clear in bringing out the oppression and the exploitation within the social systems and the political backgrounds (the political stance of *Once Upon a Time In China* is thus liberal and left-wing (as in most of Tsui Hark's films), even tho' its main protagonist, Wong Fei-hung, is a self-confessed and proud conservative, keen to uphold traditions).

The anger of Tsui Hark's two early movies (*Dangerous Encounters – First Kind* and *We're Going To Eat You*) re-surfaces many times in *Once Upon a Time In China* (and sometimes threatens to unbalance the picture). After all, *Wong Fei-hung* is quite clear that the reasons and the under-lying causes behind the degradation, the slavery, and the violence are political and ideological (and capitalist). There are forces at work in *Once Upon a Time In China* which the movie elegantly and vividly places before the viewer, and Wong Fei-hung is caught in the middle of it all.

All of this reminds us, once more, that the *script* of *Once Upon a Time In China* is very fine indeed. Or put it like this: why is *Once Upon a Time In China* a masterpiece movie? Largely because the *conception* and the *script* is excellent.

THE MIDDLE ACTS.

What's also striking about *Once Upon a Time In China* is just how much it pushes its hero into corners and heaps on the obstacles. Wong Fei-hung is on his back foot throughout the second act, as political machinations and gang warfare threaten him and his community from all sides.

It's striking because it departs from your typical action-adventure tale: *Once Upon a Time In China* is not a simple story of good guys and bad guys in a time of political turmoil. Wong Fei-hung and his crew are battling the Shaho gang and their leader Hung, the Governor and his organization, who're aligned with some of the foreigners (the Shaho gang goes to make a deal with the North Americans),[20] and even Iron Robe (plus Leung Foon) turns up to create merry hell.

Once Upon a Time In China is a movie where the hero's home and workplace is burnt in a giant conflagration, in one of the incredible fire sequences in Chinese cinema that seem far, far more dangerous than anything put on the screen in North American cinema. An American production will have corridors of fire allowing for the actors to move, but, when filmed from certain angles, it looks like they're engulfed. Not the Chinese filmmakers! They put fires all around the performers: as with rain scenes, there's no need to act! Burning arrows are shot into the midst of the performers. (One can imagine that representatives from health and safety departments are scarce on a Hong Kong film set! Or at least in the 1980s and 1990s).

The fire sequence in *Once Upon a Time In China* is a major set-piece containing numerous beats within it: of the Shaho mob dressed as ninjas in black, the flaming arrows, the attempts at defending the building, Pork Wing trying to douse the flames, Porky and Kai saving the patients, Wong Fei-hung darting up onto the roof then into an alley to confront the villains, and chasing them on horseback with a burning branch... (the *Wong Fei-hung* films, of all periods, often feature an attack on the Po Chi Lam clinic).

Instead of a single opponent, the *Once Upon a Time In China* movies tend to place Wong Fei-hung in situations where he's up against large groups of people. His powers're pretty much super-human, so it makes sense to pile up the assailants around him (one or two isn't enough). Plus placing precious characters (like Aunt Lee) in jeopardy, so Wong has to save them as well as fight the baddies.

The Peking Opera theatre[21] massacre is a remarkable sequence in *Once Upon a Time In China*, climaxing act two. It is one of the greatest action scenes in Tsui Hark's cinema, a masterpiece of construction, script-wise, and execution as film.

Staged beside the water, the set's a major construction for the crew of wood and bamboo, representing a travelling theatre company. Before the action erupts big-time, the episode starts off with some light-hearted humour, as Porky Wing and Leung Foon take to the stage in full Peking Opera make-up and costume after Porky accidentally sent the actors on their way as he sits on the gate collecting tickets. The crossdressing sidekicks and plenty of acrobatics on the stage offer a show-within-a-show in *Once Upon a Time In China*, reminding us that this is an

---
20 This is a recurring theme in movies of the time – how some of the authorities colluded with the foreigners.
21 Lisa Morton notes that it's a black joke on the part of the Americans in setting up an assassination in a theatre (LM, 78).

extravagant spectacle (theatricality, dressing up and putting on a show are a staple of the New Wave of Hong Kong cinema; of course, the traditions of the Peking Opera are significant here. This is also cinema as pure entertainment, a show just for the sake of a show).

Yes, Tsui Hark stages another of his beloved Peking Opera scenes, as if a whole act of *Peking Opera Blues* was flown in from 1986 and dropped into the second act of *Once Upon a Time In China*. Tsui can't seem to get enough of putting his actors into the extravagant Peking Opera costumes and make-up (and for Yuen Biao, one of the 'Seven Little Fortunes', the Peking Opera troupe, this is home from home).

The comedy is there partly to set-up and contrast with the far more serious sequence where the theatre audience is fired upon by the Governor's troops (the North Americans are also in attendance, and thus are colluding). The scene is yet another demonstration of Western firepower, of the gun vs. the sword, of new technology vs. old ways. That it is Chinese soldiers firing upon Chinese civilians enhances the horror (the main purpose is to kill Wong Fei-hung).

The massacre occurs towards the end of the sequence, which builds from comedy thru rapidfire *kung fu* action (where people're hurt but not killed), to the bloodshed of the deaths of Chinese civilians. That is, the sequence is carefully constructed dramatically, proceeding logically to the point of horror in the massacre (where humour would be inappropriate). Humour's used to defuse dramatic tension sometimes (there's a look between Wong and Peony when she's rather close to him as he rescues her yet again), but not too much. The humour's kept in check because the scene manifests both the gruesome power of Western technology with its guns and weapons, and also the horror of a civil war scenario.[22]

The sequence also shows that Wong Fei-hung is powerless to alter the course of events: he and his entourage are a few against many – especially when some of those (such as the Governor) have aligned themselves with the foreign powers. (The Jesuit Priest throws himself in front of a bullet meant for Wong)

THOSE NASTY WESTERNERS.

The North Americans have hired Chinese to promote work in the gold mines of the American West, reflecting historical events when many Chinese people left for the New World: at a booth rather like something out of the Wild West, hirelings hand out leaflets advertizing a paradise of gold in the Land of the Free.[23] Notice Wong Fei-hung's reaction: he watches the Chinese clustering around the booth and shakes his head: why would someone from China want to travel halfway around the world?

Meanwhile, behind the scenes, the Shaho gang, working for the Yanks, have kidnapped Chinese women to sell as prostitutes back in the U.S.A. Here, it's the Westerners who are the corrupt, twisted villains (reversing the stereotypical depiction of Asians in similar Western

[22] The slow motion evokes Akira Kurosawa (in *The Seven Samurai*) and Sam Peckinpah (in *The Wild Bunch*).
[23] This became a reality in the final *Once Upon a Time In China* movie, when Wong Fei-hung and his entourage headed to the New World.

movies). So one of Wong Fei-hung's tasks is not only to defeat the Shaho crew, but the foreigners who've taken Chinese women (including Aunt Lee).

A DARK AND RAINY NIGHT.

Most of act three of *Once Upon a Time In China* is taken up with a lengthy series of episodes set on a dark and rainy night. The highpoint of this sequence, for martial arts fans, is definitely the Wong Fei-hung versus Iron Robe Yim smackdown, situated in the courtyard of the Po Chi Lam clinic in a *mise-en-scène* of hammering rain at night. A truly remarkable feat of choreography, wire-work, lighting, editing and practical effects, this sensational sequence was *hommaged* in 2002's *Hero* (with Jet Li fighting Donnie Yen – and *Hero* was also a tribute to the last time that Li and Yen fought on screen, in *Once Upon a Time In China 2*).

The use of a flying wooden log and of slow motion enhances the grace and ferocity of this smackdown. The choreography includes lightning-quick grappling and open-handed combat, plus the incredible sight of Jet Li motionless in the rain, listening for the movement of the foe he can't see clearly.

Under house arrest, the obstacles are piled high for Wong Fei-hung: he has Iron Robe Yim coming to challenge him, and the Governor and his mob are still trying to pin him down. Which of course leads rapidly to another battle, where Wong exhorts his accomplices to fight. Porky can't believe it – 'fight?' – 'yes, fight!'. So he does.

In the chaos, Wong Fei-hung orders Bucktooth So to take Aunt Lee and a patient away from Po Chi Lam (So is back in his Western garb, and just about to leave for the U.S.A.).[24] And who do they run into? Only the Shaho gang. It's here that brave Aunt Lee takes out a pistol and shoots Hung; alas, it's not a kill shot, and Hung's crew captures our heroine.

Once Upon a Time In China's third act closes with Wong Fei-hung in prison, surrounded by his Po Chi Lam colleagues, plus many poor women unlucky enough to be captured by the Shaho Triads. It's Wong's lowest point, with the odds stacked against him. And it's completely in character that when some of the Governor's men sneak in and offer Wong a chance to escape, he should decline at first, preferring to uphold the laws of the China that he loves.

THE FINALE.

The last act of *Once Upon a Time In China* is incredibly intense: it is one of the greatest sequences in recent Chinese cinema, and certainly an outstanding act in Tsui Hark's *œuvre*.

It features multiple battles and struggles, many of which're depicted in parallel action. Aunt Lee is captured by the Shaho gang and taken, with many other Chinese women, to the vessels in the harbour of Guangdong, where they're going to be shipped to the New World as hookers (they are moved from wooden cells to the ships); Wong Fei-hung breaks out of

---

24 Tho' why So would be leaving in the middle of the night doesn't make sense.

prison to rush to her aid; Iron Robe fights Ah Foon; Aunt Lee defends herself against the Shaho leader Hung; Iron Robe challenges Wong in a storehouse; Foon tussles with the Shaho Triads; Wong, Porky and Kai battle the Shaho gang; the North Americans at their fort open fire upon the Chinese Governor and his officials; Foon and Bucktooth So sneak onto the ship to rescue Aunt Lee; and in the final *melée*, Wong saves the day and the villains're punished or killed.

In terms of martial arts and action, the storehouse sequence is one of the highlights of *Once Upon a Time In China*, and of recent Hong Kong action cinema. The duel between Wong Fei-hung and Iron Robe Yim is among the finest smackdowns ever put on celluloid – for imagination, speed, staging, ferocity and grace.

Here action directors and choreographers Lau Kar-wing, Yuen Shun-yee, Yuen Cheung-yan, Chia Yung Liu, and Bruce Law shine, letting loose the stunt team, the wire operators, and an army of assistants to create an astonishing display of cinematic virtuosity and imagination. This is what cinema was invented for – flights of fantasy and action which deliver what no other artform can do (sure theatre, concerts and ballet can do many of the same things – but not from so many camera angles! Because, once again, it is the *editing* that is the secret weapon in the huge arsenal of cinematic trickery and effects wielded by the filmmakers. Again and again, you will recognize that no matter what's happening in front of the camera, whether it's John Woo balletic shoot-'em-ups or effects-heavy *wushu* battles, it is the *editing* that orchestrates the real energy and impact. Not only that, editor Marco Mak Chi Sin (a total genius among editors) has interwoven the huge number of fights and action scenes with perfect dramatic logic. Not easy: we've all seen big action movies which mess that up, with too much time spent here, not enough there, and too many gaps or leaps in the narrative flow). And the sound design is amped up from the usual Hong Kong standards – listen to the unreal animal sounds and whooshes that accompany Iron Robe as he descends to a primitive, berserker level.

So in the finale of *Once Upon a Time In China*, it's ladders swinging all over the place (they also seesaw, spin, and break apart – many times), bales of grain being hurled across the building, high falls from towering stacks of produce, pulleys, ropes and weights being flung about (every prop is exploited), and flurries of fists, feet and arms so rapid the camera and the celluloid can barely record them. It's glorious, it's super-intense, it's ridiculous, and it's *way* beyond the demands of the story, the themes or the drama. But it works. You marvel at the sheer genius of achieving these visual effects practically.

Tsui Hark asked Yuen Woo-ping to help out with the action choreography of *Once Upon a Time In China* in its final stages: Yuen worked on the finale in the granary warehouse, where the stunts with the ladders are classic Yuenian choreography (only a handful of people could've pulled the sequence off – and they're all in the Chinese film industry). David Bordwell said there were nearly 300 different shots in the finale. 'Even for hardcore kung fu fans, the warehouse showdown between Wong and Iron Vest Yim (Yen Shi-kwan) is a dazzler', remarked Maggie Lee (2021).

The sequence employs not only every inch of the granary, it also includes every inch of the two bodies, from the hair (both men grasp each other's pigtails), down to their feet (a Yuen Woo-ping speciality). Altho' Iron Robe Yim has his own martial arts style (including a hidden blade in his pigtail), at the end, Wong Fei-hung deploys one of his famous martial arts techniques, the shadowless kick (the signature move is reprised in every subsequent *Wong Fei-hung* movie). The participants are spinning above each other, rolling and sliding along the floor, lurching at each other across great distances as well as grappling each other several times up close.

Talk about 'ecstatic cinema'!

There are numerous mini-highlights in amongst the barrage of images and sounds in the final act of *Once Upon a Time In China*, such as Iron Robe Yim dying in a hail of bullets *à la* Sam Peckinpah (*kung fu* cannot win against the gun, Yim croaks as he expires in Wong Fei-hung's arms, as martial artists in the real Boxer Rebellion hoped); Leung Foon duelling with the U.S. henchmen Tiger (Steve Tartalia) in the rigging of the ship (and hanging him); Foon defending Aunt Lee against a roomful of belligerent Triads; and of course the duel between Wong Fei-hung and Iron Robe (but even that contains countless smaller action units, like the arrival of Porky and Kai to help their *sifu*, and sending their opponents crashing thru the floor). And it's wonderful that Wong isn't using swords or staffs (it's the villains who wield guns), but fighting with his fists and legs and everything else.

❧

I've seen 100s of Western action movies and Chinese action movies, but I never feel like the Chinese action pictures are milking the finales too much: altho' they are absurdly over-cooked and over-wrought, and altho' the action scenes go on longer than Western equivalents, they are so inventive, they never out-stay their welcome. Whereas, in Western action movies, the action duplicates stunts and situations we've seen so many times before, the conflicts aren't engaging, and the finales tend to drag on too long. And that kills an action movie!

Yes, you want the final showdown between the hero and the villain to be Big and Loud and Intense, but that requires a lot of imagination and skill. Western movies repeat action beats seen elsewhere and set them within conflicts which ultimately don't grip the audience. (It's ironic, but altho' the action itself in a Chinese action flick is longer and filled with more beats and bits of business, it's the Western action finales that drag on and on. North American producers and film studios often commented from the 1980s onwards that Chinese action movies were great but wouldn't play in the U.S.A. (they often said this in relation to Jackie Chan's movies); I find it's the other way around, and it's the Western/ North American action finales that don't play. I find myself getting bored quickly by the final act of a North American/ Western action movie, but never by a Chinese action movie.)

Meanwhile, the finale of a Chinese action movie *rocks*. Not only is the action, the speed and movement, the invention of the moves and the gestures, more compelling than a Western action movie, the Chinese action movie never forgets that this is *entertainment*, that this is movie-making and Show Time. The Chinese action movie builds in pauses, and intimate moments, and pieces of comedy; it creates a *balance* of elements; and it never forgets the *magic* of cinema.

While a Western action movie plays its Big Moments as smug, look-how-clever-we-are scenes (where the hero finally manages to flick the switch to make something awe-inspiring happen), a Chinese action movie emphasizes things like graceful movement or passionate emotion. Look at how beautiful that body moves in slow motion! A Chinese action movie always puts the *body* at the centre of the show, while a Western action movie is obsessed with gadgets, guns, props, big sets, cars, and visual effects (and of course clever, quippy dialogue). The Chinese action movie knows that the greatest visual effect in front of the camera is the human body. Nothing is more fascinating, more compelling.

Another aspect worth noting about the finale of 1991's *Once Upon a Time In China* is just how *brutal* it is. It is very, very vicious. When I saw the movie again recently, I'd forgotten just how violent the treatment of Aunt Lee was at the hands of the Shaho gang and its leader, Hung. He smashes her face and body repeatedly, until he knocks her unconscious; the two are grappling and wrenching each other about. He partially strips her, his wounds drips blood over her front and then back as he gropes her . This is really nasty stuff, a rape scenario which's probably too much, too graphic, and it unbalances the picture (notice how, for instance, the filmmakers rightly drew back from putting Aunt Lee in such horrific jeopardy again in subsequent *Wong Fei-hung* movies. You just don't want to see the heroine beaten so viciously she's knocked out. Or to see actress Rosamund Kwan treated like that. Tsui Hark acknowledged that he was reluctant to go there, 'but that was the natural direction that the story moved' [LM, 82]). And even when the other women captured in the ship shove Hung into a furnace,[25] it's a satisfying demise for this psychopathic villain, true, but it doesn't quite nullify the horrors of the violence against Aunt Lee. (But then, we have to remember that Tsui has not held back from depicting men's aggression against women in his movies: men can be brutes, and Tsui isn't afraid of showing that. Also, Chinese action-adventures movies tend to be more brutal than their counterparts in the West).

A poignant piece of parallel cutting is included here, interweaving the rape of Aunt Lee with the blood-money scene between Iron Robe, the Shaho gang and Ah Foon. The message is about selling out, about one section of Chinese society selling out and exploiting another. While Foon grapples with his conscience and the money scattered on the ground (while the Shaho thugs chant, 'pick up the money!'), the film cuts repeatedly to Aunt Lee being beaten by Hung. (The message is also *not* for

---

25 What's a furnace like that doing on a wooden ship?!

a Western audience, it's for fellow Chinese. The primary audience of *Once Upon a Time In China* is *not* Americans and Europeans, it is *Chinese*).

The furious duel between Iron Robe Yim and Wong Fei-hung would be enough to cap any movie: technically, creatively, imaginatively, it has to be among the most stupendous sequences ever put on film. With its boundless energy, its use of every cinematic trick known to humans, and its forceful beauty, it's like watching a History of Cinema.

But no, there is more in the final ten minutes of *Once Upon a Time In China*: a very important scene, where the Chinese face the insane Westerners. It is played below decks in the Yanks' ship in a *very* over-the-top manner: the mad Yank has guns, the Chinese have fists, and he's stealing their women! It's simplistic but, yes, mercantile capitalism is this simple: it's about pure greed. *You have something I want – I'll buy it; if you won't sell it, I'll take it by force.*

The scene is another simplified, operatic version of the Opium War, of the slave-trading industry, and of Western capitalism: the North Americans, in possessing technology, seem to have the upper hand in the conflict (as usual – whether it's guns, gunboats, helicopters, or Rockwell B-1 bombers)[26] Wong Fei-hung takes up some pistols, but they don't work (the Chinese don't know how to use them).[27]

The scene is filled with Tsui Hark's political subtexts (such as: the villain Jackson has taken the Governor, embodiment of Chinese law, hostage at gun-point).[28] Wong Fei-hung dispatches the American slave-trader in a novel manner – by flicking a bullet with his fingers at the guy's skull. (That had already been set up in a piece of foreshadowing so deft you won't notice it: it occurs within the context of a scene where Wong is furious about his inability to find a solution to the political mess, to the alarm of Aunt Lee).

In the *dénouement*, Wong Fei-hung makes a pointed remark (standing next to the Governor on the ship): if there really is gold in the U.S.A., why do Westerners come to China? Maybe, he reckons, we are standing on gold (which's very much Tsui Hark's view).

---

26 Cost: $102 million.
27 Note that Ah Foon is fighting beside Wong now, putting the two stars together.
28 And when the Governor asks Wong and Foon to put down the guns, they obey him. Wong is portrayed as acting within the law.

Once Upon a Time In China (1991). This page and over.

3

ONCE UPON A TIME IN CHINA 2

Wong Fei-hung Je Ye – Naam Yi Dong Ji Keung

INTRO.
Once Upon a Time In China 2 (1992, *Feihong Zhi Nam'er Dang Ziqiang* in Mandarin = *Wong Fei-hung 2: Man Should Be Self-Sufficient*) is pure pleasure. This is a movie as entertainment first and foremost, whatever else it might contain. This is an hour and 56 minutes of absolute delight, a perfect piece of cinema made by a Hong Kong film crew for a Hong Kong and Chinese audience. 'It is, to be blunt, an absolutely brilliant sequel to a brilliant first film' (Lisa Morton, 85).

The cast of *Once Upon a Time In China 2* is outstanding – Jet Li, Rosamund Kwan, Max (Benny) Mok Siu-chung, Donnie Yen, Zhang Tielin, Yen Chi Tan, Xiong Xin-xin, Yan Yee-kwan and David Chiang, and the team behind the camera is incredible: Tsui Hark as director, Yuen Woo-ping as action director,[1] Shun-Yee Yuen Tsui and Ng See-Yuen as producers, Marco Mak Chi-sin, Chi Wai Chan and Angie Lam On-yee as editors, Arthur Wong Ngok Tai as DP, Ma Poon-chiu as art director, costumes by Kwok-Sun Chiu, and music[2] by Chow Gam-wing, Johnny Njo and Richard Yuen. Raymond Chow and Golden Harvest as executive producer and distributor (with Jackie Chan singing the theme song). Tsui, Hanson Chan Tin-suen and Carbon Cheung are credited with the script. Released April 16, 1992.[3] 116 minutes.

What's not to like in *Once Upon a Time In China 2*? This is one of the greatest action-adventure series ever made, boasting two of the finest finales in action cinema. Tsui Hark is at his fiercest and most visceral in his 1,0000 miles-an-hour work as director (and co-writer and co-producer),

---

[1] The other action directors were: Huan-Chiu Ku, Shun-Yee Yuen and Donnie Yen.
[2] There are several pieces of Western classical music in *Once Upon a Time In China 2*, including a scene at a society ball where a Chinese orchestra plays Mozart. These are contrasted with the Chinese music – the guy in the restaurant playing the *erhu*, and of course the famous *Wong Fei-hung* music.
[3] Only *8* months after the first *Once Upon a Time In China* movie – and this is a *giant* production! They are *fast* in Hong Kong!

and the production team *really* deliver the goods. These guys are *masters*, they are showmen who know movies and entertainment inside out.

Once Upon a Time In China 2 boasts an enormous cast, and keeping track of the multiple groups of characters and their plotlines is an impressive feat all of its own for the writers (who were Tsui Hark, Hanson Chan Tin-suen and Carbon Cheung). And not only are there many factions to juggle, *Once Upon a Time In China 2* also portrays a very wide cross-section of townspeople, from babies to old folk (so the daily demand for extras for the production was high). It's as if one of the chief ambitions of Tsui Hark and the production team was to deliver a convincing and rich portrait of turn-of-the-century China, a society teeming with people, where life is lived out on the streets.

Set in 1895 against the political background following the first Chinese-Japanese War and the signing of the Shimonoseki Treaty, which sparks demonstrations against the handing over of Formosa (Taiwan) to Japan (a student demonstration against the Treaty is part of act one).

The villains in *Once Upon a Time In China 2* are not the Western powers this time (tho' there is plenty of anti-foreign rhetoric and action on display), but elements of Chinese society: one is the White Lotus Cult, with their nationalistic, anti-Western political movement, and the other is Nap-lan Yun-seut and the military. While the White Lotus Cult (led by Master Kung) is painted in a highly cartoony fashion, the Manchu commander, Lan and his regime is more complexly depicted.[4] However, once Lan throttles the British ambassador (film critic Paul Fonoroff), he has crossed the line into arch movie villainy (from which the way is only, in movie-movie terms, death.[5] And the *Once Upon a Time In China* films are very much movie-movies).

Donnie Yen's Manchu Governor Nap-lan Yun-seut uses the chaos to take control of the British Embassy. He kills the British consulate with a stranglehold, informing him, 'This is China, not England!' Oh, how satisfying moments like that are in Chinese cinema! When, finally, the Westerners are attacked in their enclaves, and the Chinese take control of their destiny.

Apparently, Jet Li walked out of *Once Upon a Time In China 2*, due to disagreements with Golden Harvest over his contract. That left the filmmakers in the lurch, so Tsui Hark had Xiong Xin-xin do what he'd done before: shave his head and double for Jet Li.

THE VISUAL STYLE.

The attention to detail and texture in *Once Upon a Time In China 2* is outstanding. The birds in cages hanging in the stores, the lanterns swinging in the breeze at night, and the food and the restaurants, it's just marvellously rich and visceral. This is a real place filled with real people. There's a *depth* of environmental *mise-en-scène* in the *Once Upon a Time In China* series (and other historical movies produced/ directed by Tsui

---
4 *Once Upon a Time In China 2* 'may be one of the most compassionate action films ever made', remarked Lisa Morton, on account of its portrayal of race and ethnicity.
5 Or a year as a movie critic.

Hark) which goes way beyond your average costume picture. These might be film sets, but there's no feeling of costumes and props being rented for the day, or that really stilted aspect of Western historical movies, when that one car from the 1930s or that one horse and carriage that the filmmakers have rented for the day is trotted past the camera.

While we're talking about the cinematography, it should be noted that many scenes in *Once Upon a Time In China 2* take place at night (Tsui Hark is especially fond of night scenes, which're extra-demanding for film crews). These're nights that're lit by hanging lanterns, by candles, by torches, by fires, and by fireworks. *Once Upon a Time In China 2* is a masterwork of *lighting*, as DP Arthur Wong Ngok Tai, his gaffer and what must've been a large crew of sparks fill huge outdoor spaces with light at night (meanwhile, the practical effects crew would've been working non-stop to deliver the smoke, flying leaves, rain, fire, flaming torches and high wind that Tsui likes to include in every exterior shot).

Texture and atmosphere are foregrounded throughout *Once Upon a Time In China 2*. The amount of life presented on screen is hugely impressive. There is a lengthy musical montage focussing on a blind musician playing an *erhu* and singing as the 1992 movie cuts to a very large sequence of vignettes that're beautifully lit and staged. They include an opium smoker, people playing board games, Chinese customs involving ghosts and symbols, the lottery, and of course the Tsui Hark staple: people eating.

THE OPENING SCENES.

Once Upon a Time In China 2 opens with a major production value set-piece as the villains of the fiilm, the White Lotus organization, are displayed in full effect at a mass ritual in their headquarters. It's a giant sequence with acrobatics, fire, bullets, elaborate costumes, many extras and plenty of yelling and leaping about (and it's covered with many formal, carefully composed shots, many using a crane). Master Kung (Xiong Xin-xin) is introduced as the leader of the White Lotus Cult, a group dedicated to ridding China of the foreign devils (Westerners). The White Lotus Cult is a fictionalized version of real historical groups of the early 1900s which hoped to oust foreign powers and influences from China. The ultra-nationalist organizations included martial arts practitioners who believed that they could counter the technological firepower of the *gweilo* ('white devils') with Chinese magic (which's demonstrated vividly in the mass ritual). The sword vs. gun scenario is a staple of Asian action movies, but in the *Once Upon a Time In China* series it's given a blatantly political edge.

The flamboyance and extravagance of the imagery in the White Lotus Cult prologue of *Once Upon a Time In China 2* is typical of Tsui Hark's cinema, which can stage an enormous set-piece with the confidence of a David Lean or an Akira Kurosawa (the filmmakers spent a lot of time and $$$$ on this opening scene). In a symbolic gesture, the White Lotus organization pile a bunch of Western artefacts on the floor and burn them (the mound of stuff is nothing but junk, yet this is what Western capitalism produces – thousands and millions of objects, consumer goods, and trinkets (in the end, every object becomes rubbish). There is of course a clock[6] in the pile of Western crud – in later years, that junk would be computers, cel phones, tablets, DVDs, video games, and of course the ubiquitous, all-conquering television set (the average time spent watching TV in North America is over 4 hours a day).

Once Upon a Time In China 2 also finds mystery and exoticism in the White Lotus sequence, too, with its portrayal of a young girl in traditional costume who sings a pæan to China at the beginning of the ritual (a very Tsui Harkian motif). Filmed in flickering torchlight, the girl looks at the viewer with an enigmatic expression, as if she's the white lotus or the goddess of the white lotus herself (or China, or Chinese magic, or Chinese history).

One of the curious things about Xiong Xin-xin, Tsui Hark recognized, is that nobody can remember him in movies! Even tho' he plays some prominent charas (such as, in *Once Upon a Time In China 2*, the leader of the White Lotus Cult), viewers forget who he is. Tsui's solution to that was typical of Tsui: he had Xiong make himself even uglier,[7] and to walk in deformed manner, so he could play Clubfoot.

When *Once Upon a Time In China 2* combines the pro-nationalist White Lotus ritual sequence with the title sequence, which shows Wong Fei-hung, the most famous hero of recent times in China, travelling by train thru China, it is evoking very powerful political and cultural Chinese elements. The vivid representations of Chinese cultural and political icons are enhanced by the use of the traditional Wong Fei-hung music ('Under the General's Orders'), sung by George Lam, and those striking images of the Black Flag militia training on the beach at sunset (for the end credits, the song is sung by the most famous movie star of the period – Jackie Chan).

The train scene from the credits continues with the introductions of Aunt Lee and Ah Foon, and two of the stars, Rosamund Kwan and Max Mok (Wong Fei-hung has been invited to give a lecture). Foon's characterization is altered (he's still a buffoon, but lacks the stammer – and seriousness – of Jacky Cheung's Foon; in *Once Upon a Time In China 2*, Foon is secretly in love (or lust) with Aunt Lee). The dining car scene is played for comedy, and for more West-meets-East culture clashes (such as trying to eat strange Western food in a juddering railroad carriage).

The train sequence also puts Wong Fei-hung in a different environment: we are not in the Po Chi Lam clinic, and Wong is not surrounded by a large entourage.

Following the scenes where Wong Fei-hung travels on a train to Canton, there is the first fight scene of the 1992 Chinese picture. It's a classic Wong Fei-hung fight, in which he effortlessly trounces a bunch of

---
6 In the medical lecture scene, Wong Fei-hung observes in fascination someone in the audience looking at their pocket watch. In *Once Upon a Time In China 2*, time is a minor theme, with Luk Hao-tung and Sun Yat-sen consulting their watches.
7 Tsui's done that with other actors – such as Lee Fai in *Iron Monkey*.

White Lotus cultists (armed with nothing more'n a fan! – making a change from the usual umbrella!). The brawl – set on the street as Wong, Aunt Lee and Foon make their way from the railroad station to their digs – is of course the movie's finale in miniature (it crystallizes the conflict between the two key rivals in the whole of the 1992 picture: Wong Fei-hung and the White Lotus Cult).

The brawl is staged near one of the targets of the White Lotus crew: the Eastern Extension Australasia and China Telegraph Company, a Western facility. Aunt Lee is also involved when she tries to take a photograph and is set upon by White Lotus men (the camera is more devilish, Western technology). The arrival of Wong Fei-hung is played as the knight in shining armour coming to the rescue of the princess (he flies in across the heads of the crowd).

The medical lecture sequence, where Wong Fei-hung is demonstrating Chinese acupuncture, is in two halves: in the first part, Wong is invited to talk about Chinese medicine (*Once Upon a Time In China 2* features acupuncture in several scenes). The scene contains several East-West topics, such as language and translation, and tradition vs. science. Again, much of the scene is played for comedy (like the Marx Brothers-ish demonstration of the nervous system by tapping Ah Foon's knee). Wong's gentlemanly interpreter is no less than Sun Yat-sen (Zhang Tielin), a fellow Chinese doctor. The second half of the lecture episode has the White Lotus firing burning arrows and messages into the theatre.

Act one (which's short, about 25 minutes), also includes students demonstrating in the streets against the Shimonoseki Treaty, ceding Taiwan to Japan (the procession with banners is a mirror to the scene with the Catholic missionaries in the first film). Plus the introduction of one of the founders of modern China, Sun Yat-sen, in the lecture scene. *Once Upon a Time In China 2* makes several allusions to the founding of the Republic of China – it includes the figure of Sun Yat-sen (d. 1925), who founded the Republic in 1912.

Such scenes announce the much larger political context of the *Once Upon a Time In China* movies compared to many previous Wong Fei-hung films. It's part of a determination to put Wong Fei-hung into situations where major historical events are unfolding – to, no less, portray the founding of modern China.

THE MIDDLE ACTS.

In *Once Upon a Time In China 2*, Wong Fei-hung is up against multiple obstacles. One bad guy simply isn't enough for Wong (or for Jet Li!). Thus, in the second act of *Once Upon a Time In China 2* (which opens with the lengthy *erhu* musical montage), the problems mount as the White Lotus Cult cause trouble throughout the town, and Wong is struggling at first to deal with them. The White Lotus Cult are targetting Western edifices, such as the telegraph building. They assault a lecture of Western doctors. And in the middle point of *Once Upon a Time In China 2*, they burn down a school building (killing the adults, tho' the children hide and survive).

Thus, in the two middle acts of *Once Upon a Time In China 2*, Wong Fei-hung, Aunt Lee and Foon Leung are doing what they can to counter the violent tactics of the White Lotus organization. There is plenty of to-ing and fro-ing as the characters hurry around Canton, helping lost children, and doing what they can against the White Lotus mob (the heroes are thus continually reacting to the villains, and not driving the narrative).

In this section of *Once Upon a Time In China 2*, there is a society ball, where we're introduced to Governor Chung (played by Tsui regular Yan Yee-kwan, who was Iron Robe Yim in the first movie), and to Governor Nap-lan Yun-seut (Donnie Yen). The short scenes are for exposition, to define the behind-closed-doors governance of the area. We see the officials receiving orders from Hong Kong from another new-fangled machine, the telegraph.

As Bey Logan pointed out in his DVD audio commentary, the *Once Upon a Time In China* series works without martial arts: there's enough going on in terms of story and drama that it doesn't need *kung fu* sequences. However, there's no doubt that *kung fu* action enhances the dramatic conflicts in the *Once Upon a Time In China* movies no end. There's a good example of *kung fu* action in the mid-point of *Once Upon a Time In China 2*, when Wong Fei-hung in desperation goes to see the Governor at the courthouse to ask for help with the abandoned children.

The sequence begins with Governor Nap-lan Yun-seut demonstrating his prowess with wooden staff work, and launching himself against Wong Fei-hung when he enters the scene. Then follows a 'fan service' moment – Jet Li versus Donnie Yen (two of the biggest *kung fu* stars of the period – and since). It's fast and furious Shaolin staff action, in the Yuen Woo-ping manner (highly stylized, with plenty of slow motion and punchy insert shots), that of course ends in a stalemate (it's but a taster of the 1992 movie's climax, as the audience can guess. And of course, the outcome in the finale is inevitable, too).

You can have the villain threatening the hero with words, or with a show of strength from one of his henchmen, or with the demonstration of a super-weapon (*à la James Bond*), or you can have them fighting. And when you've got two stars who can move so gracefully, with an enigmatic and compelling speed and beauty, it's far better to have them duelling.

❖

The two middle acts of *Once Upon a Time In China 2* also have time for some mandatory romantic Wong Fei-hung and Aunt Lee scenes: in this one, Wong decides that Lee could do with some self-defence moves of her own. The subtext – Lee's yearning for Wong – is played for wistfulness underneath the comedy (Wong is quite rough, and also shouts at Lee, before apologizing, because that's how he talks to his students).

Aunt Lee, caught in a crouching pose by Wong Fei-hung's arm lock, looks at their shadows projected on a nearby brick wall, and imagines them dancing (so now she's bent over in a dance position). It's a reprise of the scene where Lee kissed Wong's shadow.

In the first half of act three, there are some more modest scenes – such as Ah Foon teaching the children some *kung fu* stances (and getting into a romantic clinch with Aunt Lee, much to Wong Fei-hung's fury); and another Lee-and-Wong romantic beat (filmed in burnished, intense close-up shots), where Lee confesses (some of) her feelings for Wong (to his astonishment).

In a pure Wong Fei-hung scene, the Chinese doctor assists Sun Yat-sen and Mr Luke (Lu Hao-tung – played by David Chiang) in medical operations to patch up the Brits injured in the White Lotus Cult attacks. Here Wong's skill with acupuncture performs the functions of an anæsthetic (which Sun has run out of). There's also a scene where Sun, Lu and Wong are together, and another where Sun and Lu contemplate their pocket watches. 'I never knew time was so important', Wong muses to Ah Foon (but to Tsui Hark, time is *very* important! As the characters say later: 'time is vital').

❖

In the second half of *Once Upon a Time In China 2*, the action comes thick and fast: the nighttime raid on the British Embassy by the White Lotus Cult is one of many set-pieces (it climaxes the third act, using the four-act model). Tsui Hark's genius for conjuring memorable images is to the fore throughout *Once Upon a Time In China 2*: the British Embassy sequences include the burning of a wooden cross (mocking the State religion of Britain), as well as effigies (including, to Aunt Lee's shocked, fainting dismay, one of herself!).

When the White Lotus Cult invade the British Embassy building, it's all-action as the Brits, their guards, Wong Fei-hung, Ah Foon, Aunt Lee, Mr Luke[8] and others defend themselves: this forms the climax of act three of *Once Upon a Time In China 2*. It is a very busy sequence, with action erupting in many settings in and around the Embassy. Continuing the satire on Western religion, Foon grabs a wooden cross and uses it to beat his assailants (something you don't often see in a North American action movie!). The chapel is, suitably enough, where the children hide.

The build-up to the storming contains a lot of action, with injured Westerners finding sanctuary in the Embasssy. This part of *Once Upon a Time In China 2* is a curious mixture of movie clichés (Westerners in a foreign land defending themselves from the angry locals outside); ideological and political subtexts (uneasy coalitions between the Chinese and the Brits; the regressive traditions of the White Lotus group; Wong Fei-hung discovering idealistic Chinese men who've embraced Western ways – Sun Yat-sen and Lung Hao-tung); and Tsui Hark's highly idiosyncratic way of staging all of this (it is thoroughly cinematic). It comes across as a mixture of films of the British overseas in the fading years of the Empire, like *Zulu*, *Gunga Din*,[9] and even a *Carry On* film (particularly

---

[8] With Sun Yat-sen departed on a political mission, Mr Luke (Lu) functions as his representative in the founding-of-China theme in *Once Upon a Time In China 2*.
[9] Critics such as Stephen Teo have referenced the classic action-adventure *Gunga Din* (1939) in relation to the *Wong Fei-hung* movies. *Gunga Din* was directed by George Stevens, starred Cary Grant, Victor McLagen, Sam Jaffe and Douglas Fairbanks, Jr., and was based on Rudyard Kipling's poem. A wonderful movie, *Gunga Din* is one of those classics that you can watch over and over.

Carry On Up the Khyber, about the British in India), combined with explosive Hong Kong action cinema, and Tsui's own peculiar way of filming historical stories in terms of very heightened and stylized melodrama (as if a Peking Opera troupe were making a film about Wong Fei-hung, but under the guidance of a wilfully eccentric stage director who wants to combine Western adventure flicks such as *Indiana Jones* with a Chinese sensibility).

Among the multiple gags in the storming of the Embasssy sequence are White Lotus Cult soldiers on horseback riding thru the corridors, swinging swords; Wong Fei-hung taking on a bunch of White Lotus men armed with spears on some stairs (a dance of spears); and even Aunt Lee is given a moment to shine, when she wounds a guy in the leg.

As the British Embassy is infiltrated, Governor Lan waits outside for the best chance to turn the tables – he takes advantage of the chaos created by the White Lotus Cult to wrest control from the Brits, who're in disarray. Here he kills the British Consul (witnessed by Aunt Lee, who tells Wong Fei-hung): dramatically, this sets up the finale, when Wong duels with Governor Lan (as Lan is now a murderer, it justifies, in movie-movie terms, Wong taking the fight to the death – plus the fact that Lan is trying to kill him! Repeatedly!). Thematically/ politically, Lan nobbling the Consul proves to Wong that the Chinese authorities are once again corrupting themselves (reprising the portrayal of the Governor in the first *Once Upon a Time In China* film).

THE WHITE LOTUS FINALE.

There are two major action set-pieces that climax *Once Upon a Time In China 2*: both have been signalled early on in the 1992 movie: one is Wong Fei-hung versus the White Lotus Cult, and the second is Wong going up against Governor Lan. Both action set-pieces are state of the art, fearsomely inventive and played with a ferocious, wild energy.

Jet Li is in the spotlight of both action sequences in *China 2*, and he's never looked better, moved more gracefully, or exuded such magnetism and star quality (he was 29 at the time).[10] Li is one of the most fantastically beautiful performers ever to grace the screen. (Li seems to have done far more of his stunts on this movie – on the first *Wong Fei-hung* flick he was injured). But of course, he's not working alone! There is Yuen Woo-ping and his stunt team, and there is Tsui Hark behind the camera! Hell, how can you lose?!

The action in the White Lotus temple in *Once Upon a Time In China 2* is too rapid for storyboarding, and perhaps too long for a North American audience, but any action fan is going to love it. Jet Li's Wong Fei-hung becomes a one-man army against a horde of heavies dressed in white (with some of them going into beserker frenzies). They have swords, Mr Luke has a gun, but Wong is of course unarmed (as always – he *never* walks into a battle with weapons; Wong is always the negotiator first. But when that doesn't work, he resorts to force). He might not carry weapons

---

[10] It's not all action, tho' – Jet Li acts up a storm, in a role he seems to have been born to play.

(well, he has his trusty umbrella!), but Wong does employ everything in the environment against his opponents (such as kicking the wooden platform to shards which are flung at the henchmen, or snapping off the head of one of their spears and using it).

As well as inventing numerous ways in which Wong Fei-hung can dispatch his foes (never have so many heavies been beaten with a brolly!), the action also uses multiple levels – taking the fight up onto a ledge near the roof, onto the pillars, and a stack of tables (a favourite motif in Yuen Woo-ping's form of wire-assisted *kung fu*). The gag of Kung not touching the ground, as part of his sacred function as the leader of the White Lotus Cult who must be worshipped, is exploited to the max (such as, when the tower of tables finally topple, he uses a stretched cloth to stand on an altar).

Xiong Xin-xin plays up the phony pantomime of the leader of the White Lotus Cult with relish, providing a suitably over-the-top villain for Jet Li to battle (Xiong doubles for Li in the *Once Upon a Time In China* series, and also plays Clubfoot.)

The White Lotus temple sequence is a marvel of imaginative filmmaking, a full-on, acrobatic, crowd-pleasing display of outrageous *kung fu*. Wong Fei-hung dispatches numerous henchmen, and then proceeds to duel with Gao Kung on the tables, in the air, on a ledge, on a pillar, on stretched cloth, until every inch of the temple set has been explored. The sheer velocity of physical gags is like watching all of the Marx Brothers' movies squashed into ten minutes.

As with Christianity, the 1992 Chinese movie and its heroes make fun of the more regressive and reactionary forms of Chinese religion. Wong Fei-hung lambasts the White Lotus followers for worshipping a false deity with a fake religion. In one memorable beat, Wong pretends to be taken over by the spirit of the god, standing in front of the altar, with Jet Li executing some of the incredibly rapid *wushu* moves which're one of his specialities (an action star doesn't have catchphrases like a comedian, doesn't sing like a vocalist, but has movements which become part of their signature).

The demise of Master Kung, leader of the White Lotus Cult, is tied to the historical cliché of *kung fu* versus bullets. Kung is revealed to be wearing a breastplate (for the demonstrations of *kung fu* being able to be magically deflect gunfire. Actually, Western movies use bulletproof vests all the time as cheats – usually to bring a character back to life who appears to have been shot). Mr Luke fires at Kung repeatedly, for his crimes. Kung ends up impaled, in 1930s adventure serial style, on the statue behind the altar. (And Wong is the one who hurls him there – in *Once Upon a Time In China 2,* Wong takes care of both villains).

And in the fracas, Mr Luke accidentally but symbolically also shoots the little girl, totem of the White Lotus Cult (the *Wong Fei-hung* movies never put a gun into the hands of Wong – in the films of the 1950s as well as the 1990s. However, *Once Upon a Time In China 1* does have Wong holding a gun, tho' not using it. Instead, he dispatches the slave-trader

Jackson by flicking a bullet at the villain's skull).

THE HERO VS. VILLAIN FINALE.

Foreshadowed earlier in their sparring match with staffs, the confrontation between the chief villain of *Once Upon a Time In China 2*, Nap-lan Yun-seut, and the hero, Wong Fei-hung, does not disappoint: and this is Jet Li versus Donnie Yen, two stars who can move as gracefully as anybody in the entire history of cinema. So as Mr Luke, Ah Foon and Wong hurry to the pier where a ship is about to leave (a classic countdown device, and already used in film one), they are waylaid by Lan and his men. The setting is again a warehouse, and again a place of numerous wooden poles, walkways and multiple levels. The staff duel is absolutely thrilling, filled with so many imaginative flourishes from Yuen Woo-ping and the stunt team, and Tsui Hark's eye for vivid imagery, and Arthur Wong Ngok Tai's gorgeous cinematography – and not forgetting the utterly crucial element of editing (by Marco Mak Chi-sin *et al*).

This is state of the art action cinema, fabulously over-the-top, staged with a technical bravura that few filmmaking teams have matched. In one beat, Wong Fei-hung is way up at the top of the warehouse, stretched between two walkways on outspread legs, using one of the supporting poles[11] (thirty feet long!) to imprison Nap-lan Yun-seut on the ground below like a trapped dog, preventing him from attacking Ah Foon and Mr Luke (there is no scene in Western cinema like this!).

Here the scroll of names is used as the MacGuffin, with Mr Luke hurriedly burning it as the authorities close in; Mr Luke's demise is played as a Big, Dramatic Moment (and he's given a heartfelt eulogy by Sun Yat-sen in the *dénouement*).

The complication-followed-by-complication rule is deployed (being one of the basic rules of drama as well as action), so the staff duel in the warehouse doesn't top the 1992 movie. There is more! Nap-lan Yun-seut pursues Wong Fei-hung and Ah Foon into a back alley, where the action shifts into wet rope weapon territory (Wong has a piece of bamboo, which breaks). The filmmakers excel themselves with hugely inventive scenes of long range combat in a confined space – the rope of cloth speeds thru the air, whistling past Wong (he manages to dodge it), and explodes holes in the nearby walls (clever Wong exploits that, urging Foon to make the hole bigger, and helping himself, in between beating off attacks from Lan).

Nap-lan Yun-seut seems unstoppable, exuding a manic energy. His demise occurs when he's flung the rope around Wong's neck, trapping him, and Wong slides the remains of the bamboo stick along the rope, cutting thru it, back to Lan, and embedding a splinter in Lan's neck. In a nod to samurai movies (including the famous example in *Yojimbo*, 1961), Lan expires in a spray of blood from his neck.

And *that*, folks, is how to stage a hero vs. villain fight! And *that,* folks, is how to make a movie!

Once Upon a Time In China 2 is simply glorious filmmaking, and it

---

[11] It smashes into the ground with an ominous thud, to suggest the power of the hero.

might be the finest in the first three *Wong Fei-hung* movies – until, that is, we watch the first one or the third one again!

(The *dénouement* returns to the political theme and the formation of early modern China, with evocations of the revolution, the downfall of the Qing Dynasty, and Sun Yat-sen leaving for Hong Kong, accompanied by Aunt Lee.[12] As Sun Yat-sen unfurls the flag, solemn words are delivered about sacrifice and a better future. Meanwhile, a ship leaving a dock is once again used to close a Tsui Hark movie, with its hints of travel, change, and the future).

---

12 There's a reprise of the grappling hand move, so that Aunt Lee (not Wong Fei-hung) fends off a policeman come to arrest Sun Yat-sen (which she learnt from Wong).

4

ONCE UPON A TIME IN CHINA 3

Wong Fei-hung Ji Saam – Si Wong Jaang Ba

INTRO.

Once Upon a Time In China 3 (1993, Mandarin: *Huang Feihong III Zhi San: Shiwang Zheng Ba = Wong Fei-hung 3: Lion King Struggle For Supremacy*), was filmed in Beijing, not Hong Kong, like the former two installments in the series. Ng Se-yuen and Tsui Hark were producers; Charcoal Cheung Tan, Chan Tin-suen and Tsui were the writers; action directors: Yuen Tak and Yuen Bun; music: Woo Wai-laap, William Hu and Tsui; DPs: Andrew Lau Wai-keung and Chow Man-keung;[13] editing: Marco Mak Chi-sin and Angie Lam On-yee; Sip Gam was production designer; and costumes: Tin-kiu Ching. In the cast were Jet Li, Rosamund Kwan, Max (Benny) Mok, Lau Shun, Xiong Xin-xin, John Wakefield, Chiu Chin, Wong Tak-yan, Meng Jin and Ge Cunzhuang. Released Feb 11, 1993. 105 mins.[14]

Once Upon a Time In China 3 is A Tsui Hark Production – and everyone knows it! But Raymond Chow/ Golden Harvest is an important producing partner in the enterprise, and a movie of this scale can only be produced by drawing on a *lot* of resources and expertise.

THE STORY.

The story and the characters of *Once Upon a Time In China 3* are very familiar if you've seen a few movies from Hong Kong: Wong Fei-hung is the Robin Hood hero, accompanied by Aunt Lee, who's enamoured of the West, foolish but harmless sidekick Leung Foon, Wong's father Wong Kay-ying, and other familiar characters in the Wong universe.

So in the third *Once Upon a Time In China* entry, Wong Fei-hung visits Peking[15] to see his father, to find the place in turmoil over the Lion Dance

---

13 The film was filmed in Panavision and released in Dolby.
14 The Taiwanese cut has some 15 minutes more material than the Hong Kong version (there are 26 additions, according to Wikipedia).
15 The movie recycles the train footage from film two.

competition[16] launched by the Dowager Empress Cixi, for her own political motives (a Lion Dance had opened the whole *Once Upon a Time In China* series). Martial arts groups are pitted against each other, and the bad guys, the Tai-pang Club mob, led by Master Chiu Tin-bak[17] who cackles manically in every single scene), and his henchman Iron Foot or Clubfoot (Xiong Xin-xin), a vicious psychopath, are stirring up trouble (as villains tend to do), aiming to take all of the glory of the competition (by nobbling all of the rival *kung fu* schools, including the Wongs' school).

That's the background and the large-scale story, but that isn't of course what makes *Once Upon a Time In China 3* such a pleasure, such a thoroughly entertaining movie. *Once Upon a Time In China 3* has, for a start, two enormous cinematic presences: Jet Li, one of the most charismatic and all-round beautiful stars of recent cinema, a guy so electric you can't take your eyes off him. The camera loves him, he moves like a dream, with such elegance and speed and imagination, he can act, he can emote, he can carry whole movies, he is *simply amazing!*

And the other giant presence on the production is of course producer-director-writer Tsui Hark (he even has a music co-credit!). And *Once Upon a Time In China 3* has Tsui absolutely at the top of his game, overseeing a huge production with 100s of extras, trucks full of costumes, lavish location shooting, delightful exotic colour and festivities, a vast battery of practical and visual effects, and a deliciously inventive and dynamic cinematic style.

Oh, and incendiary action – this is action filmmaking by the finest team in the world (the action directors were Yuen Tak and Yuen Bun).

Once Upon a Time In China 3 is the movie with the Lion Dances (which had appeared in the first *Once Upon a Time In China* movie) – they open the story with some costly production value scenes filmed in the Imperial palaces of Beijing (Wong Fei-hung is representing the Guangdong Association in the tournament). And there's an impressive scene with hundreds of extras in the streets watching the Lion Dance. As Stephen Teo explains:

> The lion dance is, of course, the showpiece in all Chinese festivities. To the Chinese, it is culture in its most popular form, and as a mascot for unity, brings the masses together. (1997, 173)

Once Upon a Time In China 3 is also the movie with the famous fight a-top ladders in the storeroom, a sequence of incredibly fiendish complexity, where Wong Fei-hung faces off against the villains. Another marvellous sequence has Wong going to dinner at Master Chiu Tin-bak's invitation and defending himself against multiple assailants wielding hand axes while slippin' 'n' slidin' in oil on the floor.

As if that's wasn't enough, there is also in *Once Upon a Time In China*

---

[16] The Lion Dance is a fantastically lavish sequence, a marvellous recreation of a traditional, Chinese festival. The screen is alive with colour as the paper heads jiggle and bounce thru the streets (meanwhile, at knee and foot level, fights're breaking out between the rival *kung fu* schools).
[17] Credited as Chiu Chin or Chunzhong Zhang.

3 a truly charming *lightness* and a *lightheartedness* to the proceedings. This isn't a movie bogged down by being 'weighty' or 'dark' or 'dramatic'. For instance, it's not all internecine battles in the streets and the inns between the bad guys and Wong Fei-hung and his chums, or ponderous musings on East-West geo-politics, there is plenty of romance, and plenty of humour.

THE LOOK AND STYLE.

The cinematography in *Once Upon a Time In China 3* is by Andrew Lau Wai-keung and Chow Man-keung. It is masterclass photography, with juicily saturated colouration, at its richest in the Lion Dance sequences, where the screen's alive with bright reds, yellows, golds, blues and greens. The satin blues of the nighttime scenes, the shimmering backlighting, the wafting smoke and sputtering fires, these are some of the classic images of Chinese, historical movies. Add to that very low angles, often with wide angle lenses, and rapid tracking shots along the ground – the filmmaking approach recalls Orson Welles.

The camera is often tilted in *Once Upon a Time In China 3* : to frame a street procession, the camera operators simply tilt the camera, to include more of the scene, instead of selecting a different angle or shot size. But the Dutch angles don't connote weirdness or a world off-angle, as in many movies, but simply another way of expressing the energy and freedom of the filmmaking.

Once Upon a Time In China 3 was filmed without sync sound, and was dubbed in the studio (the usual practice in Hong Kong movies. It was a long time before Chinese movies, and especially action movies, took up direct sound in significant numbers).

SUBPLOTS AND THEMES.

Romance: the lovely Rosamund Kwan once again carries the romantic subplot as Cousin/ Aunt Lee, continuing the will-they-won't-they? romance plot of the *Once Upon a Time In China* series. The self-conscious naïvety and simplicity of the romance between Aunt Lee and Wong Fei-hung is very appealing. It's a romance that has everything to do with literature and cinema, and happily sidesteps any notions of 'realism' or 'naturalism'. It is also, unlike in some other Tsui Hark movies, chaste and restrained. These are potential lovers who rarely even embrace (and when the Russian Tomanovsky (John Wakefield) kisses Aunt Lee's hand, Wong Fei-hung is outraged, and calls it unsanitary!). And yet the real Wong was married 4 times.

The motif of shadowplay is part of the romantic subplot in *Once Upon a Time In China 3*: in the previous movies, Peony imagines herself dancing with Wong Fei-hung's shadow; in the third movie, the shadows reflect the reality of Wong and Peony embracing. (And now they are seriously discussing marriage; and there's another comical moment when Ah Foon and the boys hurry in and Lee and Wong break apart, embarrassed).

That romance and eroticism is a key element in Tsui Hark's cinema often goes unremarked. And the lighthearted romances are just as much a part of Tsui's cinema as the more melodramatic or intense relationships. In *Once Upon a Time In China 3*, the courtship of Wong Fei-hung and Aunt Lee is essential to the movie, at the thematic as well as psychological and emotional level.

The romance of Wong Fei-hung and Aunt Lee is exploited many times throughout *Once Upon a Time In China 3*. In some scenes, the whole *kung fu* school is involved, like the great moment when Wong is anxious when Aunt Lee goes missing, and, re-united, he hugs her, while everybody stands there in a row, gawping (Tsui Hark is very fond of scenes where onlookers provide comical reactions).

Another subplot in *Once Upon a Time In China 3* is the Western technologies and *mœurs* that Aunt Lee brings with her (and embodies), plus items such as the steam engine. Again, the confrontations with Western science and politics are played lightly as well as seriously and dramatically. There are humorous scenes, for instance, where Aunt Lee is using an early, wind-up film camera,[18] and making a movie. During the Lion Dance sequence, the camera falls on its side, and when the *kung fu* school view the footage at a screening with a 👁, they all have their necks bent over (a classic Tsui Hark sight gag involving a crowd, recalling the gag with the street sign in *Shanghai Blues*). The celluloid becomes part of the nefarious plots of the Russians (to kill Premier Li Hongzhang), which Aunt Lee uncovers with a little detective work. (It is of course ironic that cinema itself is a Western/ European invention, and was imported into China).

The movie camera also captures Ah Foon and Wong Fei-hung going thru some *kung fu* moves. Aunt Lee calls 'action!' (yes, a female film director!) and Wong does nothing, doesn't realize what's going on. Meanwhile, Foon is monopolizing the camera, performing in front of it, while everyone else waits for their turn.

Another subplot involves Iron Foot: he's introduced as Master Chiu's chief bruiser, a formidable opponent with a nasty flying kick fighting style (Iron Foot is played by Xiong Xin-xin, Tsui Hark's regular stunt director in the 1990s, as well as a stunt double for Jet Li). But when he's injured, Iron Foot becomes the laughing stock of the Chiu mob, and is cast down some stairs. The images of Iron Foot crawling on the ground are striking, and the scene where he arrives at the Wong Fei-hung residence and is eventually helped by the doctor are moving. In cascades of heavy rain, Wong goes out to Iron Foot who spurns the sympathy of the Wong clan.[19]

Few critics foreground the elements of comedy and humour in the cinema of Tsui Hark, but it's clearly hugely important. Lengthy sections of Tsui's movies are actually lighthearted and comical (and when Tsui performs cameos, in his own or in other movies, it's often, as with Alfred Hitchcock, in a comical role).

---

18 A movie camera also features in the Lion Dance prologue.
19 It's also a reprise of the scenes of Iron Robe in the rain in film one, and Porky Wing in the rain in film two.

THE ACTS.

The opening act of *Once Upon a Time In China 3*, as in the other *Once Upon a Time In China* movies, is the whole movie in condensed form. It introduces all of the main plots, and culminates with a giant action sequence. Following the impressive production value scene of the Lion Dance in the Imperial Palace, and the introduction of the Dowager Empress (Meng Chin) and her minister, Governor Li Hongzhang (Ge Cunzhang), the movie shifts to the hero and his entourage arriving in a bustling Peking. We see the three biggest stars in *Once Upon a Time In China 3* (Li, Kwan and Mok), and some of their customary light-hearted banter (part of which involves East-West contrasts – such as Aunt Lee causing a commotion in her Western clothes, and a foreigner (the Russian man Tomanovsky) kissing Lee's hand – and also the Lee-and-Wong romance).

The confrontation between Wong Fei-hung and some locals (in which Wong effortlessly dominates them) outside the railroad station, is a prelude to several scenes in the opening act which repeat that scenario. So at the halfway mark in act one, Wong dives into a fray in the streets (literally – he leaps from the upper story of a building onto the street below). The martial arts groups are fighting over supremacy in the upcoming Lion Dance competition, and Wong plays the peace-maker, tho' by beating sense into the tussling groups. Wong is not armed, once again, and doesn't even have his trademark umbrella. So how is he going to subdue 100s of angry guys, many of whom are armed with swords? Simple – he takes off his jacket and uses it as a weapon to whack the fighters on all sides. It's another of Jet Li's familiar taking-on-all-comers action scenes, in which nobody is a match for him.

One of delights of the first act of *Once Upon a Time In China 3* is to see Xiong Xin-xin as Clubfoot in a major smackdown with Wong Fei-hung's father, Wong Kay-ying, played by Lau Shun. The setting – the Cantonese Association, where Wong senior and his colleagues are putting together (and painting) the Lion Dance masks – is once again a very traditional and very Chinese *milieu*. It's as if Tsui Hark and the team are trying to encourage their audiences not to forget Chinese traditions and customs – as well as to entertain and thrill them.

The action sequence draws on the White Lotus scenes in *Once Upon a Time In China 2* and the Embassy scenes in *Once Upon a Time In China 1*, as a local gang led by a venal commander (Master Chiu) arrives to cause trouble. The issue is simple: Chiu wants to be the sole team entering the Lion Dance competition. So he sends in his chief bruiser Clubfoot to rough up Wong senior's cohorts. The fight itself is another very acrobatic sequence, with Iron Foot parodying the famous shadowless kick of Wong Fei-hung by flying towards his opponents and kicking (including racing across the floor and up the walls, feet first).

Act one also introduces the will-they-could-they-should-they? romance plot between Aunt Lee and Wong Fei-hung. Marriage is on the cards – at least from Aunt Lee's view of things. Once again much comical juice is squeezed out of one half of a romantic couple being uptight, repressed, indignant. The scene between Wong and his father (and the misunderstanding about the marriage) is coupled with a scene featuring devilish Western technology (a steam engine), where Lee steals a kiss from Wong.

❖

The second act of *Once Upon a Time In China 3* includes several action scenes, such as Wong Fei-hung and Clubfoot battling it out in the crowded streets of Peking: Wong is chasing the rickshaw which's taken Aunt Lee off in the wrong direction, and Clubfoot is trying to stop him. It's a delight, as in film two, to see Jet Li and Xiong Xin-xin duking it out – by this time, they have worked together so often, they move with assurance and incredible high speed. They are running up walls, dancing across the top of people's heads, and performing multiple kicks as they soar through the air.

The second act of *Once Upon a Time In China 3* climaxes with a massive outdoor scene of the Lion Dance competition, in the preliminary part of the competition (thus, this is essentially a forerunner of the finale, which's set at night). These noisy, busy scenes, filmed on crowded streets filled with Lion Dancers and spectators, fireworks and smoke, might be a documentary on traditional, Chinese customs. In few other films do so many Lion Dance costumes and dancers fill the screen, in shot after shot (many shots are in slight slo-mo).

It's gloriously colourful, and extended far beyond the necessities of the drama. Tho' there *are* dramatic elements: the romantic rivalry that the Russian Tomanovsky represents, for instance (he insists on coming over to see Aunt Lee), Master Chiu's bully boys creating havoc in the Lion Dance with knives and swords, and the MacGuffin of the movie camera.

The sequence runs on and on, and includes Ah Foon being chased by Iron Foot (across the rooftops), Aunt Lee getting lost in the mob, and a stampede of horses, until finally Wong Fei-hung takes control: he rounds up the horses, and puts the Lion Dancers in their place. How? By beating them with staffs – yes, it's another example of Jet Li's astonishing ability to control long, wooden poles (two this time!), and flail them with lightning speed.[20]

The third act of *Once Upon a Time In China 3* keeps several plot strands spinning in the air, which have already been a part of acts one and two: the romance/ marriage plot (Aunt Lee looking on as Wong Fei-hung confides in his father and tells him that he's marrying Cousin Lee); more Westernization (Aunt Lee teaching Wong some English words, including 'man', 'woman' and 'I love you'); the scene where Clubfoot is ostracized from the Tai-pang gang; and a moving sequence where Clubfoot rejects the help of Wong and co., until he relents.

Act three climaxes with one of the great sequences in the *Once Upon a Time In China* series: Wong Fei-hung visiting Master Chiu for dinner, which rapidly descends into an elaborate bust-up with the gimmick of an oil-slicked floor, which has everybody skidding helplessly all over it (in a

---

[20] He also uses the poles like stilts, hopping over the Lion Dancers.

fun gag, the Tai-pang heavies have spiked shoes, so they can grip in the sea of oil). Dodging flying axes and flailing swords, this is another scene of Jet Li taking on all comers, and triumphing, accompanied, inevitably, by the *Wong Fei-hung* signature music.

The fight moves out onto the streets, as the Po Chi Lam brigade run down Master Chiu, who's revealed to be a mean martial artist. As Chiu departs, chuckling as always, across the roofs, there is another 'to be continued' hung in the air, which leads us directly into the finale.

THE FINALE – THE LION DANCE COMPETITION.

The finale of *Once Upon a Time In China 3* is of course the Lion Dance competition, a giant action sequence set at night involving the Lion Dance teams competing for the trophy, overseen by Governor Li Hongzhang and numerous officials (plus the foreign – Russian – contingent). The Russians want to kill Governor Li over the treaty which will cede the Liandong Peninsula to Japan.

The Lion Dance sequence begins with stately festivities,[21] but gradually escalates into in-fighting down at the level of the dancers, and ultimately all-out fight scenes as Master Chiu and his Tai-pang mob take on Wong Fei-hung and Iron Foot (Ah Foon gets injured early on, and has to wait out the fight). Wong and Iron Foot work together to win the competition, while fighting off henchmen on all sides (they're armed with swords, small shooting spears, and banners fitted with blades at the top).

In the Lion Dance finale the assassination plot also plays out. The Russian Tomanovsky confronts Aunt Lee about the movie camera in a dark alley, which rounds off the subplot of flirtation between Lee and Tomanovsky (he commands her to return the footage she filmed, then he decides that he'll have to kill her). Tomanovsky foolishly raises his pistol to shoot the Governor himself, when the assassination plot is foiled, and is killed by his own side (they tell the Chinese officials that he was a Japanese spy). Here, Lee voices the familiar nationalistic mantra: China is for the Chinese, and it can sort out its own problems, without foreign intervention.

In amongst the colourful dancing lion masks and bodies, Wong Fei-hung's Lion Dance mask is white, like most of his costumes, which makes it stand out. Master Chiu, meanwhile, of course has the largest lion head in the competition (four times as big as the others).

The centrepiece of the competition is a tall, wooden tower, decorated with red cloth (similar to the one in *Fong Sai-yuk*, 1993). The winner is the one who snaffles the golden trophy. As expected, it's soon tottering, with wooden poles being snapped or kicked across the square as missiles. Much of the action occurs on top, inside or halfway up the tower – a very challenging sequence for the stunt team, filming over many nights. Jet Li and Xiong Xin-xin are very fine here, with Xiong generously giving all of the glory to Li (tho' he has his own moments to shine).

After an impressive duel with Master Chiu amid twirling staffs and

---

21 Wong Fei-hung handles the exposition, to explain how the Lion Dance competition works.

banners, Wong Fei-hung saves the day, as usual, and gets to say his piece about peace to the Governor (who has nothing to offer in reply). In the finale of *Once Upon a Time In China 3*, as Stefan Hammond and Mike Wilkins sum up, Wong does everything:

> enters the Lion Dance competition in order to win the crown, defeat Chiu, frustrate the Russian assassination, produce more film evidence against the Russians, and lecture President Li on how his policies are dividing the country. (87)

❖

This is filmmaking that simply bursts out all over the place with energy. The dynamism of this 1993 movie, and much of Hong Kong New Wave cinema, is breathtaking: the camera is all over the place, but it's always moving with a function. Altho' it seems showy (well, it *is*!), it is also utterly unlike MTV or pop promo or commercials filmmaking in the West, or the Western movies trumpeted with the meaningless word 'stylish',[22] where the camera moves independently of the action and the drama, has little real dramatic value other than offering a different (and pointless) view of the same action (like the over-editing of Western movies, where four different shots will be used of a single action, for no other reason than using a variety of images of the same thing, in a desperate attempt at making something more interesting. The rapid editing and the multiple, brief views of the same action disguise the fact that the *storytelling* and the *pacing* are pretty much the same as they're always been in Western cinema. It seems 'faster', but it *isn't*. For ex, acts *still* run to 25-30 minutes, as usual in cinema since the 1920s, and there *aren't* more characters than in previous cinema, and the stories are often *exactly* the same. Sure, there might be more scenes, and more events, or action within scenes, but the storytelling isn't quicker – indeed, you can argue, with Hollywood movies now regularly running to two hours, or 140 mins, that storytelling today is *slower* than in earlier films. Certainly many movies today are longer than the average feature in the Classical Hollywood era).

Chinese action filmmaking is completely different: it is tied in to the action to an incredibly strong degree. Even tho' the filmmakers are using the same tools – cameras, tripods, microphones, dollies, cranes, Kodak film stock, etc – their approach to filmmaking is so different.

Once Upon a Time In China 3 celebrates the body in space, the body in movement, the body beautiful. The very low angle tracking shots, with a wide angle lens, across a row of people watching a Lion Dance... the tilted camera views of the fights, as Wong Fei-hung batters the participants in a street fight between rival martial arts organizations using his clothes as a weapon... the compositions that emphasize the huge, blue bowl of the sky... *Once Upon a Time In China 3* is a dream of a movie, a marvellous succession of colourful images.

Again, in looking at *Once Upon a Time In China 3*, I'm struck by the feeling that *anything can happen!* That a scene could move in all sorts of directions, with the same openness towards drama that the movie shows

---
22 All art, nay, everything has a 'style'.

towards movement and bodies. Even tho' the tale the movie's telling is familiar and genre-based, and very much drawing on the Wong Fei-hung legend, and even tho' the characters're predictable and as familiar as character types in any genre fiction, there's still a feeling of total freedom.

And it's this emphasis on freedom that makes *Once Upon a Time In China 3* and Hong Kong New Wave cinema, and so much of Chinese action cinema, so appealing. Even when you've seen these movies many times, they still manage to surprise you each time. These movies really are as light on their feet as their characters. The way the figures leap onto a table as if it's the easiest thing in the world, or suddenly strike a memorable pose (how does Jet Li crouch down to the floor, with his legs spread wide and almost parallel with it, *so* quickly?!), is reflected by the 1993 movie itself, by its graceful and quickfire motion, its ability to sketch in a scene with a few elegant brushstrokes (now we're in a moonlit street, now we're in the upstairs room of an inn), and by its seemingly boundless ability to re-invent itself as it goes along.

A movie like this is surely what cinema was invented for. This is true cinema, the total opposite of 'filmed theatre' or 'talking heads', which comprises most cinema and all television.

5

ONCE UPON A TIME IN CHINA 4

Wong Fei-hung Ji Sei – Wong Je Ji Fung

INTRO.

The fourth installment in the *Once Upon a Time In China* series was released the same year as the third movie – 1993 (this was a period when the Hong Kong film industry was in a massive renaissance – look at how many movies the actors and filmmakers were working on in 1993! Did they ever sleep?!).

Once Upon a Time In China 4 (1993, Mandarin: *Huang Fei Hong Zhi Si: Zhe Zhi Feng*), was produced by Tsui Hark and 'N.G.' (Ng See Yuen) for Film Workshop/ Paragon Films Ltd.; Tsui and Tang Pik-yin scripted; and Yuen Bun directed (and was action choreographer). Music was by William Hu; the DPs were Arthur Wong Ngok Tai, Ko Chiu-lam, Chow Man-keung and Cheung Man-po. Edited by Marco Mak Chi-sin. Hong Kong gross: HK $11,301,790.00. Released only 4 months after *Once Upon a Time In China 3*: June 10, 1993. 101 minutes.

Among the cast were Vincent Zhao as Wong Fei-hung, Jean Wang as 14th Aunt, Max Mok as Ah Foon, Xiong Xin-xin as Clubfoot, Billy Chow as Iron Fist, Chin Kar-lok as Tuen Tin-lui, Lau Shun as Wong's father, Wong Kei-ying, Louis Roth as Father Thomas, and Wang Zhiwen as the deputy Governor.[23]

Once Upon a Time In China 4 was the first *Once Upon a Time In China* movie which changed the actor playing the title role – Jet Li stepped out, to pursue other projects (Li made a *lot* of movies in 1993), and Vincent Zhao (also known as Zhao Wenzhou, a.k.a. Chin Man Chuek, b. 1972) was hired.[24]

There was talk about Jet Li in the first *Once Upon a Time In China*

---

[23] You can see in numerous scenes that it was *very* cold during the making of *Once Upon a Time In China 4*, and that even many of the interiors, filled with lights, were still cold (partly because many scenes were filmed at night).
[24] Vincent Zhao was apparently discovered by Corey Yuen Kwai in a martial arts school in Beijing. But director Ann Hui claims that she discovered Zhao (F. Dannen, 90).

picture, wondering if he was too young to play the much-loved character of Wong Fei-hung (who had been played in the *Wong Fei-hung* series by a much older actor, Kwan Tak Hing). Well, Vincent Zhao looks even younger than Li (he was only 21). And he is, you have to admit, a less appealing actor all-round (tho' he moves like a dream in the action scenes). Zhao is superb (very wonderful in *The Blade*), but he doesn't heat up the screen like a superstar such as Jet Li.[25] Zhao also seems uncomfortable in the scenes which require real acting, including the comical scenes and the romantic scenes[26] – both vital ingredients in the *Once Upon a Time In China* franchise. (However, as the villain Governor Oryeetor in *Fong Sai-yuk*, filmed the same year, where Zhao goes up against Jet Li, Zhao was more impressive. And, to be fair, Zhao did have the challenge of following a big star like Li, and in movies which had been very successful locally).

Fortunately, in *Once Upon a Time In China 4* Vincent Zhao is surrounded by a host of familiar and dependable Chinese actors, many of whom are part of the *Once Upon a Time In China* family: Max Mok, Xiong Xin-xin,[27] Lau Shun, etc. So that even if Zhao is somewhat wooden, he has many people around him who can deliver the goods.

Once again, *Once Upon a Time In China 4* is a gorgeous production photographically. But then, with the DPs being headed up by Arthur Wong Ngok Tai, it's going to look great (plus Ko Chiu-lam, Chow Man-keung and Cheung Man-po). Of course, you can't lose visually with so many luxurious costumes and colours in the Lion Dances, the Red Lantern Society, and the outfits of early, modern China.

Tsui Hark's input in *Once Upon a Time In China 4* included production and co-writing (plus it was produced by his company, Film Workshop – along with Paragon Films and Golden Harvest). *Once Upon a Time In China 4* is wholly A Tsui Hark Movie in pretty much every respect, despite him handing over the directorial reins to Yuen Bun (one of Tsui's regular action choreographers). Not least because it is the fourth entry in a series which had been directed and produced and co-written (and, crucially, *conceived*) by Tsui. That is, Tsui's stamp is all over the first three *Once Upon a Time In China* films, and the fourth film is actually directed – by Yuen Bun – like Tsui (right down to the movement of the camera).

YUEN BUN.

Director Yuen Bun (b. 1954) is an actor who has been in pretty much everything, and an action director who has worked with Tsui Hark on many productions, as well as numerous Hong Kong classics. Bun was one of the 'Seven Little Fortunes', the Peking Opera School group that included future Hong Kong legends such as Jackie Chan, Sammo Hung, Yuen Wah, Corey Yuen Kwai and Yuen Ting.

By 2014, Yuen Bun had action director credits on 102 films! (Going back to 1974, a remarkable career). Plus 107 acting credits. However,

---

25 And those thick eyebrows! Oh dear. Where were the make-up girl's scissors?!
26 Zhao 'seems completely at sea when it comes to the right Wong mix of stoicism and emotion', complained Lisa Morton (LM, 196).
27 Clubfoot is a much cleaned-up, much less angry guy from the third *Once Upon a Time In China* movie.

Yuen has only directed three films,[28] preferring to work as a choreographer or actor: *Once Upon a Time in China 4* (1993), *Tough Beauty and the Sloppy Slop* (1995) and *Fearful 24 Hours* (2004).

Yuen Bun is without question one of the great action directors of recent times, with a list of credits that includes many masterpieces (and Yuen's contribution, in choreographing the action, is absolutely pivotal to those films being masterpieces): such as, for Tsui Hark: *Time and Tide, Dragon Gate Inn, Swordsman 2, The Blade, Flying Swords of Dragon Gate* and the three *Detective Dee* movies.

Yuen Bun is one of the unsung heroes of Hong Kong action cinema. The limelight is hogged by other action directors – Yuen Woo-ping, Tony Ching, Corey Yuen Kwai and Jackie Chan, but Yuen has choreographed some of the greatest action in all Hong Kong cinema (and therefore all world cinema).

In sum, the collaborations between Yuen Bun and Tsui Hark have been among the finest in action cinema: they clearly work well together (you've got be *really* good to keep up with a director as amazing as Tsui).

THE STORY, ACT-BY-ACT.

Once Upon a Time In China 4 opens with two lengthy prologue/ title sequences (one wonders if these were included to bump up the running time): Wong Fei-hung practising kung fu in an Imperial China setting (with the customary 'Under the General's Orders' martial music, to introduce the new star), followed by the main titles (set against the Lion Dance competition footage, which climaxed the previous *Once Upon a Time In China* film – a cheap option, and a standard tactic for increasing the running time).

Once Upon a Time In China 4 seems like a chronological continuation of *Once Upon a Time In China 3* (and from the Lion Dance finale of *Once Upon a Time In China 3*): the first act contains many scenes of Lion Dances and colourful parades (production value scenes, yes, and also scenes asserting Chinese national culture, a particular passion for Tsui Hark).

Once again, nationalist politics, national cultures, and the conflicts between nations are foregrounded in *Once Upon a Time In China 4*, emphasizing yet again just how intensely *political* the *Once Upon a Time In China* series is. Altho' they are movies about a great Chinese hero, and they're colourful action movies, it's surprising just how much of their setting and background is ideological, cultural and political. *Once Upon a Time In China 4* is set in 1900.

Once again, any group or individual that's 'foreign' is negatively typed: here, it's Germans and Brits. And the battleground? Only another Lion Dance competition! (How can any group from outside China possibly be victorious in a traditional, Chinese event like a Lion Dance?! Especially when Wong Fei-hung is involved!). But the Lion Dance competition is a mere sideshow to the Eight Nation Alliance, which's moving against China.

---

28 It might've been daunting to follow Tsui Hark in directing his first film, and having his first film as director being a big picture and part of a successful franchise.

Meanwhile, the organization within China that's shifting too far towards radicalism or nationalism in *Once Upon a Time In China 4* is a group of nationalistic feminists, the Red Lantern Society. The *Once Upon a Time In China* series doesn't create narratives where only 'foreigners' are rivals/ enemies – there is always a group inside China which is descending into a radical ideology which unbalances the status quo. The *Once Upon a Time In China* series doesn't side with rebels or activists – its politics are ultimately conservative and pro-State.

After all, let's not forget that the hero of the 1990s *Wong Fei-hung* movies is... Wong Fei-hung! That is, an upright citizen of society, if ever there was one! Wong is almost too perfect, too righteous. And he needs big villains, whole organizations, not single individuals (because an individual, even if they're played by martial arts masters like Donnie Yen or Xiong Xin-xin, are ultimately no match for Wong).

Thus, in the action climax of act one of *Once Upon a Time In China 4* – a terrorist attack on a German church by the Red Lantern Society – it's Wong Fei-hung defending law and order. Well, that's the over-arching, political setting – but the filmic reality is actually one young man beating off a whole troupe of female martial artists! Bang goes the taboo against hitting women! (And yet, there are differences between the way this scene is filmed – no blood, for a start, and Wong beats the women with a piece of rolled-up cloth, not swords or spears).

The Red Lantern Society are very likely wholly created by Tsui Hark. A band of young women who're taking nationalistic fervour to terrorist extremes is a classic, Tsuian motif. Radical feminism plus terrorism plus martial arts! – it's the perfect combination for Tsui! In terms of action and choreography and staging, the Red Lantern Society sequences are predictable – it is, after all, young women kicking ass, which Hong Kong cinema has been trotting out for decades. They throw lanterns filled with ether (which explode like fire-bombs), and they have an attractive leader, Miao Sanniang (played by Elaine Lui Siu-Ling). In the procession sequence, the leader somersaults down from a human pyramid to have a little time in amongst the crowds with Wong Fei-hung (with a little moment of rivalry with 14th Aunt).

But beyond the cheesy action cinema trappings, politically and ideologically, the Red Lantern Society is fascinating. *Once Upon a Time In China 4* is clearly aiming to evoke some deeper undercurrents in contemporary Chinese society and politics. And in this quasi-historical setting (rather than a fantasy context), seeing a group of women acting so aggressively in public, and in a very patriarchal and traditional society like China *circa* 1900, is very unusual.

❖

Act one of *Once Upon a Time In China 4* includes the aftermath of the Lion Dance competition from the third film (with much self-congratulation), the invitation to participate in another Lion Dance festival, a procession and Lion Dance in the streets, and the finale: the procession from the Red Lantern Society followed by the raid on the German church.

Act one also contains the requisite comical scenes from Ah Foon, and the introduction of the romantic interest (in the second part of act one): with Rosamund Kwan stepping down, her role is now taken up by Jean Wang, playing what is essentially the same character. As well as the romantic elements (one-sided, as usual – Wong Fei-hung is not interested in 14th Aunt like that – yet), the scenes also feature the character's fascination with Western technology (here, it's printing presses).[29] But Wang's 14th Aunt has little to do in *Once Upon a Time In China 4,* and doesn't contribute to the plot as much as 13th Aunt did in the previous installments. One wonders if more was filmed but left out, due to Vincent Zhao coming across as uncomfortable in the romantic scenes.

❖

Act two includes two stunning sequences featuring the nationalistic feminists of the Red Lantern Society. Like the White Lotus Cult in film two of the *Once Upon a Time In China* series, the Red Lantern Society is very fond of putting over their ideological messages using pageantry and co-ordinated acrobatics. The twist here in *China 4* is seeing an all-women team, clad in matching white costumes (with red trimming). So we know, for a start, that when the fighting starts (as it must!), there will be no murders (tho' the women will be pushed, kicked and battered about).

The two set-pieces are staged at the Po Chi Lam clinic at night, when the Wong Fei-hung group returns (minus Wong, however), to find that the Red Lantern Society have overwhelmed the building with their banners and deadly lanterns (the Red Lantern Society certainly have an eye for decoration). The inevitable bust-up is spectacular, intense, and wildly acrobatic, like the Cirque du Soleil meets Peking Opera. If there's a circus trick to be used, the *Once Upon a Time In China* series will use it (they include a lengthy duel on wires, a call-back to the White Lotus Cult sequence, where touching the ground is avoided, and the famous ladders scene in the first *Once Upon a Time In China* movie).

In the first Red Lantern Society set-piece, our heroes are overcome by the powder wielded by the warriors in their lanterns (no one is immune to it). In the second set-piece, Wong Fei-hung turns up (accompanied by Miao Sanniang), having escaped jail. The scene involves an over-elaborate game of dominoes,[30] using large blocks of wood (again with balancing and not touching the ground as a rule, as in a children's game), and the staple of the *Once Upon a Time In China* series: Wong Fei-hung versus numerous assailants. The second part is a highwire act, with Wong going up against Miao, the leader of the Red Lantern Society (cue close-ups of feet on wires, and the commander being kicked to the ground. Oh no, we couldn't have Wong being bested by a woman!).

There's no shortage of ideas here – or energy: indeed, these movies look like the filmmakers could go on and on coming up with new moves, new twirls, new ways of using wires, or new ways of nobbling an opponent. I bet if they were allowed to, Hong Kong action directors could fill out an

---

29 But 14th Aunt isn't such a passionate proponent of Western science as 13th Aunt.
30 Plenty of celluloid is reversed to provide the trick shots of the domino pieces being returned upright by Wong Fei-hung.

entire movie with tumbling, jumping, slashing and flying. This is moviemaking as a Peking Opera performance. The stamina seems endless – these guys and girls just don't quit! – and the use of the body in space is without equal anywhere on the planet.

❖

With so much of *Once Upon a Time In China 4* taking place during Lion Dances or street processions, it's like watching a travelogue about Chinese folklore and customs: cinema of course adores festivals, carnivals, fairgrounds, anything where there's a multitude of people, colour, movement, performance, rides, etc. The *Once Upon a Time In China* series contains a striking amount of theatre and performance, of processions thru the old town set, or from the tumbling acrobats of the Red Lantern team at the Po Chi Lam clinic. Indeed, one of Wong Fei-hung's alternative careers is as a Lion Dancer and street performer (of course, Wong turns out to be the finest of all Lion Dancers, and always does something heroic at a Lion Dance show. Sometimes, Wong seems like an expert and famous Lion Dancer who just happens to run a clinic and be a martial arts star, too).

Thus, *Once Upon a Time In China 4* contains not only several Lion Dances, but also a street procession from the Red Lantern Society, a funeral for General Chengdu, and even Ah Foon performs to a crowd. The *Once Upon a Time In China* series is very fond of combining the pageantry and tradition of China (in the Lion Dances) with martial arts choreography: thus, as in previous *Once Upon a Time In China* outings, the Lion Dance staged by the Eight-Nation Alliance in Peking is an excuse for the foreigners to attack the General and his team (with new-fangled technology – a Gatling gun). So, once again, it's the foreigners inside China who turn on the Chinese and assault them.

❖

As usual in the *Once Upon a Time In China* series, there isn't a single sequence for the finale in *Once Upon a Time In China 4*, but several. The first climax rounds off the Red Lantern Society plot: once again, it's those nasty foreigners (here, Germans) who are the villains, firing on the Red Lantern Society girls with rifles. Well, we know that *kung fu* and swords are no match for firearms (which are, as Akira Kurosawa noted, too easy – you just stand there and shoot).

The violence exerted against women is striking in *Once Upon a Time In China 4* (one of the members of the Red Lantern Society, for instance, is lacerated with bullets like Sonny Corleone in *The Godfather*, and the leader is decapitated, much to her followers' dismay). These acts are carried out by the two heavies (Tuen Tin-lui (Chin Kar-lok) and Iron Fist (Billy Chow)) hired by the foreign powers to deal with the locals. (One of the henchmen (Iron Fist) is given the ability to punch out a horse (a staple of the cowboy genre) – Clubfoot encounters these guys on horseback, and only just manages to get away).

There is re-match of the Lion Dance competition back in the capital, with Wong Fei-hung, Clubfoot, Wong senior and their chums turning out victorious (of course). This supplies the setting for the last part of the finale of *Once Upon a Time In China 4*, which's fantastically chaotic and visceral – everybody is being flung around in the dust of the parade ground (right into the night). In the finale, the stunt team stage every gag they can think of – the screen is frantic with fighters in festival costumes leaping about, amazing images of lions, eagles, centipedes, bulls and crabs,[31] guns blazing and swords flashing (Wong chooses a walking stick this time). Quite rightly, the movie depicts the clashes of animals among the Lion Dancers as if they are real, mythical creatures – thus, the lion heads attack the bodies of the birds, crabs and centipedes, as if this is a smackdown between huge, Japanese monsters (*kaiju*).

For action fans, some of the finest moments are in the closing minutes, when Wong Fei-hung and Clubfoot go up against the two bruisers sent by the foreign powers, Iron Fist and Tuen Tin-lui (here, Vincent Zhao's strength as a *wushu* performer pays off. Zhao and Xiong make a great team – the highlight of their collaboration being the truly extraordinary duel that closes *The Blade*, two years later).

Once Upon a Time In China 4 does suffer from the downsides of sequelizing – that we have seen all of this before: the same sort of characters, the same sort of action, the same sort of spectacle and effects, the same sort of romance, and the same sort of comedy. Part of the feeling of *déja vu* comes from the use of the Lion Dance motif – which ran throughout the third *Once Upon a Time In China* movie (and featured in the first movies, too); film four thus not only continues the Lion Dance theme of the third movie, it feels like a remake of it.

Starting a Wong Fei-hung movie with some new actors in the lead roles (such as Wong Fei-hung and 14th Aunt) might've been better served with a different *milieu* for the story. (Being released 4 months after film three maybe didn't leave time to develop new material).

---

31 The Lion Dance costumes are a delight.

Once Upon a Time In China 2 (1992).

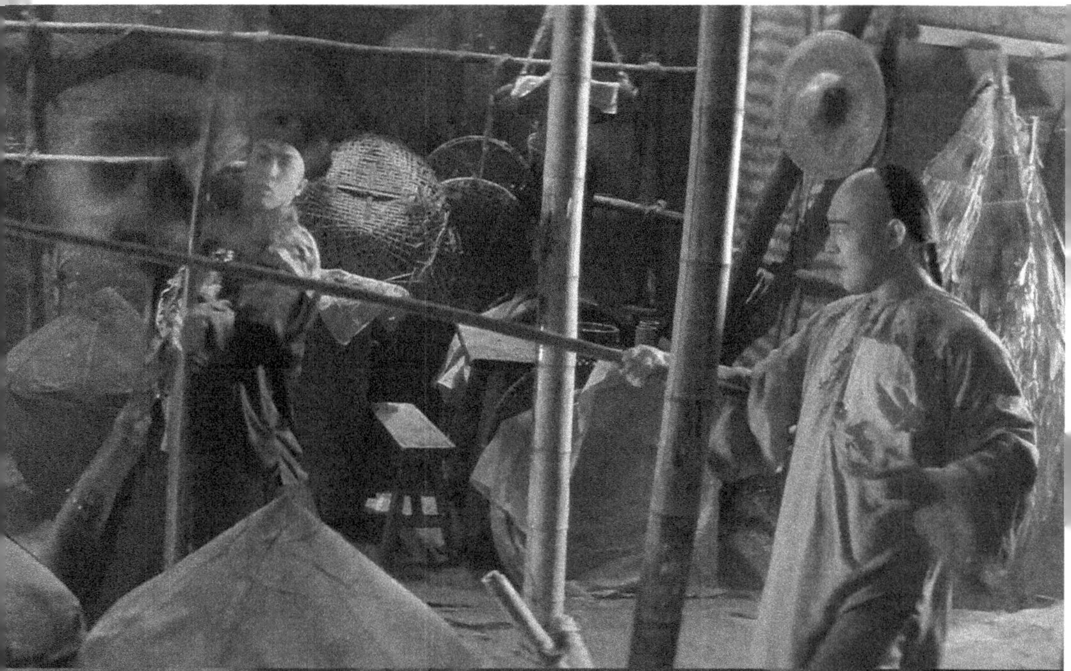

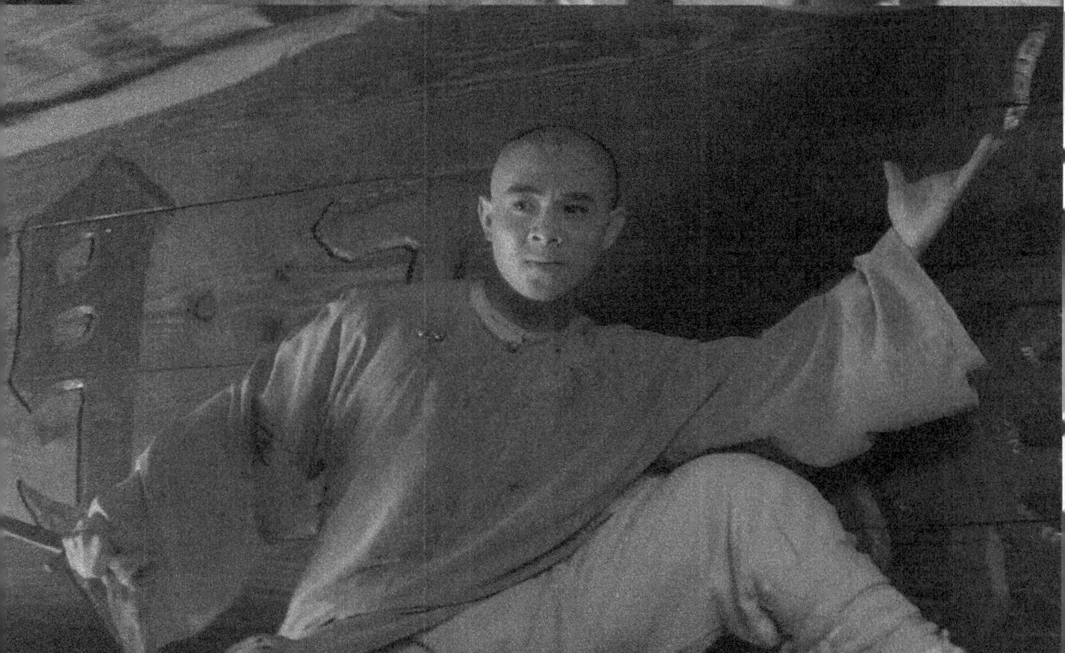

AMAZIA
A FILM BY TSUI HARK
ONCE UPON A TIME IN CHINA II
2
FSK 16
JET-LI

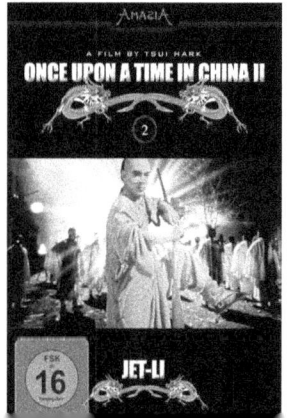

Once Upon a Time In China 3 (1993). This page and over.

Once Upon a Time In China 4 (1993). This page and over.

6

ONCE UPON A TIME IN CHINA 5

Wong Fei-hung
Ji Ng Lung Sing Chin Ba

Once Upon a Time In China 5 (1994, *Shiàonián Huáng Feihóng Zhi Tie Maliú* in Mandarin = *Wong Fei-hung 5: Dragon City's Exterminator Tyrant*), was produced by Tsui Hark and Ng See-yuen. It was written by Tsui, Lau Daai-muk and Lam Kee-to. The DPs were: Ko Chiu-Lam, Derek Wan, Peter Pau Tak-Hai, Tom Lau Moon-tong and Andy Lam. Art dir. by Bill Lui. Costumes: Kwok-Sun Chui. Action dir.: Yuen Bun. Edited by Marco Mak Chi-sin. Music by William Hu. It was produced by Film Workshop/ Paragon Films Ltd. (The home box office was disappointing – HK $4,902,426, compared to the HK $11 million-plus of *Once Upon a Time In China 4,* and it's disappointing for a Tsui Hark movie, and a *Once Upon a Time In China* movie). Released November 17, 1994. 101 minutes.

In the cast of *Once Upon a Time In China 5* were the full compliment of Wong Fei-hung regulars: Vincent Zhao as Wong Fei-hung, Rosamund Kwan as 13th Aunt, Max Mok as Leung Foon, Kent Cheng as Porky Wing, Roger Kwok as 'Bucktooth' So, Xiong Xin-xin as Clubfoot, Jean Wang as 14th Aunt, Lau Shun as Wong Kei-ying, Tam Bing-man as Boss, Yee Tin-hung as Devil Cheung, Elaine Lui Siu-Ling as 'Single-eyed' Ying, Zhang Tie-lin[1] as Chief Constable, Stephen Tung as Junior Cheung, and Dion Lam as Flying Monkey.

Music: as with *Once Upon a Time In China 4*, you have to admit that some of the music composed and produced for *Once Upon a Time In China 5* is rather generic and so-so (it is credited to William Hu and Tsui Hark). And too much of it is cheaply and cheesily orchestral – using synthesizers to emulate strings in an orchestra, but not in an impressive or imaginative manner. Visuals and set-pieces this grand really do demand (and deserve) a higher grade of musical composition.

---

[1] He played Sun Yat-sen in *Once Upon a Time In China 2*.

Once Upon a Time In China 5 is Tsui Hark's pirate[2] movie.[3] The 1994 movie goes all-out in its depictions of pirates at work and play. Battles on ships, treasure chests, a treasure horde, cascading gold, bandoleros, etc. From the Prologue, where pirates menace a hapless petty criminal, *Once Upon a Time In China 5* celebrates movie-movie pirates – the more grizzled, belligerent and OTT the better. Nobody can do a pirate movie straight since, well, probably the 1940s: *Once Upon a Time In China 5* is no different (but this time combines the pirate genre with the *kung fu* genre). The pirate genre is sent up while it's exalted (and yet, pirating perfectly describes the aggression and rampant capitalism of new economies like Hong Kong and the Pacific Rim, where real pirates, in the form of organized syndicates, flourish. And pirates still prey on ships today). Tsui is especially fond of no-goods with a scuzzy, eccentric appearance – he enjoys villains and rebels with a punky or post-punk look (they crop up in *New Dragon Gate Inn, The Blade* and *Seven Swords* for instance. Indeed, parts of *Once Upon a Time In China 5* look like a dry run for the teeming scenes of rough-and-ready banditos in *The Blade*).

The comedy in *Once Upon a Time In China 5*, which takes up a *lot* of screentime (the first act contains several purely comical scenes), is largely carried by the four goofs who surround Wong Fei-hung: Ah Foon, Porky Wing, Bucktooth So and Clubfoot. In numerous scenes this foursome of hapless, accident-prone fools delivers comical business, under-cutting the action and the drama, lightening the narrative, and reminding us, once again, that *comedy* is actually one of Tsui Hark's major concerns. And you can see that Tsui enjoyed the interplay of the four actors (Max Mok, Kent Cheng, Xiong Xin-xin and Roger Kwok), dwelling on their humorous antics at length.

In the 1990s conception of the Wong Fei-hung Legend, the group that gathers around the Robin Hood figure of Wong is absolutely fundamental. They are simple-minded, naïve, brave and utterly devoted to Wong. When Wong enters the room, squabbling ceases instantly, and things become serious.

Once Upon a Time In China 5 seems to be an attempt at a different kind of Wong Fei-hung movie, or a self-conscious departure by the filmmakers from the pattern already established. Thus, the visual approach steps away from the bright, colourful images of the first three movies, and into a much murkier, shadowier realm. The first act takes place, for instance, largely at night, or in reduced light, with the customary oranges and blues of night scenes in Hong Kong movies taken way down (actors play scenes with their faces moving into shadow. The low levels of light also mean that Wong seems interchangeable now with the many members of his coterie who look similar).

Once Upon a Time In China 5 delivers the familiar Tsui Hark visual flourishes – like the rainstorm in the opening scenes, with the first Big

---
2 The pirate setting allows our heroes to dress up differently, as pirates (all in black), as they go in disguise.
3 Pirates had appeared in Jackie Chan's *Project A* movies, among other Hong Kong pictures.

Fight occurring at night in a heavy downpour, and the rapidly mobile camera, the shadowplay, and penchant for capturing unusual camera angles, or telling close-ups and insert shots. (Despite five DPs being credited, *Once Upon a Time In China 5* has a seamless look).

Once Upon a Time In China 5 continues Tsui Hark's penchant for staging scenes in a *tableau* format with lengthy takes: he and his DPs will frame a bunch of actors (typically grouped around Wong Fei-hung), and keep the camera on them without cutting, while they deliver the dialogue.

There is a larger group of characters surrounding Wong Fei-hung in this movie – such as Porky Wing (Kent Cheung), Ah Foon (Max Mok), Bucktooth So (Roger Kwok) and Clubfoot (Xiong Xin-xin). 14th Aunt (Jean Wang) is retained from the previous *Once Upon a Time In China* movie, but Rosamund Kwan is back as 13th Aunt. (This is largely the cast that appeared in the 1996 *Once Upon a Time In China* TV series).

Sometimes, *Once Upon a Time In China 5* looks as if it's more of a team format than a Wong Fei-hung format – it's Wong Fei-hung plus his four trusty fighting assistants: Porky Wing, Foon Leung, Bucktooth So and Clubfoot. Wong is still the commander, leading the team into battle, and making all of the key decisions, but often he's offscreen, and we're watching Mok, Cheng, Kwok and Xiong do their stuff as four martial artists.

It's true that *Once Upon a Time In China 5* doesn't have the grandly political sweep of the earlier *Once Upon a Time In China* movies. *Once Upon a Time In China 5* is much more like a television episode, or a small-scale film, in which the heroes tackle a single foe (here, it's pirates).

Once Upon a Time In China 5 opens with action that continues directly from the ending of *Once Upon a Time In China 4*, where our heroes were travelling away from Peking after the Lion Dance competition (the movie even uses the main titles sequence wholesale from *Once Upon a Time In China 4*). They are travelling to Foshan, a step away from moving to Hong Kong. So, at the start of *Once Upon a Time In China 5*, they are waylaid on their trip, in a similar manner to the beginning of *Once Upon a Time In China 4* (and also *Once Upon a Time In China and America*).

The world of China evoked in *Once Upon a Time In China 5* is a more troubled place than in previous *Once Upon a Time In China* films. Food is scarce, and people are hungry (many scenes in the first act are set at meal times, and in a food store). The sombre tone is evoked in the opening action scene involving pirates (led by Stephen Tung), where a victim's hands're whipped off by the villains. Not long after this archetypal piece of Chinese horror (which doesn't really fit in the *Once Upon a Time In China* series), a chest of human fingers is delivered by the pirates to the food store.

It's in this atmosphere of socio-economic unrest that Wong Fei-hung and his entourage arrive, and are ambushed by the guys from the food store (of course, they are no match for Wong, Clubfoot, Foon and co.). This begins the story in *Once Upon a Time In China 5* – with Wong acting in his guise as Robin Hood, the Hero of the Oppressed.

The first act of *Once Upon a Time In China 5* also features the other regular ingredients of a *Wong Fei-hung* outing: several comical scenes (often at Ah Foon's expense), the romantic subplots, and the introduction of the principal groups or communities (the pirate gang, the Chief Constable and his team, the food store employees, etc).

A romantic triangle is set up in the first act of *Once Upon a Time In China 5*, between the two Aunts (the 14th and the 13th Aunts), played by Jean Wang and Rosamund Kwan[4] (once again, Vincent Zhao doesn't look quite at home in the romantic scenes, and Jet Li's portrayal in the romantic scenes was lighter and more playful). The erotic rivalry is of course between the two women – it's the women who're desiring Wong Fei-hung, not the other way around. Because in the 1990s *Once Upon a Time In China* series, Wong is fairly indifferent to matters of the heart. Or at least, to playing the romantic heartthrob in a romantic melodrama (or anyway, in pursuing women, whereas the real Wong had four wives).

❖

Opening act two of *Once Upon a Time In China 5* is a *lot* of comedy exploring the romantic triangle, using the motif that Tsui Hark and the filmmakers had developed for the romance in the first three *Once Upon a Time In China* movies: shadowplay. So we have the bunch of Wong Fei-hung's followers (Porky Wing, Ah Foon, Clubfoot *et al*) seeing what appears to be some romantic goings-on in a nearby room between Wong and the 14th Aunt (in fact, they are picking up a pearl necklace that's Daddy Wong's broken and scattered on the floor). The 13th Aunt also turns up and sees what appears to be a kiss (and maybe more) with her beloved Wong and 14th Aunt next door.

The comical interplay in the romantic triangle carries over into the following scene, where pirates're sneaking around town at night brandishing swords, up to no good. Aunt Yeo storms out in a huff, and in her anger she's able to easily overcome the pirates who intimidate her (this offers a welcome bit of action for Rosamund Kwan – it reprises the grappling hand move that Wong Fei-hung taught her in film two). Earlier, a two-hander scene had Aunt Yeo persuading Wong Fei-hung to exchange rings, in preparation for a Western-style marriage (Aunt Yeo already has the confetti, too. The soundtrack plays Felix Mendelssohn's *Wedding March*, which Aunt Yeo also hums). Needless to say, Wong is baffled, as ever, with Aunt Yeo's romantic overtures.

Act two of *Once Upon a Time In China 5* properly begins, however, with the commencement of the pirate theme, as Wong Fei-hung and co. decide to take some action against the bandits disrupting Southern China. There are scenes at the port of Foshan, with our heroes in disguise, as they manœuvre into place to pin down the pirates.

Some movies sag in their middle acts like bloated bellies full of beer and burgers. Not *Once Upon a Time In China 5* – this is a trim, agile movie that leaps about from foot to hand to toe to finger to elbow and back again. Thus, following the comical scenes in the kitchen, involving the romantic

---

[4] Kwan's introduction receives a *big* build-up; 14th Aunt looks on jealously as 13th Aunt embraces Wong closely.

triangle and Aunt Yeo's huff, *Once Upon a Time In China 5* explodes into two (really three) absolutely outstanding action sequences (with a short training scene, where our heroes try their hand at firing guns – with, of course, comical results. Bucktooth So, unexpectedly, turns out to a crackshot, and performs two-gun acrobatics, in a send-up of John Woo's films, a bit of the kooky humour from the *Aces Go Places* and *All the Wrong Clues* series).

The first action sequence takes place on boats at sea: this is Tsui Hark's version of the swashbucklers and action-adventure movies he loved as a youth (Oriental ones as well as Western ones). If Tsui were directing the *Pirates of the Caribbean* movies (if only!), this is what they would look like. The stunts and action choreography are glorious – again the feeling of freedom, of movement into any area of the frame, from any direction, is pure delight. (Tsui explored this territory in the *Detective Dee* series).

(The girls are left behind now: true, *Once Upon a Time In China 5* brings the romantic subplots and the action plots together, but not as convincingly as in previous *Once Upon a Time In China* outings. This time, the men and the women are separated, and it's the boys who go into battle).

The pirate den sequence is really two action sequences smashed together. *Once Upon a Time In China 5* revels in putting cartoon-like outcasts and criminals on screen, drinking and carousing.5 It's another saloon/ nightclub/ restaurant scene where the heroes enter in disguise, and you know there's going to be a Giant Fight. It takes place in one of the densely layered sets that regularly turn up in Tsui Hark's movies (the lighting job by one of the five cinematographers is outstanding and very intricate). The set is crammed with stuff – principally, of course, for the stunt team to bounce around in, manipulate on wires (boxes and poles are thrown around all over the place), and smash to bits. It seems as if every wooden chest, every suitcase, and every box in Hong Kong was carted in just for this scene.

Our heroes (Wong Fei-hung, Clubfoot, Ah Foon, Porky Wing and Bucktooth So) are up against countless pirates in this sequence, which segues into the treasure trove scene. Notice how the filmmakers concentrate completely on the five heroes, always shooting action from their point-of-view, with the opponents being piled up one after another as henchmen to be dispatched in countless imaginative ways. The pirates aren't personalized at all (beyond generic, piratey carousing) – except for the female pirate ('Single-eyed' Ying) that Wong encounters.

Yes, *Once Upon a Time In China 5* pits Wong Fei-hung against a formidable woman pirate (played by Elaine Lui Siu-Ling, the Red Lantern Society heroine Miao Sanniang in the previous film). And the setting eroticizes their relationship, with 'Single-eyed' Ying leading Wong into her boudoir. As the romantic clinch seems about to take place, of course the

---

5 There is some comedy before the bust-up: the drink (beer?) tastes disgusting and is spat out, and our heroes are clad in cool black costumes that seem much more like the 1990s than the 1900s.

action starts up (no, not even a kiss with the wrong woman for the ever-chaste Wong! The movie always sticks to the formula!).

The struggle on the bed between Wong Fei-hung and 'Single-eyed' Ying recalls the equally amazing scene in *New Dragon Gate Inn* between Jade and Yuan Mo-ya. The bed fitted with a variety of weaponry (like spikes and rows of spears, which suddenly burst upwards phallically) is reminiscent of an early *James Bond* movie. The choreography has a rapidity and invention which is never seen in Western movies – it's love-making as action as dance.

The final section of the seemingly continuous action sequence in the middle of *Once Upon a Time In China 5* involves a remnant from another era, Flying Monkey (Dion Lam). This is Tsui Hark putting a bit of the Monkey King on screen (which he's always wanted to do – and finally did in *Journey To the West*). So Flying Monkey is a mandarin who can leap about and is beyond the capabilities of anybody among the heroes, except for – yes – Wong Fei-hung.

Once again, the duel employs gravity-defying stuntwork and reprises the motif of not touching the ground. This time, the participants are balancing atop large vases, which teeter-totter like the wooden dominoes in film four and the ladders in film one. It's marvellous stuff, purely – solely – crowd-pleasing, a movie as a circus act in which the audience can admire the stunts and agility of the performers, gasp when Wong Fei-hung is hit, boo-hiss the villain, and cheer when Flying Monkey disappears under an avalanche of chests, vases, and treasure.

❖

The climactic action sequence of *Once Upon a Time In China 5* is essentially a reprise of previous action scenes in the movie: it's Wong Fei-hung and his cohorts going up against the pirates (the bunch from the opening scenes). There are battles and duels all over the place, entirely filmed at night (Tsui Hark is especially fond of filming at night – one imagines that film crews find this exhausting, but Tsui, with his boundless energy, keeps them enthused thru the night).

The finale is given a suitably lengthy build-up, with the filmmakers taking their time in covering the preparations that Wong Fei-hung and company have made to counter the attack of the pirates (for example, going to the lengths of staging a Lion Dance on wires, but without people, to fool the pirates, and to set off fireworks, to make the pirates think they're out celebrating. Meanwhile, our heroes have set up gun emplacements with sandbags, as if they're staging a war. It's *The Seven Samurai* narrative format again, preparing to defend a village).

The action sequences run thru numerous outdoor spaces (such as Porky Wing's mob, with their canons), all over the roofs (several times), across the festive decorations on a balcony, in the upper levels of the warehouse (and the jail), and back onto the streets, with the filmmakers exploiting every inch of the sets. Again, there is that feeling that the filmmakers can and will zoom their actors and stunt guys into any part of the frame and any corner of the set. Total freedom of movement – if a pirate grabs a rope and skitters upwards like a monkey onto the roofs, then the heroes will follow him instantly (there are incredible scenes where Wong Fei-hung and Clubfoot are leaping from pillar to wall to roof, kicking off from one wall to fly thru the air to land on a post, then launching themselves upwards).

'Single-eyed' Ying escapes from prison by unpicking the locks on her wrists using her feet *through* the cell bars (she is a very flexible girl), a guy has a gun hidden in a spear, and everybody is running and flying about like crazy. The movie comes up with surprising elements and textures – billowing gunpowder, cascades of rice, sacks of food hurled across the set. Ying is dispatched with a gunshot to the head (the *Battleship Potemkin* shot thru the glasses), and a victim receives a cannon ball at close range (it's Wong Fei-hung, of course, who kicks the cannon round).

Part of the finale culminates in the food storehouse – an elaborate set that contains multiple levels and plenty of props to throw about (boxes and sacks of rice), and plenty of wooden structures to smash. Instead of sand or dust, rice is used (by Wong Fei-hung) to hurl at the enemy to temporarily blind them. Very impressive fire effects are employed again, as the warehouse burns down; actors are set on fire; when the action moves outside, gunpowder is bursting over the performers (from out of a barrel), and filling the air, with a guy clambering about trying to reach a lamp to ignite it (and everyone trying to stop him).

It really is astonishing cinema – purely in terms of the orchestration of movement in space in conjunction with outstanding camerawork, gorgeous and *very* intricate lighting, razor-sharp editing and pacing, and a total confidence in exploiting the technical weaponry of modern cinema.

7

ONCE UPON A TIME IN CHINA AND AMERICA

Wong Feihong Ji Sai Wik Hung Si

INTRO.
Sammo Hung + Tsui Hark + Jet Li + an idea supposedly stolen from Jackie Chan! It can't fail, can it?! For this 1997 *Wong Fei-hung* outing, the sixth in the *Once Upon a Time In China* movie series, Tsui opted for the producer role (but we know for Tsui that can mean co-direction!), and asked his friend Hung Kam-bo to helm a 'Chinaman in America' story,[6] complete with cowboys, Native Americans, guns, shoot-outs, horses, one-street towns, saloons, deserts, dust, sunsets, Sherrifs and Mayors, and just about everything else from the mythical American West that the Chinese filmmakers had imbibed back in Hong Kong as kids.

Actually, an 'Eastern Western' – a Chinaman in the Wild West – wasn't original to Jackie Chan. Bruce Lee, for example, had pitched an 'Eastern Western' called *The Warrior* to Warners in 1971, with himself in the lead role:

> It's a really freaky adventure series about a Chinese guy who winds up in the American West in 1860 [Lee explained]. Can you dig that? All these cowboys on horses with guns and me with a long, green hunk of bamboo, right?[7]

But according to Bruce Lee's biographer Matthew Polly, Lee didn't originate the idea: it was Ed Spielman and Howard Friedlander, two New York comedy writers, who developed the concept of a Shaolin monk who comes to America in the 1880s in a Western.[8]

❖

The sixth *Once Upon a Time In China* (*Huang Feihong Zhi Xiyu*

---

6 *Once Upon a Time In China and America* is also an early 20th century version of another Tsui Hark 'Chinaman in America' story, *The Master* (which also starred Jet Li).
7 Quoted in M. Polly, 334.
8 Ibid., 277f.

Hongshi in Mandarin = *Wong Fei-hung: West Territory Mighty Lion*), brought Jet Li back to the series with a tale that went to the U.S.A. The concept apparently came from Jackie Chan, who had told Sammo Hung Kam-bo, his former Peking Opera buddy, about it years before. *Shanghai Noon* (2000) was Chan's version of the Chinaman in the American Old West idea (with Owen Wilson playing the Yank he teams up with).

Roy Szeto Cheuk-hon, Shut Mei-yee, Sharon Hui Sa-long, Philip Kwok and So Man-Sing co-wrote the script of *Once Upon a Time In China and America*; Tsui Hark and Dick Cho Kin-nam produced, thru Film Workshop (Lau Kar-wing is sometimes credited with co-direction, and/ or second unit direction);[9] the DPs were Walter Gregg, Lam Fai-tai and Koo Kwok-wah; Marco Mak Chi-sIn and Angie Lam On-yee edited; and music was by Lowell Lo.[10] The 98-minute movie grossed a healthy HK $30,268,415 in Hong Kong (it was shot quickly in time for a traditional, Chinese New Year release (Feb 1, 1997) – you can see how cold it was on location in Texas). The budget was very high for a Hong Kong movie (some $8 million (no doubt due to filming in the U.S.A.)

The crew of *Once Upon a Time In China and America* was largely from Hong Kong – *Once Upon a Time In China and America* is very much a Chinese movie made in the U.S.A. (based in Texas, filming at the Alamo Village, built for the movie *The Alamo*).[11] The cast, headed up by Jet Li and Rosamund Kwan, included Xiong Xin-xin (a big part of the *Once Upon a Time In China* franchise), back as Clubfoot (a.k.a. Seven), Power Chan (Chan Kwok Pong) as Bucktooth So, Richard Ng as Han, Jeff Wolfe as Billy, Joe Sayah as a Mexican bandit, and T.J. Storm as a Native American brave. Plus Mars, Lau Kar-wing, Patrick Lung, Ron Ring, Crystal Bell, Ryon Marshall, Freddy Joe, and William Fung.

Tsui Hark had wanted to do a Western, and *Once Upon a Time In China and America* was a golden opportunity. The whole Old West mythology is thrown into the mix, and totally in a movie-movie manner. (Of course, the *Once Upon a Time In China* movies draw on plenty of American Western movies which the filmmakers grew up watching – *Once Upon a Time In China and America* is another of Tsui's movie-movies).

Hong Kong cinema had already produced Westerns in China, or *kung fu* and historical movies which took motifs from American Western movies: *Blood Money* (1974) and *Kung Fu Brothers In the Wild West* (1973), for example. In the 1990s, Chow Yun-fat had starred in *The Peace Hotel* (1995), and later there was *Warriors of Heaven and Earth* (Ping He, 2003). However, Hong Kong productions which went to the U.S.A. to film *kung fu/* Western hybrids were much rarer (partly because of cost).

Once Upon a Time In China and America is filmed in the textured, rough-and-ready style of Hong Kong filmmaking: plenty of smoke and rain, and an emphasis on visceral, rough-and-tumble action.[12] With Sammo

---

9 Lau Kar-wing also played a Lion Dance Drummer.
10 Lowell Lo delivered some impressive versions of Native American-ish music – even the famous *Wong Fei-hung* cue in a percussive, Native American style.
11 In the entertaining 'making of' documentary, every actor and crew member notes how cold it was filming in Texas in December, 1996, for a Chinese New Year's release.
12 In some scenes, Jet Li moves thru many fighting styles – from *wushu* to Northern mantis to chen tai chi.

Hung Kam-bo holding the directorial reins, *Once Upon a Time In China and America* inevitably displays Hung's penchant for martial arts action which stays close to the ground, involves lots of fists and kicks, and is what a human could realistically achieve (however, there is wirework a-plenty). Action choreographers were Hung, plus Cho Wing and Xiong Xin-xin. Visual effects, as usual in a Tsui Hark movie (or any Hong Kong action movie), are everywhere, from exploding glasses of beer to vats of water that blow up.

THE SCRIPT.

In terms of plot and character, *Once Upon a Time In China and America* is certainly a less engaging outing in the *Once Upon a Time In China* series than the earlier movies. Many of the characters are either types or one-dimensional (they coast along on characterizations already created in the earlier films), and the white Americans are relentlessly caricatured as ugly, violent, racist bores. The 1997 movie also runs thru similar scenarios to the previous five movies (inevitable, really, for the sixth outing in a series). And it does seem, despite the colossal talents involved, a lesser work than the earlier *Once Upon a Time In China* flicks. (But that's only, really, if you compare the movie to the earlier pictures. On its own terms, *China and America* is rousing stuff).

There *is* a story in *Once Upon a Time In China and America*, but the movie is more about exploiting the clash of cultures, in mining the action (and the comedy) of throwing a bunch of Chinese guys in amongst some (mainly unfriendly) North Americans. Five writers are credited (Roy Szeto Cheuk-hon, Shut Mei-yee, Sharon Hui Sa-long, Philip Kwok and So Man-Sing), and you'd have to add Sammo Hung and Tsui Hark, artists who aren't shy about adding their own input.

Critics complained that *Once Upon a Time In China and America* was largely 'plotless'. Not true, of course: but *Once Upon a Time In China and America* does lack an over-arching plot, or a series of clearly-defined goals which the heroes have to achieve. Rather, *Once Upon a Time In China and America* is episodic, it's a 'Wong Fei-hung's Adventures in the U.S.A.' story: there's 'the Wong Fei-hung Among the Native Americans' in the first act of *Once Upon a Time In China and America*; there's 'Chinese In the Old West' in the first two acts; and there's the 'Robbery and Imprisonment of the Heroes' plot in the third act. Those episodes are not quite melded together satisfactorily, but they all fit under the over-arching 'Chinese folk in America' story, which's what *Once Upon a Time In China and America* is at heart.

In defence of the screenwriting of *Once Upon a Time In China and America*, some of the characters *do* under-go 'story arcs', that favourite narrative device of North American screenwriting gurus (and film studios). Thus, Billy, down on his luck in the 1997's movie's opening scene (he's just about to kill himself), becomes the Mayor of the town by the end of the movie. (Billy, as played by Jeff Wolfe, is a rather plastic version of a do-gooder cowboy. With his blond locks, tho', and very contemporary acting style, he is clear forerunner of Owen Wilson in *Shanghai Noon*. But Wolfe moves well, and blends in with the ensemble nicely).

The 1997 movie, however, does sideline Wong Fei-hung for too long, and we miss Jet Li when he's not on screen. The script also doesn't find much for Aunt Yeo to do in the third act of *Once Upon a Time In China and America* (other than be tossed into jail along with all of the other Chinese folk). Aunt Yeo does get involved in some of the action sequences, tho' (she's thrown around in a galloping coach, for instance, and performs several versions of the Wongian shadowless kick), and she's a fetching sight in her Chinese version of a cowgirl costume (Rosamund Kwan as a cowgirl? What's not to like!?).

POLITICS.

For the critics and theorists who like to analyze everything that comes out of the Hong Kong film industry in terms of politics and ideology, *Once Upon a Time In China and America* could be seen as another rumination on the 1997 Hand-over (it was released several months b4 the Hand-over), with its evocations of Chinese immigrants in the American West of the early 20th century (thus, Wong Fei-hung literally becomes an 'Overseas Chinese', a social/ national identity that has consumed quite a bit of Tsui Hark's interest – being one himself. And we recall that of course Tsui had studied cinema in two universities where the movie was filmed – good ol' Texas, back in the Seventies – the 1970s, that is, not the 1870s!).

The xenophobia of the American West is brought out very strongly and crudely in *Once Upon a Time In China and America* in the early scenes involving the Chinese doctor Bucktooth So and his chums. The (white) Americans are portrayed as ultra-violent thugs, who'll whip out a pistol at the slightest provocation: they shoot out the glass of beer that Bucktooth So holds in a bar (given to him by one of the ladies of the saloon); they draw guns on the doctor and his pal when they put up posters for Wong Fei-hung; and they manhandle Aunt Yeo really roughly. Yup, pardner, no Chinamen are allowed in the saloon, and they cain't drink beer, neither – hell, not anywhere in the goddam town, outside-a their own alley!

Once Upon a Time In China and America delights in portraying the racism that seethes everywhere in the U.S.A. – then as now. The xenophobia is depicted with many comedic touches, but there's no denying the intensity of it, and what the filmmakers think of the bigoted, intolerant (and corrupt) Sheriff and the Mayor. (Even so, racism and classism was also a key ingredient of the *Wong Fei-hung* movies based in China, with different sections of the Chinese community being set against each other. However, the North Americans were also vividly derided as slave-traders and aggressive oiks).

Meanwhile, one of the aims of the *Once Upon a Time In China* series was to cover or allude to historical events: *Once Upon a Time In China and America* is notable for *not* making much of North American politics or history (other than the generic, Old West context). *Once Upon a Time In China and America* isn't much interested in North America or the American people (and the Native Americans, too, are really just generalizations). Instead, the Americans of all types are simply cast as 'foreigners' (intolerant, crude, corrupt), as far as the Chinese within the movie, and the Chinese in the primary audience for the movie in Hong Kong, are concerned.

In their book on Hong Kong cinema, L. Stokes and M. Hoover remind us that Chinese were forbidden to be naturalized citizens in the U.S.A. until 1952, and that they were prohibited from entering the country in a 1882 law (which was in place until 1943).

Yes – the 1882 Chinese Exclusion Act aimed to control Chinese immigration and fears of the 'Yellow[13] Peril'. Chinese came to the U.S.A. for many reasons – one was the rigours of the Qing dynasty; another was the lure of the California Gold Rush.

COMEDY AND ROMANCE.

Once Upon a Time In China and America contains more of the gentle comedy that Tsui Hark explores many times in his cinema deriving from cultural differences. So there's a lengthy sequence in the stagecoach at the beginning where Wong Fei-hung once again attempts to understand another language (English). And once again lovely Aunt Yeo is on hand to correct him. And when Wong sits down to talk with Billy at a rest-stop, he smiles and pretends to understand him, as people have done for thousands of years. You nod, you smile, you say the only words you know in the language (like 'yeah!'), and you get by.

Once Upon a Time In China and America also contains other examples of Tsui Hark's sense of humour: a scene where a bunch of Chinese workers huddle round a doorway, looking in awe at Aunt Yeo – it's a *woman*! (There are very few Chinese women Out West).

Much comedy (very much of the Tsui Harkian kind) is squeezed out of Wong Fei-hung losing his memory: Jet Li's talent for humour is often unappreciated by film critics. It *is* funny seeing Jet Li as a Native American. Not as funny as Mel Brooks or Woody Allen, admittedly (!), but still amusing. Certainly, he's a much finer comic actor than many action stars in the West. The view that Li is too often too serious and stoic isn't true – if you look at movies he made around this time, such as *Tai Chi Master, Fong Sai-yuk, Last Hero In China* and the *Once Upon a Time In China* series, there are many humorous scenes (and Li has a beautiful smile, which pops out of the screen). For action fans, maybe the comical scenes – like the romantic scenes – slow the movies down. But they are vital in maintaining an appealing mix: this is one of Tsui's fundamental formulas of movie-making – his form of entertainment (like Wong Jing's) is designed to take in romance and comedy as well as action and thrills.

Among the Native Americans, there is a teensy hint of a mild flirtation btn an attractive, young woman, Sarah (Chrysta Bell Eucht) and Wong Fei-hung. However, in keeping with Tsui Hark's characterization of Wong (and that of Wong in the movies and TV in general), it is a very chaste,

---
13 Wong Fei-hung is given the name 'Yellow' by the Native Americans.

restrained and barely evoked liaison (and it's mostly from the woman's point-of-view. She is much fonder of 'Yellow', as she calls him, than he is of her. He gives her a ring in jest, but it means more to her (and to Aunt Yeo later on). Jackie Chan's relations with white women in the *Shanghai Noon* films were much racier, in keeping with Chan's screen image. And Chan wasn't playing Wong Fei-hung, of course).

The romantic subplot plays into the Wong-losing-his-memory subplot, with Aunt Yeo sinking into a huff when she discovers that Wong as 'Yellow' and the Native American woman Sarah seem to have a relationship (the rings are used as a token of love). Even when Wong Fei-hung recovers his memory, and claims he doesn't remember anything that happened, Aunt Yeo is not convinced.

ACTION.

The first Big Action Sequence in *Once Upon a Time In China and America* is not the Chinese versus the Americans, but an attack on the Chinese as they travel in the desert by some Native Americans. (Made in 1997, *Once Upon a Time In China and America* might've been responding to movies such as *Dances With Wolves* (1990), in portraying Native Americans in a more sympathetic light. But in a way the Native Americans are caricatured just as simplistically as the white Americans). For a Chinese audience (the primary audience for this movie), they are all *gweilo,* 'foreign', whether they're white Americans, or Native Americans, or Mexicans, or African Americans.

But nothing much changes, either, when it's a North American production depicting Chinese immigrant workers in the American West – in *The Lone Ranger* (2013), a giant ($215m) Walt Disney movie produced by Jerry Bruckheimer (where the Chinese are depicted from a white, American perspective). However, American movies are sometimes more careful about offending audiences overseas (partly because such a huge amount of their revenue is made in foreign territories). The Chinese immigrants issue would be reprised in *Shanghai Noon.*

Anyhoo, *Once Upon a Time In China and America* takes up one of the staples of the revisionist Western genre – the white hero who holes up with a Native American community (which, of course, lives in teepees in a rural setting, evoked in several formal crane shots worthy of *Heaven's Gate*, 1981). It worked for *Dances With Wolves*[14] (1990) and *The Last of the Mohicans* (1992), and before that, *Little Big Man* (1970) and *Buffalo Bill and the Indians* (1976). But this time, it's a Chinese guy in amongst the Native Americans, not a white guy from back East (with the added gimmick of it being the most famous Chinese hero of all, Wong Fei-hung, and of Wong having lost his memory, which handily delays his reunion with his Chinese chums).

With Jet Li's Wong Fei-hung spending half of the 1997 movie in the Native American village, much of the action back in town is handled by

---

14 David Chou called *Once Upon a Time In China and America* 'a noodle Western' – like 'the original *King Fu* series colliding head on with *Blazing Saddles* and *Dances With Wolves*' ("Once Upon a Time In China and America", S.M.R. Home Theatre, Nov, 1998.

Clubfoot, Aunt Yeo and Bucktooth So, as they come into constant conflict with the boorish, backward Yanks.

Once Upon a Time In China and America delivers more of the martial-arts-versus-the-gun theme, the aggressive manifestation of the West v.s East issue that the *Once Upon a Time In China* series has explored (along the very simple ideological lines of: West = guns = bad, and East = martial arts = good). Notice that no Chinese fire a gun in this movie (handily, they have Billy on their side to do that – Billy's invited to be a deputy). Instead, they use *kung fu* and athletic prowess to run rings around the Yanks (and as the white Americans're all depicted as burly cowboys who seem to spend all of their time slouching about in the saloon, drinking and smoking, that isn't difficult).

There's a satisfying Chinese/ Hong Kong version of the stereotypical bar-room brawl in a Western movie where Clubfoot (a.k.a. Seven) takes on not one but all of the no-goods loitering there. Here, a single, small Chinese guy fights all of the hulking cowboys and knocks them flat. It's doubly satisfying, because in the dramatic build-up, poor Aunt Yeo is pretty harshly treated (she is pushed about, insulted, and has alcohol poured over her before Clubfoot and Bucktooth So come to the rescue).

Xiong Xin-xin is superb as Clubfoot (you can see why he doubled Jet Li for so long, and why he is an accomplished action director himself) – he is given a *lot* of screentime. Indeed, after making such an impact as Clubfoot in the second installment of *Once Upon a Time In China*, Xiong was given more prominence (and in the *Wong Fei-hung* TV series, too).

One of the highlights of *Once Upon a Time In China and America* is a lengthy duel between Jet Li and Xiong Xin-xin, with Clubfoot trying to encourage Wong Fei-hung to remember who he is.

The robbery is a clichéd piece of dramatic business which's not interesting in the slightest: it's there to provide the impetus for the finale of *Once Upon a Time In China and America*. What it does do, tho', is offer a context for yet more racism and brutality from the Yanks. To the point where the Chinese at the Po Chi Lam clinic are raided, searched and imprisoned. Once again, Westerners are depicted as crooked all the way through: in this town, both the Mayor and the Sherrif are dishonest. The blackmailing (it's a fellow Chinaman who plants the sacks of money in the clinic), allows for more malicious treatment of the poor, innocent Chinese by the crude, horrible Americans. (In *Once Upon a Time In China and America*, the Chinese are portrayed as hard-working, close-knit, compassionate, with only small-scale gambling[15] as their vice[16]).

❖

THE FINALE.

Once Upon a Time In China and America creates a rather preposterous villain in the figure of the Mexican bandit (Joe Sayah): he's the classic cowboy bad guy dressed in black out of Spaghetti Westerns and post-1960s horse operas. He has razor-sharp spurs which he uses to

---
[15] But even Wong Fei-hung joins in (when he's still hazy after his regaining his memory).
[16] However, in the *dénouement*, there's a new arrival in town: a hooker, which delights the Chinese guys. That gag seems very Tsui-ian.

slice open victims. In his absurd introductory scene, the bandito is loitering in the woods at night (as you do); he sees a pack of wolves approaching; he slashes open his chest, to let the animals smell the fresh blood; when they attack, he demolishes one hound, and the others flee.

Well, anyway, the Mexican bandito is created solely for Jet Li to have someone suitably accomplished as a warrior to duel in the finale (that Signor Mexico is a nasty piece of work all-round – he kills several people, including unnecessarily and in cold blood – is par for the course).

Thus, the finale is exactly as expected, and the same as all of the previous *Wong Fei-hung* movies: a Big Battle, with the centrepiece being a Long Duel between the hero and the villain. The prelude to the smackdown has our heroes about to be executed: Wong Fei-hung and the Po Chi Lam crew are strung up with nooses around their necks on a wooden scaffold, a particularly gruesome sight (Wong escapes using his martial arts skills).

The action in the finale includes the usual elements (lightning kicks, stuff smashing to bits, brief pauses, slo-mo, high falls, height and a wooden tower, etc). The camerawork is especially wild, careening off the horizontal all over the place. To address the vexed issue of guns versus fists, the 1997 movie includes some visual effects to portray how the Chinese martial artists could elude bullets. And, much cheaper than effects and opticals, simple cuts are employed to suggest that Wong Fei-hung can move *very* fast.

Everyone gets their moment to shine in *Once Upon a Time In China and America*, with pride of place being given to Jet Li and Joe Sayah. By this point in the *Once Upon a Time In China* franchise (film six, plus the TV series), it was very challenging topping the finales in the previous movies (indeed, the benchmark was set impossibly high in the first *China* movie, with the fight on ladders in the warehouse). Not to mention the endings in the other *Once Upon* flicks – the Lion Dance competition finale, the White Lotus Cult finale, the pirate ships finale, etc). As this is Sammo Hung Kam-bo in the director's chair, the action is wonderful.

In the duel in *Once Upon a Time In China and America*, Wong Fei-hung is depicted as never being in serious trouble – the Mexican bandit is no match for him in any respect, really (morally, spiritually, ethically, politically, socially, culturally). Now it's all about Wong teaching the villain the true meaning of Chinese *kung fu*, of training for years, of being effortlessly brilliant.

Also, the finale of *Once Upon a Time In China and America* is smaller in scale, and doesn't have the big, political-ideological cargo of the previous *Once Upon a Time In China* films. The vicious racism of the Yanks has been exposed throughout the movie, and hardly needs embellishing in the action of the finale. So there are no extra dramatic elements, apart from Wong Fei-hung needing to beat the Mexican bandit to clear his name of the crime of the bank robbery. And with Aunt Yeo gone to fetch the Native Americans to help out, there are no Princesses to be rescued, either (that gives Aunt Yeo something to do in the finale, but also cleverly takes her away from danger. But, shoot, it's nice to see the Native

American characters brought back for their curtain call).

As is customary in the *Once Upon a Time In China* series, *Once Upon a Time In China and America* closes with an affirmation of Chinese values and traditional, Chinese culture – with a favourite Tsui Hark motif, the Lion Dance[17] (to celebrate the establishment of a Chinatown in the community). Wong Fei-hung performs the dance, as usual (being the finest Lion Dancer in history), and the *Wong Fei-hung* music sounds off. (A Lion Dance is the perfect scene for a movie released in China during Chinese New Year, of course). And after that, Wong, Aunt Yeo, Clubfoot and co. are heading back home, to Guangdong.

ONCE UPON A TIME IN CHINA AND AMERICA AND *SHANGHAI NOON*

Filmed chiefly in Canada, on a budget of US $55 million (20 or 30 times more than a Hong Kong movie!), *Shanghai Noon* garnered favourable reviews, in the main. (*Shanghai Noon* also filmed in the Forbidden City in Beijing).[18] It was produced by Touchstone/ Spyglass/ Jackie Chan Films; Roger Birnbaum, Jackie Chan and Gary Barber were producers; it was written by Alfred Gough and Miles Millar;[19] Tom Dey was director; the music was by Randy Edelman; the DP was Dan Mindel; and the editor was Richard Chew. Released May 19, 2000. 110 minutes.

In the cast of *Shanghai Noon* were Lucy Liu (b. 1968) as Princess Pei Pei (then a rising star in movies like *Charlie's Angels, Payback* and *Chicago*), Xander Berkeley was nasty Marshal Nathan Van Cleef, rodeo star and model Brandon Merrill (as Jackie Chan's wife, Falling Leaves), Jason Connery (son of Sean) was the Princess's English tutor Calvin Andrews, Walton Goggins was goofy, dim outlaw Wallace, and stalwarts of the Hong Kong film industry, such as Yu Rong Guang, Eric Chen, and Roger Yuan (as Chan's uncle). Yuen Biao has a cameo in the barroom brawl.

Shanghai Noon (2000) was Jackie Chan's version of the story he apparently told Sammo Hung about a Chinaman in the Old West.[20] *Shanghai Noon* is a Jackie Chan movie, yes – but like other Chan flicks aimed at a North American and international audience, he is teamed up with a Western actor – Owen Wilson (Chan has also been paired with Chris

---

17 Lau Kar-wing has a cameo as a Lion Dancer.
18 As director Tom Dey put it, *The Last Emperor* had 8 months in the Forbidden City, but they had only six hours.
19 Gough and Millar were veterans of the business, working on TV series such as *Smallville, Martial Law, Charlie's Angels, Timecop,* and *Wednesday*, and movies such as *Beetlejuice 2, Spider-man 2, The Mummy 3* and *Lethal Weapon*.
20 Chan said that he'd had the idea of a Chinaman in the Old West for 15-20 years. But it wasn't original to Chan.

Tucker, Lee Evans, Jennifer Love Hewitt and Steve Coogan).

It's striking just how much *Shanghai Noon* runs over the same dusty tracks of *Once Upon a Time In China and America*: there's a journey from China to America, in roughly the same time period (late 19th century), including train and carriage treks. Jackie Chan is separated from his fellow Chinese travellers, just like Jet Li in *Once Upon a Time In China and America*, and he also ends up in a Native American community in the first act (and has a mate, too – called Falling Leaves, and played by the lovely Brandon Merrill, a Mid-West rodeo star – a real Native American girl who really can use ropes and lassos!). The same jokes about language are delivered in both movies (and both use the staple of subtitles translating quips in Native American at the expense of the Chinese visitors. A similar Old West town (in *Shanghai Noon,* it's Carson City). Chan also fights with a bunch of invading warriors, like Li (even the setting – of dusty, grassy woodland – is similar to *Once Upon a Time In China and America*). As in *Once Upon a Time In China and America*, our heroes're strung up to be hung, and make a daring escape (the similarities even include horses, and the execution scaffold being demolished). Owen Wilson is his usual blond, surfer type, and even his look is similar to the character of Billy (Jeff Wolfe) in *Once Upon a Time In China and America*. There's a barroom brawl.

One could go on listing the similarities btn the 1997 Chinese picture and the 2000 N. American picture (one thing's for sure – if *Shanghai Noon* had been made within the Hong Kong film industry, it would've been released the same year! – not three years later). And the North American producers knew that no Hong Kong producer would sue them for copyright (altho' Disney, famous for its aggressive pursuit of litigation, might well have done if it was vice versa!).

The Disney *Shanghai Noon,* however, is much more P.C. than the Hong Kong *Once Upon a Time In China and America*. The brutal racism of the North Americans in *Once Upon a Time In China and America* is portrayed in a vivid manner (tho' in both films Chinese immigrants are being used as workers. But notice how the manager of the railroad company using Chinese labour is also Chinese – thus letting white Americans off the hook). In the Disney Jackie Chan movie, racism and xenophobia is treated humorously in the main; *Once Upon a Time In China and America* also used plenty of humour (tho' sometimes cruder).[21] The Disney version of *The Lone Ranger*, released in 2013, covered some of the same ground.

Shanghai Noon is a crisper, technically slick production than *Once Upon a Time In China and America* – the sound mix, for example, is instantly noticeable as a multi-channel mix favoured by North American productions (and the music (by Randy Edelman) is sawing away non-stop, quoting some melodies and orchestrations familiar from cowboy movies: the brassy fanfares, for instance, or the bluesy guitar for the desert scene where Roy O'Bannion is buried in the sand. Composer Edelman also includes some pastiches of traditional Chinese music. There are songs,

---

21 However, *Shanghai Noon* does include a bordello scene, some deaths, drugs references (the peace pipe gag), and plenty-a cussin'.

too, such as 'La Grange' by ZZ Top and 'Cowboy' by Kid Rock).

Both *Shanghai Noon* and *Once Upon a Time In China and America* of course feature famous exponents of Hong Kong action – and both Jackie Chan and Sammo Hung favour tussles which humans could realistically accomplish. It is some 8 or 9 minutes into *Shanghai Noon* before the first action sequence occurs – a very traditional chase and fight on a speeding railroad train (which O'Bannon and his inept mob are holding up). The second one is the running battle btn Wang and several Native Americans (of the Crow tribe).

The narrative of *Shanghai Noon* is slightly more complicated than the story in *Once Upon a Time In China and America*, but both orchestrate simple oppositions: Chinese vs. Americans, Chinese vs. Native Americans, modern America with traditional China, etc. To get the story rolling in *Shanghai Noon,* the dramatic hook is slightly more complex than in *Once Upon a Time In China and America* (where Wong Fei-hung are his companions are visiting the Po Chi Lam clinic and 'Bucktooth' So). In *Shanghai Noon,* Princess Pei Pei (Lucy Liu) is the prize that must be saved: she flees from an arranged marriage with an oaf in the Imperial City in Peking. Unfortunately, the Westerner that arranges for Pei Pei to escape on a ship turns out to be an opportunist, who delivers Pei Pei to Lo Fong, the railroad manager. Meanwhile, Jackie Chan's Chon Wang volunteers to bring back Pei Pei from the U.S.A. to China (a second, complicating event occurs during the botched heist on the train – this is true to Disney's very formulaic kind of screenwriting, which follows *very* strict patterns: at the turning point in act one, Wang's uncle Lo Fong is murdered. Thus, Wang has a second goal – to seek revenge for his uncle's death – as soon as Wang discovers his uncle, for example, he races away to find and catch the perpetrators).

❖

In *Shanghai Noon,* Jackie Chan plays his usual underdog/ everyman character on the side of right (he's an Imperial guard in the Forbidden City). Chan's Chon Wang isn't given much characterization – because, one assumes, Chan is such a gigantic movie star, that all you need to know is that a character is played by Chan. Indeed, Chan is one of the few movie stars where that occurs, in a similar manner to John Wayne or Marilyn Monroe.

Owen Wilson plays his usual goofy, laid-back stoner character – in *Shanghai Noon,* he's a wannabe Butch Cassidy or Billy the Kid, an outlaw with big aspirations but saddled with a bunch of dopey sidekicks. Roy O'Bannion is also a womanizer (there are several bordello scenes).

The pairing of Owen Wilson and Jackie Chan is appealing, tho', in *Shanghai Noon*, and the their interplay is amusing (Chan's Imperial guard is rather uptight and serious, tho' that doesn't harm the comedy – partly so that his personality can provide more of a contrast with Wilson's chilled-out, wannabe outlaw). There's no romantic subplot in *Shanghai Noon* – so that the bonding of the male leads is by far the strongest relationship (tho' the homoerotic undertones are, as usual in the cowboy genre, and in the *kung fu* genre, not addressed.22 Yet the guys do bathe together). Actually, yes, there *is* a romantic subplot. Of sorts – when Wang marries the Native American Falling Leaves (she doesn't disappear entirely from the story, as is usual, however – she pops again, for instance, to aid our heroes escape the hangman's noose).

Shanghai Noon is wholly a movie-movie, with numerous references to earlier cowboy flicks – John Wayne (Chon Wang is a joke on John Wayne), Van Cleef, Spaghetti Westerns, Billy the Kid, Wyatt Earp, *High Noon, Little Big Man, Dr Quinn, Red Sun, Dances With Wolves, Butch Cassidy and the Sundance Kid*,23 etc – yes, and even *Once Upon a Time In China and America* (there are also references to some of Jackie Chan's earlier pics, such as *Drunken Master*).

Shanghai Noon is a *much* talkier movie than *Once Upon a Time In China and America* – it's filled with page after page of dialogue in some stretches. Also, some scenes wend on far longer than their equivalents would do in a Hong Kong action picture (the escape from the jail, for instance, which's a boring scene that out-stays its welcome).

❖

The finale24 of *Shanghai Noon* is set in, of all places, a Catholic church25 in the middle of nowhere (it just happens to have a tower and scaffolding which offers the necessary multiple levels to make the fights interesting, plus ropes, statuary, pillars and props for the stunt and practical effects guys to smash up). There are the usual multiple fights in the climax: the hero vs. the bad guy, the Princess vs. the bad guy, the hero vs. the other Imperial guards, Roy O'Bannion vs. the crooked Marshall Van Cleef, etc. Among the finest mini-fights in the finale is the one between the wonderful Yu Rong Guang and Jackie Chan (Yu has of course been in many action movies). It uses the traditional spear of Chinese martial arts, and very rapid exchanges of blows (you have to bring in another Chinese performer to have someone sufficiently skilful for Jackie Chan to duel).

Curiously, the romantic subplots are switched round at the end of *Shanghai Noon*: now Roy O'Bannion is kissed by Chon Wang's wife Falling Leaves. Eh? But Chon isn't bothered at all, because Princess Pei Pei takes his hand (much to Chon's surprise – this is Chinese royalty that Chon can't even bear to look in the face!). However, the Princess has opted to stay in the U.S.A. and not return to Asia (and Chon, going against his Imperial orders, aids her). That the white, American stars enjoys a kiss but the Asian star doesn't is typical of the differences between the way they are used in Western movies.

---

22 When Chan puts his hand on Wilson's arm, Wilson asks him to remove it.
23 Our heroes opting to blast their way out of the church into the brilliant light is yet another reference to *Butch Cassidy* (this time with the *deus ex machina* of the Native Americans arriving to Save The Day).
24 The movie closes with the customary Jackie Chan montage of outtakes.
25 The *Once Upon a Time In China* series includes scenes set in churches, including fights.

SHANGHAI KNIGHTS.

In *Shanghai Knights* (2003), production companies Disney/ Birnbaum/ Barber Prods./ Jackie Chan Films/ All Knight Prods./ Spyglass produced More Of The Same as *Shanghai Noon*.[26] The sequel to *Shanghai Noon* was released 3 years later (a typical gap) – if this was Hong Kong, it would be three months later! Screenwriters Alfred Gough and Miles Millar were back, as were the producers (the executive producers were: Jackie Chan, Willie Chan, Stephanie Austin, Edward McDonnal and Solon So; the producers were: Gary Barber, Roger Birnbaum and Jonathan Glickman, plus 3 others). The director was David Dobkin. Released: Feb 7, 2003. 114 mins.

Shanghai Knights featured pretty much the same elements as *Shanghai Noon,* in the same sort of story: so Roy O'Bannion and Chon Wang are teamed up again to track down another dastardly villain – this time it was Rathbone (Aidan Gillen), the killer of Wang's father (Kim Chan). The Lucy Liu character was replaced by Fann Wong as Wang's sister Chon Lin. Now Wang is working as a Sheriff in Carson City, while O'Bannion has frittered away his part of the loot, and is working as a waiter at a fancy hotel in Gotham.

Pure popcorn, undemanding and delightfully old-fashioned, *Shanghai Knights* made producing an action-adventure film look so easy. *Shanghai Knights* is 'a Chinaman in London' story, instead of 'a Chinaman in the Old West'. A third installment was rumoured in 2003, and later in 2016, tho' it hasn't appeared yet.

---

26 *Shanghai Knights* was filmed in Prague, London, Canada, and L.A.

Once Upon a Time In China 5 (1994).

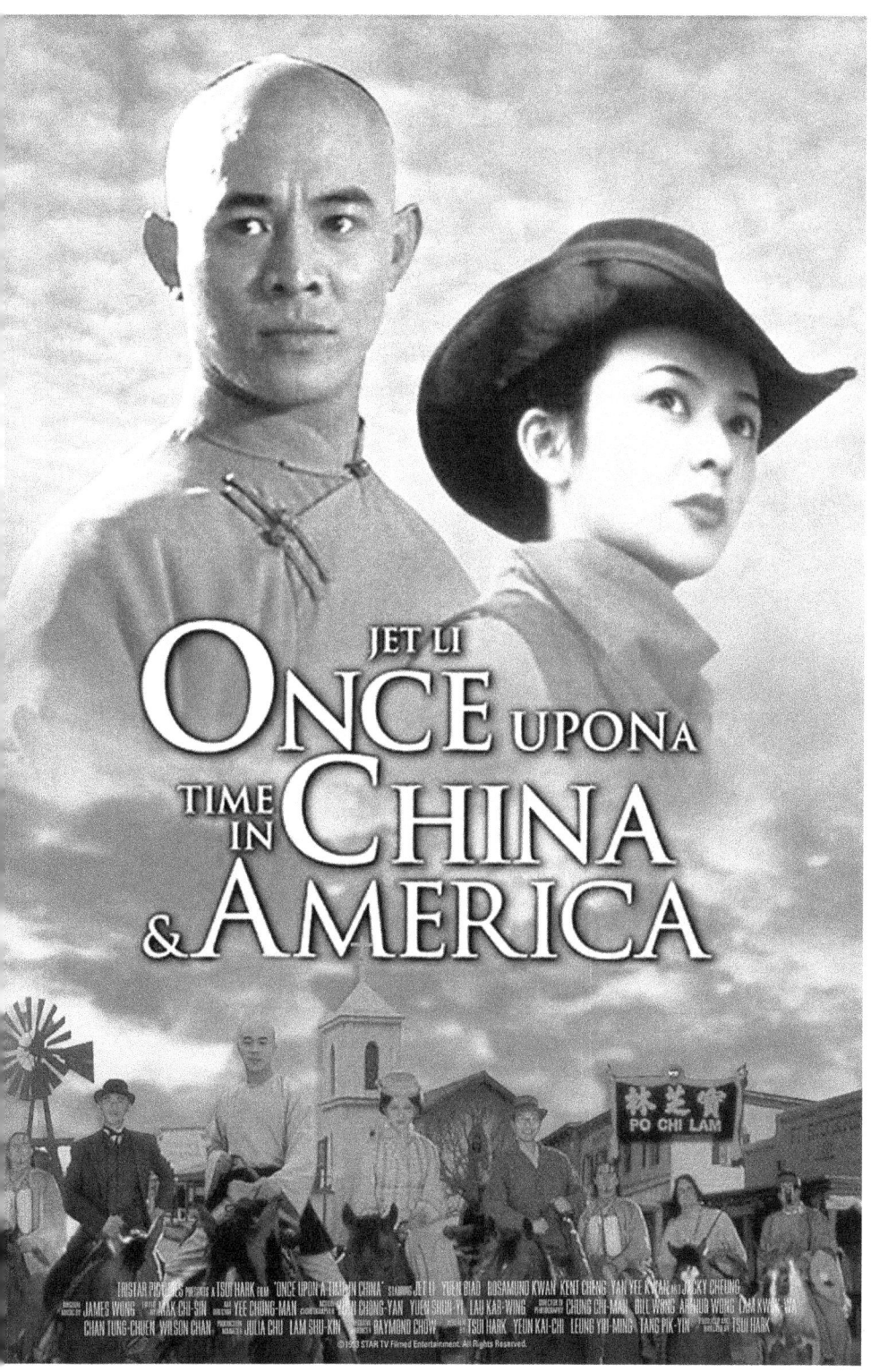

Once Upon a Time In China and America (1997).
This page and over.

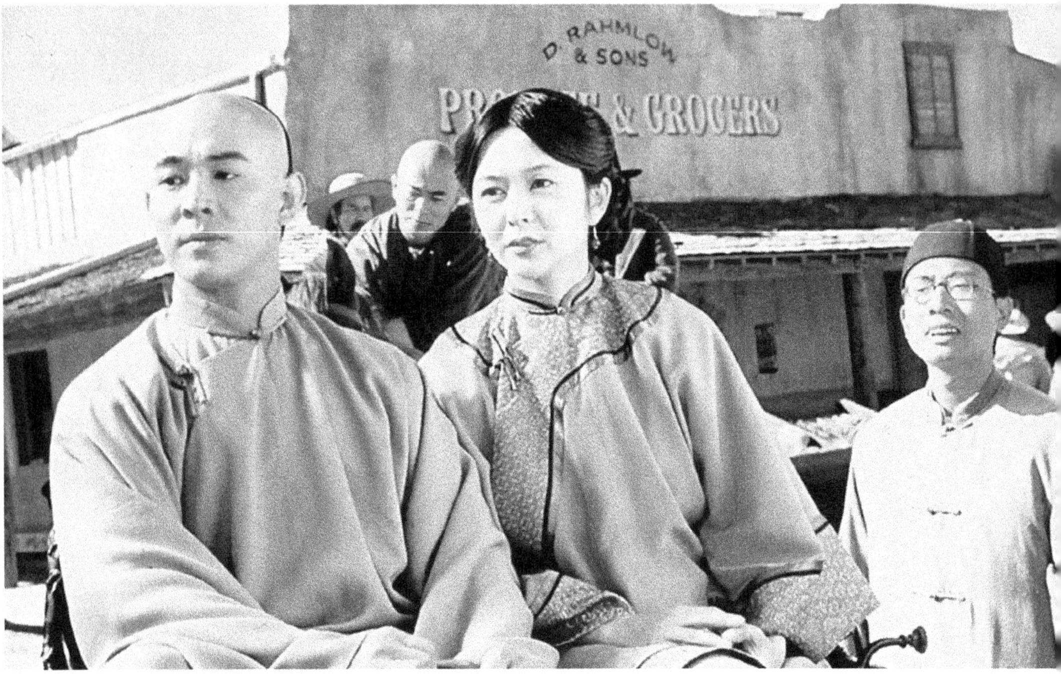
D. RAHMLOW
& SONS
& GROCERS

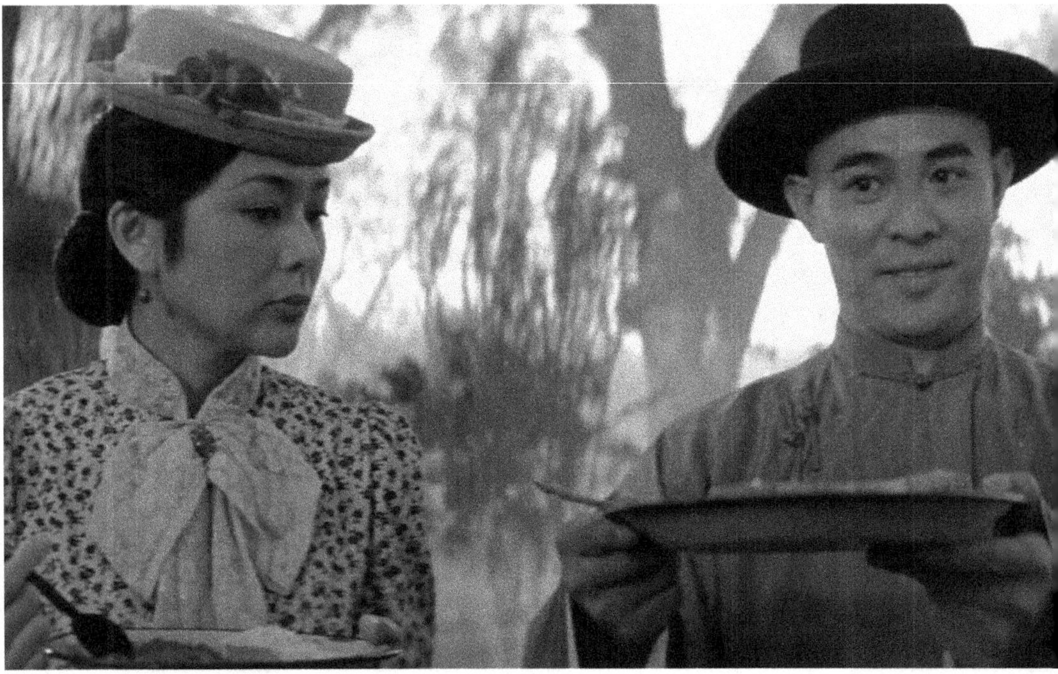

Shanghai Noon (2000).

APPENDIX

LAST HERO IN CHINA

The *Once Upon a Time In China* series was the focus of cash-in movies and comical send-ups. One of the funniest is *Last Hero In China*, which stars Jet Li himself.

Last Hero In China (*Wong Fei-hong Zi Tit Gai Dau Ng-gung*, 1993, a.k.a. *Iron Rooster vs. Centipede,* a.k.a. *Claws of Steel*), was made by Win's Movie Productions, prod. by Jet Li, wr. and dir. by Wong Jing, music by James Wong Jim, Mark Lui and Sherman Crow, DPs: Jingle Ma, Tom Lau Moon-tong, Ma Goon-wa and Chan Kwong-hung, and ed. by Poon Hung. Also in the cast were Sharla Cheung-man, Anita Yuen, Gordon Liu, Lau Kar-fai, Leung Kar-yan,[1] Chan Bak-cheung and Yan King-tan. Released: Apl 1, 1993. 108 mins.

Last Hero In China could be described as *Once Upon a Time In China 3 1/2*, or *Once Upon a Time In China 3B*: it is another movie about Wong Fei-hung, and it also stars Jet Li. *Last Hero In China* is a case of Hong Kong cinema seeing a good thing and cashing in on it: the *Once Upon a Time In China* series led to a number of other movies about Wong Fei-hung or similar legendary heroes (such as Fong Sai-yuk); altho', let's not forget, films about Wong Fei-hung have been made in every era of Hong Kong cinema since at least the 1940s.

Last Hero In China is one of the better ones: for a start, it stars Jet Li. And that's enough to be going on with! And the action director is one of the finest in the world: Yuen Woo-ping. And that's more than enough! Add to that the exploitation director Wong Jing, and you have an impressive trio of talents at the top of the production tree.

With Yuen Woo-ping and Yuen Cheung-yan overseeing the action and Jet Li performing it, *Last Hero In China* cannot possibly disappoint, and cannot possibly be less than entertaining (Li and Yuen had worked together on the *Once Upon a Time In China* series). Even if the story, the characters, the themes, the issues, the romance, the psychology, the drama and everything else sucked, you know the action is going to be great! And it is!

---

[1] Ah Foon is played by Leung Kar-yan, whose career goes back through the gangster brotherhood films of the late 1980s to the *kung fu* boom of the 1970s.

This is Yuen Woo-ping and Jet Li at their silliest and most over-the-top: the gags come thick and fast, there is a wildly bawdy and slapstick sense of humour, and the tone is far dumber than *Once Upon a Time In China* and much cruder.

Grisly, too – the opening teaser depicts a bunch of young women hurrying away from a gang of kidnappers at night in a forest (cue the smoke and the backlighting). Out of the darkness hurtles an iron claw which grabs and pierces the women one by one (one victim is torn in two, in mid-air, a Hong Kong speciality). A huge, flying, red lotus flower hovers overhead sinisterly (only later is the master villain[2] revealed to be inside it, wielding the iron claw). Then we shift into the main titles, in red ideograms over black.

So the nefarious plot at the heart of *Last Hero In China* is slave trading – as in *Once Upon a Time In China* (and other movies of the 1990s) – and once again it's young women who're being sold as prostitutes. Grim stuff. Very grim stuff. (But this is a comedy, a spoof, in the main, with the slave-trading plot used as a means of maintaining the narrative pace).

This time, it's not the 'white devils', the foreigners, who're behind it, but fellow Chinese (part of the Boxer Society). Corruption is rife, however – because the authorities are colluding with the slave-traders. The portrayal of the villains is madly OTT – the young women are placed in cages hanging from ropes in the air in the dark bowels of a Buddhist temple, and the madman overseeing this operation is a Shaolin Temple-trained psycho who floats around in a red lotus flower. (So even tho' it sends up the *Once Upon a Time In China* movies, it is also actually very close to them).

In *Last Hero In China*, Wong Fei-hung is the usual do-right, nice guy hero, and his cast of lackeys (Buck-tooth So, Foon, etc), are on hand to enhance proceedings with comedy. Meanwhile, there are many secondary characters, including Ti Yiner (Sharla Cheung-man) and her father (Jue Tit-woh), who're trying to discover the secret of the slave traders, pervy monks, corrupt judges, and wannabe *kung fu* acolytes.

The flipside of the white slave trade plot has Wong Fei-hung moving his Po Chi Lam clinic (because of high rents), and ending up next to a brothel. This's presented humorously, with the famously prudish Wong confronting a stern brothel madam and her giggling, attractive charges at every turn. (The film doesn't waste an opportunity for Wong *sifu* to get up close and personal with the hookers, for comical effect).

❋

After the prologue, *Last Hero In China* swiftly introduces our hero, Wong Fei-hung, and the film's star (and producer), Jet Li. And what is Li as Master Wong going to do? Fight! He's at the railroad station where a bunch of Boxer Society no-goods make trouble: he deals with them in a furiously staged smackdown. Even if it's played for comedy, the action is still intense. Using props like wooden benches, Master Wong trounces the heavies; soon they're falling through glass-windowed walls.

Marvellous is the filmmakers' energy and willingness to entertain in

---

[2] He's played by Lau Kar Fai, the star of *36th Chamber of Shaolin* (1978), one of the classic *kung fu* movies.

every beat of *Last Hero In China*. This is funnier than the *Once Upon a Time In China* movies, with Wong Jing, Yuen Woo-ping and the team delivering some great knockabout comedy, including some really surreal moments (which Yuen is known for – have a look at his early films!). Some of the jokes have the simplicity and crudity of a group of 11 year-old schoolkids thinking up gags.3 But they're delivered with such charm and lightness, you can't help but be won over (*Last Hero In China* doesn't hang around to see if an effect or a gag has worked – it's already moved on to the next bit of business. Again and again, this one of the primary appeals of Chinese action cinema: it *races* along). Jet Li is also willing to be the butt of some of the jokes, which pricks that familiar stern, monk-like exterior (of course, being an authority figure, Wong Fei-hung is inevitably going to be the target of some of the humour. If gag writers have a range of characters that they want to send up, anybody in authority is top of the list).

Last Hero In China is a thorough spoof of the *Once Upon a Time In China* movies – it was released after the first three Wong Fei-hung flicks (in between *3* and *4*). *Last Hero In China* takes many of the icons and elements of the Wong Fei-hung mythology and sends them up. In fact, *Last Hero In China* has the lot, pretty much everything in the historical movies of the Chinese New Wave era: alcohol, prostitution, sex, Westernization, slave trading, political corruption, Lion Dances, harbour scenes, inn scenes, Buddhist temple scenes, seduction scenes, ghostly, forest night scenes, silly costumes, acupuncture and healing, drunken fighting, the shadowless kick, crane and animal martial arts, and of course the famous Wong Fei-hung music, 'Under the General's Orders' (the only element missing really is the presence of Aunt Lee4 – but the lovely Sharla Cheung-man as Yiner makes up for that. She was Ren Yingying, leader of the Sun Moon Sect, in the *Swordsman* movies).

Last Hero In China is great fun – everyone seems to be having a good time, including Jet Li, spoofing the rather po-faced, do-gooder characterization of Wong Fei-hung in the *Once Upon a Time In China* series. One of the finest and funniest scenes is the song-and-dance number, when the women in the brothel take on the famous 'Under the General's Orders', the Wong Fei-hung music, and deliver their sexed-up version of it, waggling their boobs at the camera. (This is swiftly followed by one of the staples of the *Once Upon a Time In China* movies, a Lion Dance. Inevitably, the lion that emerges from the brothel is female, and the scene is played for farce).

And in the final battle, Jet Li is dressed up as a chicken! It's a spoof of the solemn moment of revelation, when the hero discovers the way in which he can defeat the villains. In *Last Hero In China*, it has Wong Fei-hung observing some chickens making short work of a centipede, when he's in exile from his Po Chi Lam clinic; so Wong enters the Lion Dance to defeat the villains in their centipede costume in a red rooster outfit. (Perhaps the Lion Dance competitions in the later *Once Upon a Time In*

---

3 Such as bodies bent over a wooden post like a floppy doll.
4 Her absence is explained in a letter delivered to Wong at the top of the movie.

China movies are a nod to this, because they include all sorts of creatures – crabs, birds, bulls, etc).

In the early part of the third act, *Last Hero In China* takes some unusual turns, narrative-wise: Wong Fei-hung is banished, and heals his hearing (following a poison attempt), aided by Yiner and her father (similar interludes of exile occur in *Tai Chi Master*, directed by Yuen Woo-ping). The Lion Dance competition is won by the rival team with their centipede costume, and Wong muses on this during his (brief) exile (we know that Wong will return to triumph, being the best Lion Dancer as well as the best everything else). There are further action scenes, including one where Bucktooth So and Ah Foon take on the villains (the slave trade plot continues in the background).

Altho' *Last Hero In China* is a lesser-known outing in Chinese action cinema compared to the *Once Upon a Time In China* series or the *Legend of Fong Sai-yuk* series or the *Swordsman* series of the same early Nineties period, boy does it deliver some terrific action! The finale takes place at the Lion Dance competition (of course!), with Wong Fei-hung in a scarlet rooster costume battling the villains dressed as a centipede, complete with flame thrower and blades (only in a Chinese action movie!). It's played for laughs but also thrills, with incredible wirework and stunts. Ladders, logs, towers, ropes – the environment as well as the performers are hurtling about on wires.

And that's not all: there's the marvellous smackdown between Wong Fei-hung and the second chief villain, Liu Yat-siu (set in – where else?! – a warehouse! Mant elements of the finale come from the *Once Upon a Time In China* movies, including the fiendishly complicated ladder fight, which Yuen Woo-ping helped to choreograph). Here comes the shadowless kick, the trading of rapidfire fists and insults, smashing timber, hurled logs, blood seeping out of the mouth, and more varieties of body movement than you'll see in 500 action movies made in the West. (*Last Hero In China* reprises the drunken fist style, as Wong gulps down wine).[5]

And in the second act of *Last Hero In China*, there is action a-plenty: a terrific showdown on the streets where Yiner[6] and her father are introduced (performing martial arts for money);[7] a scene where Ah Foon and Bucktooth plus the brothel manager invade the Buddhist temple to save the women; and a remarkable face-off in the bowels of the temple between Wong Fei-hung and the super-villain, Liu Hung, played by the very wonderful Gordon Liu, star of one of the great *kung fu* films, *The 36th Chamber of Shaolin* (Liu is a suitably formidable opponent for Jet Li). They duelled again in *Flying Swords of Dragon Gate* (2011).

For this fight, the film set is elaborate: it's filled with smoke, there's a wooden walkway way above the ground, supported by chains (which leads to a raised island where one of the hookers from the brothel has been tied

---
5 And of course the flasks of wine are also used as weapons.
6 Sharla Cheung also performs some great fight scenes later on.
7 Yiner beats off government soldiers in yet another action sequence – the raid on Yiner and her father's home in the countryside. Here Wong Fei-hung and co. defend themselves against storms of arrows. One of Jet Li's signature motifs, the long piece of cloth as a weapon, is used here.

to a wooden cross), and other prostitutes are kept in cages hanging in space. It's the villain's highly improbable fantasy lair in an *Indiana Jones* movie. As expected, the choreography of the action traverses the space, and also takes place under as well as on top of the walkway (which also falls apart).

Yuen Woo-ping is especially fond of staging up action in the air, where there is more room to move, where poses look even more impressive, and where the jeopardy is increased (of falling, of structures collapsing). The action combines rapid open-handed fighting, plenty of kicks, leaps into the dark, smashing props, shadows, and several fire gags. It would suffice as the climactic battle in many a movie, but it's only one of several sequences in the second act of *Last Hero In China*.

Generously, it's Ah Foon and Bucktooth So who get to defeat the super-villain Master Liu Hung, in another amazing showdown (because the other villain of piece, Boxer Association officer Liu Yat-siu, is saved for the finale, against Jet Li). This is another classic Yuen Woo-ping duel, with Foon and Bucktooth combining their skills to take on Liu Hung (like running up their partner's body, to use it as a springboard, an acrobatic gag that's reprised elsewhere).

This is an action comedy, or a comical action film – but that doesn't mean that the action is any less impressive than in a straight, dramatic piece. *Last Hero In China* is full of Yuen Woo-ping's motifs, such as open-handed combat, and keeping the action close to the ground (not all of the time, of course – for the famous shadowless kick of Wong Fei-hung, Jet Li is up in the air).

Everyone knows that making a comedy movie can be even more challenging for the stunt team than a dramatic movie, that comedies often require even more stunt people than a drama, and that just as many people can be injured on a comedy movie set.

Last Hero In China is no different: when the fighting starts, it's as fierce and intense as in a drama (when the scene isn't played for comedy). To make the thriller plot work, for example (the abduction and slave-trading), the villains have to be formidable. And they are – Wong Fei-hung and his pals have to work hard to defeat them.

In fact, *Last Hero In China* is a giant action movie – and, as Wong Jing happily admits, he is no *kung fu* expert, so half of the movie is action, half of the movie is a Yuen Woo-ping production.

Last Hero In China (1993).

FILMOGRAPHY

TSUI HARK: MOVIES AS DIRECTOR

The Butterfly Murders, 1979
We're Going To Eat You, 1980
Dangerous Encounters of the First Kind, 1980
All the Wrong Clues, 1981
Zu: Warriors From the Magic Mountain, 1983
Search For the Gods, 1983
Aces Go Places 3, 1984
Shanghai Blues, 1984
Working Class, 1985
Peking Opera Blues, 1986
Spirit Chaser Aisha, 1986
The Master, 1989
A Better Tomorrow 3, 1989
The Swordsman, 1990
Once Upon a Time in China, 1991
The Banquet, 1991
The Raid, 1991
Once Upon a Time in China 2, 1992
Twin Dragons, 1992
Once Upon a Time in China 3, 1993
Green Snake, 1993
Once Upon a Time in China 5, 1994
The Lovers, 1994
The Chinese Feast, 1995
Love In the Time of Twilight, 1995
The Blade, 1995
Tristar, 1996
Double Team, 1997
Knock Off, 1998
Time and Tide, 2000
The Legend of Zu, 2001
Black Mask 2: City of Masks, 2002
In The Blue, 2005
Seven Swords, 2005
Triangle, 2007
Missing, 2008
All About Women, 2008
Detective Dee and the Mystery of the Phantom Flame, 2010
The Flying Swords of Dragon Gate, 2011
Young Detective Dee: Rise of the Sea Dragon, 2013

Catching Monkey 3-D, 2013
The Taking of Tiger Mountain, 2014
Journey To the West: The Demons Strike Back, 2017
Detective Dee and the Four Heavenly Kings, 2018
The Battle At Lake Changjin, 2021
The Battle At Lake Changjin 2, 2022

TSUI HARK: MOVIES AS PRODUCER

All the Wrong Spies, 1983
A Better Tomorrow, 1986
The Laser Man, 1986
A Chinese Ghost Story, 1987
A Better Tomorrow 2, 1987
The Big Heat, 1988
Gunmen, 1988
Diary of a Big Man, 1988
The King of Chess, 1988/ 1992
The Master, 1989
A Better Tomorrow 3, 1989
The Killer, 1989
Just Heroes, 1989
The Terracotta Warrior, 1989
The Swordsman, 1990
A Chinese Ghost Story 2, 1990
A Chinese Ghost Story 3, 1991
Once Upon a Time in China, 1991
New Dragon Gate Inn, 1992
The Swordsman 2, 1992
The Wicked City, 1992
Once Upon a Time in China 2, 1992
Once Upon a Time in China 3, 1993
Green Snake, 1993
The Swordsman 3/ The East Is Red, 1993
Once Upon a Time in China 4, 1993
Once Upon a Time in China 5, 1994
The Lovers, 1994
Burning Paradise, 1994
The Chinese Feast, 1995
The Blade, 1995
Shanghai Grand, 1996
A Chinese Ghost Story: The Tsui Hark Animation, 1997
Once Upon a Time in China and America, 1997
Time and Tide, 2000
The Legend of Zu, 2001
Old Master Q, 2001
Tsui Hark's Vampire Hunters, 2002
Black Mask 2: City of Masks, 2002
Xanda, 2004
Seven Swords, 2005
The Warrior, 2006

Triangle, 2007
Missing, 2008
All About Women, 2008
Detective Dee and the Mystery of the Phantom Flame, 2010
The Flying Swords of Dragon Gate, 2011
Young Detective Dee: Rise of the Sea Dragon, 2013
Christmas Rose, 2013
The Taking of Tiger Mountain, 2014
Sword Master, 2016
The Thousand Faces of Dunjia, 2017
Journey To the West: The Demons Strike Back, 2017
Detective Dee and the Four Heavenly Kings, 2018
The Climbers, 2019
The Battle At Lake Changjin, 2021
The Battle At Lake Changjin 2, 2022

RECOMMENDED BOOKS AND WEBSITES

One of the finest general introductions to the history of Hong Kong cinema, and a great place to start, is *Hong Kong Cinema* (1997) by Stephen Teo. David Bordwell and Kristin Thompson are consistently excellent commentators on film, in books such as *Film History: An Introduction* (2010) and Bordwell's account of Hong Kong cinema, *Planet Hong Kong: Popular Cinema and the Art of Entertainment* (2000).

Bey Logan's *Hong Kong Action Cinema* (1995) is an entertaining introduction to the action side of Hong Kong cinema (with many valuable illustrations). *Kung-fu Cult Masters: From Bruce Lee To 'Crouching Tiger'* (2003) takes a more theoretical approach to the same subject.

For surveys of films, Jeff Yang's *Once Upon a Time In China* (2003) is superb, as is *Hong Kong Babylon* (1997) by F. Dannen & B. Long (this book also features many interviews with the key players in the Hong Kong industry). Lisa Morton's *The Cinema of Tsui Hark* (2001) is an important early study.

Jackie Chan has attracted many studies and biographies, including *Jackie Chan* by C. Gentry (1997), *The Essential Jackie Chan Sourcebook* by J. Rovin & K. Tracy (1997), and *Dying For Action: The Life and Times of Jackie Chan* by R. Witterstaetter (1997). And Chan's own memoirs: *I Am Jackie Chan* (1998) and *Never Grow Up* (2018).

Among critical essays, I would recommend *At Full Speed: Hong Kong Cinema In a Borderless World* (1998, edited by E.C.M. Yau) and *The Cinema of Hong Kong* (2002), edited by P. Fu & D. Desser.

The Warrior, 2006

    Hong Kong Movie Database
    Love Hong Kong Film
    Hong Kong Cinemagic
    Film Workshop
    Jet Li   jetli.com

BIBLIOGRAPHY

ON TSUI HARK

B. Accomando. "Army of Darkness: Hong Kong Director Tsui Hark Takes On the West", *Giant Robot*, 8, 1997
G. Hendrix. "Tsui Hark: Great Directors", *Senses of Cinema*, July, 2013
Howard Hampton. "Once Upon a Time In Hong Kong", *Film Comment*, 33, 1997
Hal Hinson. "*Peking Opera Blues*," *Washington Post*, Oct 14, 1988
D. Houx. "The Underrated Insanity of Tsui Hark and Jean-Claude van Damme's *Knock Off*', *Badass Digest*, 2014
A. Hwang. "The Irresistible: Hong Kong Movie *Once Upon a Time In China* Series", *Asian Cinema*, 10, 1, 1998
Y. Lee. "Artist Provocateur – On Tsui Hark", Hong Kong International Film Festival, 23, 1999
P. Macias. "Animerica Interview: Tsui Hark", *Animerica*, 7, 10
The Making of A Chinese Ghost Story: The Tsui Hark Animation, Hong Kong, 1997
L. Morton. *The Cinema of Tsui Hark*, McFarland, Jefferson, North Carolina, 2001
C. Reid. "Interview With Tsui Hark", *Film Quarterly*, 48, 3, 1995
S. Short. "Tsui Hark", interview, *Time*, CNN, 2000
Chuck Stephens. "Tsui Hark's Planet Hong Kong", *Village Voice*, May 1, 2001
S. Tan. "Ban(g)! Ban(g)! *Dangerous Encounter – 1st Kind*', *Asian Cinema*, 8, 1, 1996
Stephen Teo. "Tsui Hark: Filmography", *Senses of Cinema* 17, Nov, 2001
Tsui Hark. Interview, in F. Dannen, 1997
Ben Umstead. "An Interview With Tsui Hark", *Twitch*/ N.Y.A.F.F., 2011, July 11, 2011

OTHERS

A. Abbas. *Hong Kong*, University of Minnoestoa Press, Minneapolis, 1997
J. Abert. *A Knight At the Movies: Medieval History On Film*, Routledge, London, 2003
G. Adair. *Vietnam on Film*, Proteus, New York, NY, 1981
—. *Hollywood's Vietnam*, Heinemann, London, 1989
R.C. Allen, ed. *Channels of Discourse: Television and Contemporary Criticism*, Methuen, London, 1987
R. Altman, ed. *Sound Theory, Sound Practice*, Routledge, London, 1992
—. *Film/ Genre*, British Film Institute, London, 1999
M. Anderegg, ed. *Inventing Vietnam*, Temple University Press, Philadelphia, PA, 1991
G. Andrew. *The Film Handbook*, Longman, London, 1989
—. *Stranger Than Paradise: Maverick Filmmakers In Recent American Cinema*, Prion, 1998
J. Arroyo. *Action/ Spectacle Cinema*, British Film Institute, London, 2000
A. Assister & A. Carol, eds. *Bad Girls and Dirty Pictures: The Challenge To Reclaim Feminism*, Pluto Press, London, 1993
A. Auster. *How the War Was Remembered: Hollywood and Vietnam*, Praeger, New York, NY, 1988
R. Baker & T. Russell. *The Essential Guide To Hong Kong Movies*, Eastern Heroes, London, 1994
—. *The Essential Guide To the Best of Eastern Heroes*, Eastern Heroes, London, 1995
—. *The Essential Guide To Deadly China Dolls*, Eastern Heroes, London, 1996
M. Barker, ed. *The Video Nasties: Freedom and Censorship In the Media*, Pluto Press, London, 1984
—. & J. Petley, eds. *Ill Effects: The Media/ Violence Debate*, Routledge, London, 1997
L. Bawden, ed. *The Oxford Companion To Film*, Oxford University Press, Oxford, 1976
J. Baxter. *George Lucas*, HarperCollins, London, 1999

J. Beck, ed. *Animation Art*, Flame Tree Publishing, London, 2004
M. Beja. *Film and Literature: An Introduction*, Longman, London, 1979
R. Bergan & R. Karney. *Bloomsbury Foreign Film Guide*, Bloomsbury, London, 1988
I. Bergman. *Talking With Ingmar Bergman*, Dallas, TX, 1983
—. *Bergman on Bergman, Interviews with Ingmar Bergman*, eds. S. Björkman, *et al*, tr. P. B. Austin, Touchstone, New York, NY, 1986
—. *The Magic Lantern: An Autobiography*, London, 1988
C. Berry. *Perspectives On Chinese Cinema*, B.F.I., London, 1991
P. Biskind. *Easy Riders, Raging Bulls: How the Sex 'n' Drugs 'n' Rock 'n' Roll Generation Saved Hollywood*, Bloomsbury, London, 1998
—. *Down and Dirty Pictures: Miramax, Sundance and the Rise of Independent Film*, Bloomsbury, London, 2004
M. Bliss. *Between the Bullets: The Spiritual Cinema of John Woo*, Scarecrow Press, Lanham, MD, 2002
A. Block & L. Wilson, eds. *George Lucas's Blockbusting*, HarperCollins, New York, 2010
D. Bordwell & K. Thompson. *Film Art: An Introduction*, McGraw-Hill Publishing Company, New York, NY, 1979
—. *et al. The Classical Hollywood Cinema: Film Style and Mode of Production To 1960*, Routledge, London, 1985
—. *Narration In the Fiction Film*, Routledge, London, 1988
—. *Making Meaning*, Harvard University Press, Cambridge, MA, 1989
—. & N. Caroll, eds. *Post-Theory: Reconstructing Film Studies*, University of Wisconsin Press, Madison, WI, 1996
—. *Planet Hong Kong: Popular Cinema and the Art of Entertainment*, Harvard University Press, 2000
—. "Aesthetics in Action: *Kungfu*, Gunplay and Cinematic Expressivity", in E. Yau, 2001
—. *The Way Hollywood Tells It*, University of California Press, Berkeley, CA, 2006
J. Bower, ed. *The Cinema of Japan and Korea*, Wallflower Press, London, 2004
D. Breskin. *Inner Voices: Filmmakers In Conversation*, Da Capo, New York, 1997
A. Britton *et al. American Nightmare: Essays On the Horror Film*, Toronto, 1979
A. Brown. *Directing Hong Kong: The Political Cinema of John Woo and Wong Kar-Wai*, Routledge/ Curzon, 2001
R. Brown. *Overtones and Undertones: Reading Film Music*, University of California Press, Berkeley, CA, 1994
N. Browne *et al*, eds. *New Chinese Cinema*, Cambridge University Press, 1994
S. Bukatman. *Terminal Identity: The Virtual Subject In Postmodern Science Fiction*, Duke University Press, Durham, NC, 1993
G. Burt. *The Art of Film Music*, Northeastern University Press, 1994
B. Camp & J. Davis. *Anime Classics*, Stone Bridge Press, CA, 2007
J. Campbell. *The Power of Myth,* with B. Moyers, ed. B.S. Flowers, Doubleday, New York, NY, 1988
J. Chan. *I Am Jackie Chan*, with Jeff Yang, Pan Books, 1998
—. *Never Grow Up*, Simon & Schuster, London, 2018
J. Charles. *The Hong Kong Filmography: 1977-1997*, McFarland, 2000
R. Chu. "*Swordman II* and *The East Is Red*", *Bright Lights*, 13, 1994
C. Chun-shu & Shelley Hsueh-lun Chang. *Redefining History: Ghosts, Spirits, and Human Society in Pu Sung-ling's World, 1640–1715*, University of Michigan Press, Ann Arbor, 1998
D. Chute & Cheng-Sim Lim, eds. *Heroic Grace: The Chinese Martial Arts Film*, University of California, Los Angeles, Film and Television Archive, 2003
P. Clark. *Chinese Cinema: Culture and Politics Since 1949,* Cambridge University Press, 1987
J. Clements & H. McCarthy, eds. *The Anime Encyclopedia*, Stone Bridge Press, Berkeley, CA, 2001/ 2007/ 2015
S. Cohan & I.R. Hark, eds. *Screening the Male: Exploring Masculinities In Hollywood Cinema*, Routledge, London, 1993
J. Collins *et al*, eds. *Film Theory Goes To the Movies*, Routledge, New York, NY, 1993
D.A. Cook. *A History of Narrative Film*, W.W. Norton, New York, NY, 1981, 1990, 1996
P. Cook, ed. *The Cinema Book*, British Film Institute, London, 1985/ 1999
S. Cornelius & I. Smith. *New Chinese Cinema*, Wallflower Press, London, 2002
J. Crist, ed. *Take 22: Moviemakers On Moviemaking*, Continuum, New York, NY, 1991
F. Dannen & B. Long. *Hong Kong Babylon*, Faber, London, 1997
G. Deleuze & F. Guattari. *Cinema 1: The Movement Image*, Athlone Press, London, 1989
—. *Cinema 2: The Time Image*, Athlone Press, London, 1989
C. Desjardins. *Outlaw Masters of Japanese Film*, I.B. Tauris, London, 2005
D. Desser. *Eros Plus Massacre: An Introduction to the Japanese New Wave Cinema*, Indiana University Press, Bloomington, IN, 1988
L. Dittmar & G. Michael. *From Hanoi To Hollywood*, Rutgers University Press, NJ, 1991
J. Donald, ed. *Fantasy and the Cinema*, British Film Institute, London, 1989
K.J. Donnelly, ed. *Film Music*, Edinburgh University Press, Edinburgh, 2001
C. Ducker & Stuart Cutler. *The H.K.S. Guide To Jet Li*, Hong Kong Superstars, London, 2000

M. Eagleton, ed. *Feminist Literary Theory: A Reader*, Blackwell, Oxford, 1986
—. ed. *Feminist Literary Criticism*, Longman, London, 1991
A. Easthope, ed. *Contemporary Film Theory*, Longman, London, 1993
P. Ettedgui. *Production Design & Art Direction*, RotoVision, 1999
D. Fairservice. *Film Editing*, Manchester University Press, Manchester, 2001
K. Fang. *John Woo's A Better Tomorrow, The New Hong Kong Cinema*, Hong Kong University Press, Hong Kong, 2004
C. Finch. *Special Effects*, Abbeville, 1984
J. Finler. *The Movie Director's Story*, Octopus Books, London, 1985
—. *The Hollywood Story*, Wallflower Press, London, 2003
C. Fleming. *High Concept: Don Simpson and the Hollywood Culture of Excess*, Bloomsbury, London, 1998
J. Fletcher & A. Benjamin, eds. *Abjection, Melancholia and Love: The Work of Julia Kristeva*, Routledge, London, 1990
K. Fowkes. *Giving Up the Ghost: Spirits, Ghosts and Angels In Mainstream Comedy Films*, Wayne State University Press, Detroit, MI, 1998
A. Frank. *Horror Films*, Hamlyn, London, 1977
—. *The Horror Film Handbook*, Barnes & Noble, 1982
K. French, ed. *Screen Violence*, Bloomsbury, London, 1996
P. Fu & D. Desser, eds. *The Cinema of Hong Kong*, Cambridge University Press, Cambridge, 2002
Lisa Funnell. *Warrior Women: Gender, Race, and the Transnational Chinese Action Star*, State University of New York Press, 2014
M. Gallagher. "Masculinity In Translation: Jackie Chan", *Velvet Light Trap*, 39, 1997
—. *Tony Leung Chiu-wai*, British Film Instititute, 2018
L. Gamman & M. Marshment, eds. *The Female Gaze: Women as Viewers of Popular Culture*, Women's Press, London, 1988
J. Geiger & R. Rutsky, eds. *Film Analysis*, Norton & Company, New York, NY, 2005
K. Gelder & S. Thornton, eds. *The Subcultures Reader*, Routledge, London, 1997
—. ed. *The Horror Reader*, Routledge, London, 2000
J. Gelmis. *The Film Director as Superstar*, Penguin, London, 1974
C. Gentry. *Jackie Chan*, Taylor, Dallas, TX, 1997
Jean-Luc Godard. *Godard On Godard*, eds. J. Narobi & T. Milne, Da Capo, New York, NY, 1986
—. *Interviews*, ed. D. Sterritt, University of Mississippi Press, Jackson, 1998
L. Goldberg et al, eds. *Science Fiction Filmmaking In the 1980s*, McFarland, Jefferson, 1995
M. Goodwin & N. Wise. *On the Edge: The Life and Times of Francis Coppola*, William Morrow, New York, NY, 1989
B.K. Grant, ed. *Film Genre*, Scarecrow Press, Metuchen, NJ, 1977
—. ed. *Planks of Reason: Essays On the Horror Film*, Scarecrow Press, Metuchen, NJ, 1984
—. *Film Genre Reader II*, University of Texas Press, Austin, TX, 1995
—. ed. *The Dread of Difference: Gender and the Horror Film*, University of Texas Press, Austin, TX, 1996
E. Grosz. *Sexual Subversions*, Allen & Unwin, London, 1989
—. *Jacques Lacan: A Feminist Introduction*, Routledge, London, 1990
—. *Volatile Bodies*, Indiana University Press, Bloomington, IN, 1994
—. *Space, Time and Perversion*, Routledge, London, 1995
K. Hall. *John Woo: The Films*, McFarland & Co., Jefferson, N.C., 1999
L. Halliwell. *Halliwell's Filmgoer's Companion*, 7th edition, Granada, London, 1980
D. Hamamoto & S. Liu, eds. *Countervision: Asian-American Film Criticism*, Temple University Press, Philadelphia, PA, 2000
S. Hammond. *Hollywood East*, Contemporary Books, Lincoln, IL, 2000
P. Hardy, ed. *The Aurum Encyclopedia of Science Fiction*, Aurum, London, 1991
C. Heard. *Ten Thousand Bullets: The Cinematic Journey of John Woo*, Lone Eagle Publishing Co., L.A., 2000
S. & N. Hibbin. *The Official James Bond Movie Book*, Hamlyn, London, 1989
G. Hickenlooper. *Reel Conversations: Candid Interviews With Film's Foremost Directors and Critics*, Citadel, New York, NY, 1991
J. Hillier. *The New Hollywood*, Studio Vista, London, 1992
—. *American Independent Cinema: A Sight & Sound Reader*, British Film Institute, London, 2001
L.C. Hillstrom, ed. *International Dictionary of Films and Filmmakers: Directors*, St James Press, London, 1997
Sam Ho, ed. *The Swordsman and His Juang Hu: Tsui Hark and Hong Kong Film*, Hong Kong University Press, Hong Kong, 2002
Hong Kong Film Archive. *The Making of Martial Arts Films*, Hong Kong Provisional Urban Council, 1999
Hong Kong International Film Festival. *Hong Kong Panorama*, Leisure and Cultural Services Department
Hong Kong International Film Festival. *Hong Kong New Wave: Twenty Years After*, Provisional Urban Council of Hong Kong, 1999

Hong Kong International Film Festival. *Hong Kong Cinema '79-'89*, Leisure and Cultural Services Department, 2000
D. Hudson. *Draculas, Vampires, and Other Undead Forms*, Rowman & Littlefield, 2009
D. Hughes. *Comic Book Movies*, Virgin, London, 2003
L. Hughes. *The Rough Guide To Gangster Movies*, Penguin, 2005
L. Hunt. "Once Upon a Time In China: Kung Fu From Bruce Lee To Jet Li", *Framework*, 40, 1999
—. *Kung-fu Cult Masters: From Bruce Lee To 'Crouching Tiger'*, Wallflower Press, London, 2003
J. Hunter. *Eros In Hell: Sex, Blood and Madness In Japanese Cinema*, Creation Books, London, 1998
J. Inverne. *Musicals*, Faber, London, 2009
L. Irigiaray. *The Irigaray Reader*, ed. M. Whitford, Blackwell, Oxford, 1991
S. Jackson & J. Jones, eds. *Contemporary Feminist Theories*, Edinburgh University Press, Edinburgh, 1998
S. Jaworzyn, ed. *Shock: The Essential Guide To Exploitation Cinema*, Titan Books, London, 1996
S. Jeffords. *Hard Bodies: Hollywood Masculinity In the Reagan Era*, Rutgers University Press, New Brunswick, NJ, 1994
E. Jeffreys & L. Edwards, eds. *Celebrity In China*, Hong Kong University Press, Hong Kong, 2010
K. Kalinak. *Settling the Score: Music and the Classical Hollywood Film*, University of Wisconsin Press, Madison, WI, 1992
B.F. Kawin. *Mindscreen: Bergman, Godard and First-Person Film*, Princeton University Press, Princeton, NJ, 1978
—. *How Movies Work*, Macmillan, New York, NY, 1987
P. Keough, ed. *Flesh and Blood: The National Society of Film Critics on Sex, Violence, and Censorship*, Mercury House, San Francisco, CA, 1995
M. Kinder. *Playing With Power In Movies*, University of California Press, Berkeley, CA, 1991
P. Kolker. *The Altering Eye: Contemporary International Cinema*, Oxford University Press, New York, NY, 1983
—. *A Cinema of Loneliness: Penn, Stone, Kubrick, Scorsese, Spielberg, Altman*, Oxford University Press, New York, NY, 2000
P. Kramer. *The Big Picture: Hollywood Cinema From Star Wars To Titanic*, British Film Institute, London, 2001
—. *The New Hollywood*, Wallflower Press, London, 2005
J. Kristeva. *About Chinese Women*, tr. A. Barrows, Marion Boyars, London, 1977
—. *Desire In Language: A Semiotic Approach To Literature and Art*, ed. L.S. Roudiez, tr. T. Gora *et al*, Blackwell 1982
—. *Powers of Horror: An Essay on Abjection*, tr. L.S. Roudiez, Columbia University Press, New York, NY, 1982
—. *Revolution In Poetic Language*, tr. M. Walker, Columbia University Press, New York, NY, 1984
—. *The Kristeva Reader*, ed. T. Moi, Blackwell, Oxford, 1986
—. *Tales of Love*, tr. L.S. Roudiez, Columbia University Press, New York, NY, 1987
—. *Black Sun: Depression and Melancholy*, tr. L.S. Roudiez, Columbia University Press, New York, NY, 1989
—. *Strangers To Ourselves*, tr. L.S. Roudiez, Harvester Wheatsheaf 1991
J. Kwok Wah Lau. "Imploding Genre, Gender and History: *Peking Opera Blues*", in J. Geiger, 2005
M. Lanning. *Vietnam At the Movies*, Fawcett Columbine, New York, NY, 1994
R. Lapsley & M. Westlake, eds. *Film Theory: An Introduction*, Manchester University Press, Manchester, 1988
Shing-hou Lau, ed. *A Study of the Hong Kong Martial Arts Film*, Hong Kong International Film Festival, 1980
—. *A Study of the Hong Kong Swordplay Film, 1945-80*, Hong Kong International Film Festival, 1981
Law Kar, ed. *Fifty Years of Elecric Shadows*, Hong Kong International Film Festival, 1997
M. Lee. "*Once Upon a Time In China*", Criterion, 2021
J. Lent. *The Asian Film Industry*, Austin, TX, 1990
T. Leung Siu-hung. "Mastering Action", Hong Kong Cinemagic, March, 2006
E. Levy. *Cinema of Outsiders: The Rise of American Independent Film*, New York University Press, New York, NY, 1999
J. Lewis. *The Road To Romance and Ruin: Teen Films and Youth Culture*, Routledge, London, 1992
—. *Whom God Wishes To Destroy: Francis Coppola and the New Hollywood*, Duke University Press, Durham, NC, 1995
—. ed. *New American Cinema*, Duke University Press, Durham, NC, 1998
—. *Hollywood v. Hard Core: How the Struggle Over Censorship Created the Modern Film Industry*, New York University Press, New York, NY, 2000

J. Leyda. ed. *Film Makers Speak: Voices of Film Experience*, Da Capo, New York, NY, 1977
V. LoBrutto. *Sound-On-Film*, Praeger, New York, NY, 1994
B. Logan. *Hong Kong Action Cinema*, Titan, London, 1995
S. Lu, ed. *Transnational Chinese Cinemas*, University of Hawaii Press, Honolulu, 1997
H. Ludi. *Movie Worlds: Production Design In Film*, Mengers, Stuttgart, 2000
B. McCabe. *The Rough Guide To Comedy Movies*, Rough Guides, London, 2005
R. Maltby. *Harmless Entertainment: Hollywood and the Ideology of Consensus*, Scarecrow Press, Metuchen, NJ, 1983
—. & I. Craven. *Hollywood Cinema: An Introduction*, Blackwell, Oxford, 1995
—. *Hollywood Cinema*, 2nd ed., Blackwell, Oxford, 2003
E. Marks & I. de Courtivron, eds. *New French Feminisms: an anthology*, Harvester Wheatsheaf, Hemel Hempstead, 1981
G. Mast et al, eds. *Film Theory and Criticism: Introductory Readings*, Oxford University Press, New York, NY, 1992a
—. & B Kawin. *A Short History of the Movies*, Macmillan, New York, NY, 1992b
C. Marx. *Jet Li, Martial Arts Masters*, Rosen Publishing Group, 2002
T.D. Matthews. *Censored*, Chatto & Windus, London, 1994
F. McConnell. *Storytelling and Mythmaking*, Oxford University Press, New York, NY, 1979
S.Y. McDougal. *Made Into Movies: From Literature To Film*, Holt, Rinehart and Winston, New York, NY, 1985
M. Medved. *Hollywood vs. America*, HarperCollins, London, 1992
R. Meyers. *Martial Arts Movies*, Citadel Press, NJ, 1985
—. *Great Martial Arts Movies*, Citadel Press, NJ, 2001
D. Millar. *Cinema Secrets: Special Effects*, Apple Press, 1990
T. Miller et al, eds. *Global Hollywood*, British Film Institute, London, 2001
T. Moi. *Sexual/Textual Politics: Feminist Literary Theory*, Methuen, London, 1983
J. Monaco. *The New Wave: Truffaut, Godard, Chabrol, Rohmer, Rivette*, Oxford University Press, New York, NY, 1977
—. *American Film Now*, New American Library, London, 1979
—. *How To Read a Film*, Oxford University Press, Oxford, 1981
R. Murray. *Images In the Dark: An Encyclopedia of Gay and Lesbian Film and Video*, Titan Books, London, 1998
S. Neale. *Cinema and Technology*, Macmillan, London, 1985
—. & M. Smith, eds. *Contemporary Hollywood Cinema*, Routledge, London, 1998
—. *Genre and Contemporary Hollywood*, Routledge, London, 2002
J. Nelmes, ed. *An Introduction To Film Studies*, Routledge, London, 1996
D. Neumann, ed. *Film Architecture: From Metropolis To Blade Runner*, Prestel-Verlag, New York, NY, 1996
K. Newman. *Nightmare Movies*, Harmony, New York, NY, 1988
—. *Millennium Movies*, Titan Books, London, 1999
G. Nowell-Smith, ed. *The Oxford History of World Cinema*, Oxford University Press, Oxford, 1996
D. O'Brien. *Spooky Encounters: A Gwailo's Guide To Hong Kong Horror,* Headpress, 2004
T. Ohanian & M. Phillips. *Digital Filmmaking*, 2nd ed., Focal Press, Boston, MA, 2000
J. Orr. *Contemporary Cinema*, Edinburgh University Press, Edinburgh, 1998
B. Palmer et al. *The Encyclopedia of Martial Arts Movies*, Scarecrow Press, NJ, 1995
A. Paludan. *Chronicle of the Chinese Emperors*, Thames & Hudson, 1998
L. Pang. *Masculinities and Hong Kong Cinema*, Kent State University Press, 2005
D. Parkinson. *The Rough Guide To Film Musicals*, Penguin, London, 2007
J. Parish. *Jet Li: A Biography*, Thunder's Mouth Press, New York, 2002
F. Patten. *Watching Anime, Reading Manga*, Stone Bridge Press, CA, 2004
D. Peary & G. Peary, eds. *The American Animated Cartoon*, Dutton, New York, NY, 1980
—. *Cult Movies 2*, Vermilion, London, 1984
—. *Cult Movies 3*, Sigwick & Jackson, London, 1989
C. Penley, ed. *Feminism and Film Theory*, Routledge, London, 1988
D. Petrie. *Screening Europe: Image and Identity In Contemporary European Cinema*, British Film Institute, London, 1992
P. Phillips. *Understanding Film Texts*, British Film Institute, London, 2000
M. Pierson. *Special Effects*, Columbia University Press, New York, NY, 2002
L. Pietropaolo & A. Testaferri, eds. *Feminisms In the Cinema*, Indiana University Press, Bloomington, IN, 1995
D. Pollock. *Skywalking: The Life and Films of George Lucas*, Crown, New York, NY, 1983, 1990, 2000
M. Polly. *Bruce Lee*, Simon & Schuster, New York, 2018
S. Prince, ed. *Screening Violence*, Athlone Press, London, 2000
D. Prindle. *Risky Business: The Political Economy of Hollywood*, Westview, Boulder, CO, 1993
N. Proferes. *Film Directing Fundamentals*, Focal Press, Boston, MA, 2001
M. Pye & Lynda Myles. *The Movie Brats: How the Film Generation Took Over Hollywood*, Faber, London, 1979
T. Reeves. *The Worldwide Guide To Movie Locations*, Titan Books, London, 2003

P. Rice & P. Waugh, eds. *Modern Literary Theory: A Reader*, Arnold, London, 1992
D. Richie. *The Films of Akira Kurosawa*, University of California Press, Berkeley, CA, 1965
R. Rickitt. *Special Effects*, Aurum, London, 2006
B. Robb. *Screams and Nightmares*, Titan Books, London, 1998
J. Robertson. *The British Board of Film Censors*, Croom Helm, 1985
D. Robinson. *World Cinema*, Methuen, London, 1981
W.H. Rockett. *Devouring Whirlwind: Terror and Transcendence In the Cinema of Cruelty*, Greenwood Press, New York, NY, 1988
S. Rohdie. *The Passion of Pier Paolo Pasolini*, British Film Institute, London, 1995
J. Romney & A. Wootton, eds. *Celluloid Jukebox: Popular Music and the Movies Since the 50s*, British Film Institute, London, 1995
P. Rosen, ed. *Narrative, Apparatus, Ideology: A Film Theory Reader*, Columbia University Press, New York, NY, 1986
J. Rosenbaum. *Placing Movies*, University of California Press, Berkeley, CA, 1995
R. Rosenblum & R. Karen. *When the Shooting Stops... The Cutting Begins: A Film Editor's Story*, Da Capo Press, New York, NY, 1979
J. Ross. *The Incredibly Strange Film Book: An Alternative History of Cinema*, Simon and Schuster, 1993
The Rough Guide To China, Penguin, 2017
R. Roud. *Jean-Luc Godard*, Thames & Hudson, London, 1970
J. Rovin & K. Tracy. *The Essential Jackie Chan Sourcebook*, Pocket Books, New York, 1997
M. Rubin. *Thrillers*, Cambridge University Press, Cambridge, 1999
K. Russell. *A British Picture: An Autobiography*, Heinemann, London, 1989
V. Russo. *The Celluloid Closet: Homosexuality In the Movies*, Harper & Row, New York, NY, 1981
K. Sandler. *Reading the Rabbit: Explorations In Warner Bros. Animation*, Rutgers University Press, Brunswick, NJ, 1998
A. Sarris. *The American Cinema*, Dutton, New York, NY, 1968
T. Sato. *Currents In Japanese Cinema*, Kodansha, New York, 1982
D. Schaefer & L. Salvato, eds. *Masters of Light*, University of California Press, Berkeley, CA, 1984
T. Schatz. *Hollywood Genres,* Random House, New York, NY, 1981
—. *Old Hollywood/ New Hollywood*, UMI Research Press, Ann Arbor, MI, 1983
—. *The Genius of the System: Hollywood Filmmaking In the Studio Era*, Pantheon, New York, NY 1988
F. Schodt. *Inside the Robot Kingdom: Japan, Mechatronics and the Coming Robotopia*, Kodansha, Tokyo, 1988
—. *Manga! Manga! The World of Japanese Magazines*, Kodansha International, London, 1997
—. *Dreamland Japan: Writings On Modern Manga*, Stone Bridge Press, Berkeley, CA, 2002
P. Schrader. *Transcendental Style In Film: Ozu, Bresson, Dreyer*, Da Capo Press, 1972
A. Schroeder. *Tsui Hark's Zu: Warriors From the Magic Mountain*, Hong Kong University Press, Hong Kong, 2004
R. Schubart. *Super Bitches and Action Babes: The Female Hero In Popular Cinema, 1970-2006,* McFarland, 2007
M. Schumacher. *Francis Ford Coppola*, Bloomsbury, London, 2000
M. Scorsese. *Scorsese On Scorsese*, ed. D. Thompson & I. Christie, Faber, London, 1989, 1995
Screen Reader I: Cinema/ Ideology/ Politics, Society for Education in Film & TV, 1977
Screen Reader II: Cinema and Semiotics, British Film Institute, London, 1982
C. Sharrett, ed. *Crisis Cinema*, Maisonneuve Press, Washington, DC, 1993
—. *Mythologies of Violence In Postmodern Media*, Wayne State University Press, 1999
M. Shiel & T. Fitzmaurice, eds. *Screenng the City*, Verso, London, 2003
D. Shipman. *The Story of Cinema*, Hodder & Stoughton, London, 1984
T. Shone. *Blockbuster: How the Jaws and Jedi Generation Turned Hollywood Into a Boom-Town*, Scribner, London, 2005
E. Showalter, ed. *The New Feminist Criticism*, Virago, London, 1986
E. Siciliano. *Pasolini: A Biography*, Bloomsbury, London, 1987
L. Sider et al, eds. *Soundscapes: The School of Sound Lectures 1998-2001*, Wallflower Press, London, 2003
M. Singer. *A History of the American Avant-Garde Cinema*, American Federation of the Arts, New York, NY, 1976
P. Adams Sitney, ed. *The Film Culture Reader*, Praeger, New York, NY, 1970
—. ed. *The Avant-Garde Film: A Reader of Theory and Criticism*, New York University Press, New York, NY, 1978
—. *Visionary Film: The American Avant-Garde, 1943-1978*, 2nd ed., Oxford University Press, New York, NY, 1979
G. Smith. *Epic Films*, McFarland, Jefferson, NC, 1991
J. Smith. *Looking Away: Hollywood and Vietnam*, Scribner's, New York, NY, 1975
T.G. Smith. *Industrial Light and Magic: The Art of Special Effects*, Columbus Books, 1986

E. Smoodin. *Animating Culture: Hollywood Cartoons From the Sound Era*, Roundhouse, 1993
—. ed. *Disney Discourse: Producing the Magic Kingdom*, Routledge, London, 1994
V. Sobchack. *The Limits of Infinity: The American Science Fiction Film*, A.S. Barnes, New York, NY, 1980
—. *Screening Space: The American Science Fiction Film*, Ungar, New York, NY, 1987/ 1993
J. Squire, ed. *The Movie Business Book*, Fireside, New York, NY, 1992
J. Staiger. *Interpreting Films*, Princeton University Press, Princeton, NJ, 1992
—. *Perverse Spectators: The Practices of Film Reception*, New York University Press, New York, NY, 2000
N. Stair. *Michelle Yeoh*, Rosen Publishing Group, 2001
B. Steene. *Ingmar Bergman*, Twayne, Boston, MA, 1968
L. Stern. *The Scorsese Connection*, British Film Institute, London, 1995
D. Sterritt. *The Films of Jean-Luc Godard*, Cambridge University Press, Cambridge, 1999
G. Stewart. *Between Film and Screen: Modernism's Photo Synthesis*, University of Chicago Press, Chicago, IL, 1999
M. Stokes & R. Maltby, eds. *Identifying Hollywood Audiences*, British Film Institute, London, 1999
J. Storey, ed. *Cultural Theory and Popular Culture*, Harvester Wheatsheaf, Hemel Hempstead, 1994
J.M. Straczynski. *The Complete Book of Scriptwriting*, Titan Books, London, 1997
J. Stringer. "Problems With the Treatment of Hong Kong Cinema As Camp", *Asian Cinema*, 8, 2, 1996
—. ed. *Movie Blockbusters*, Routledge, London, 2003
C. Sylvester, ed. *The Penguin Book of Hollywood*, Penguin, London, 1999
K. Tam & W. Dissanayake. *New Chinese Cinema*, Oxford University Press, Hong Kong, 1998
A. Tarkovsky. *Sculpting In Time: Reflections On the Cinema*, tr. K. Hunter-Blair, Faber, London, 1989
C. Tashiro. *Pretty Pictures: Production Design and the History Film*, University of Texas Press, 1998
Y. Tasker. *Spectacular Bodies: Gender, Genre and the Action Cinema*, Routledge, London, 1993
R. Taylor *et al*, eds. *The B.F.I. Companion To Eastern European and Russian Cinema*, British Film Institute, London, 2000
S. Teo. *Hong Kong Cinema*, British Film Institute, London, 1997
—. "Tsui Hark", in C. Yau, 1998
B. Thomas. *Video Hound's Dragon: Asian Action and Cult Flicks*, Visible Ink Press, 2003
K. Thompson & D. Bordwell. *Film History: An Introduction*, McGraw-Hill, New York, NY, 1994/ 2010
—. *Storytelling In the New Hollywood*, Harvard University Press, Cambridge, MA, 1999
D. Thomson. *A Biographical Dictionary of Film*, Deutsch, London, 1995
S. Thrower, ed. *Eyeball: Compendium: Sex and Horror, Art and Exploitation*, F.A.B. Press, Godalming, Surrey, 2003
C. Tohill & P. Tombs. *Immoral Tales: Sex and Horror Cinema In Europe 1956-1984*, Titan Books, London, 1995
J. Trevelyan. *What the Censor Saw*, Michael Joseph, London, 1973
A.D. Vacche. *Cinema and Painting*, Athlone Press, London, 1996
K. Van Gunden. *Fantasy Films*, McFarland, Jefferson, NC 1989
—. *Postmodern Auteurs: Coppola, Lucas, De Palma, Spielberg and Scorsese*, McFarland, Jefferson, NC 1991
M.C. Vaz. *From Star Wars To Indiana Jones*, Chronicle, San Francisco, CA, 1994
—. & P.R. Duignan. *Industrial Light & Magic*, Virgin, London, 1996
G. Vincendeau, ed. *Encyclopedia of European Cinema*, British Film Institute, London, 1995
—. ed. *Film/ Literature/ Heritage: A Sight & Sound Reader*, British Film Institute, London, 2001
P. Virillio. *War and Cinema*, Verso, London, 1992
D. Vivier & T. Podvin. "Through the Lens of Arthur Wong", Hong Kong Cinemagic, Jan 2005
H. Vogel. *Entertainment Industry Economics*, Cambridge University Press, Cambridge, 1995
C. Vogler. *The Writer's Journey: Mythic Structure For Storytellers and Screenwriters*, Pan, London, 1998
J. Wasko. *Movies and Money*, Ablex, NJ, 1982
—. *Hollywood In the Information Age*, Polity Press, Cambridge, 1994
E. Weiss. & J. Belton, eds. *Film Sound: Theory and Practice*, Columbia University Press, New York, NY, 1989
T. Weisser. *Asian Cult Cinema*, Boulveard Books, New York, NY, 1997
O. Welles. *This is Orson Welles*, HarperCollins, London, 1992
P. Wells. *Understanding Animation*, Routledge, London, 1998
D. West. *Chasing Dragons: An Introduction To the Martial Arts Film*, I.B. Tauris, London, 2006
L. Williams, ed. *Viewing Positions: Ways of Seeing Film*, Rutgers University Press, New

Brunswick, NJ, 1995
T. Williams. "To Live and Die In Hong Kong", *Cineaction*, 36, 1995
—. "Kwan Tak-hing and the New Generation", *Asian Cinema*, 10, 1, 1998
—. "Space, Place and Spectacle: the Crisis Cinema of John Woo", in P. Fu, 2002
R. Witterstaetter. *Dying For Action: The Life and Times of Jackie Chan*, Warner Books, New York, 1997
M. Wolf. *The Entertainment Economy*, Penguin, London, 1999
P. Wollen: *Signs and Meaning In the Cinema*, Secker & Warburg, London, 1972
J. Woo. Interview, in J. Arroyo, 2000
—. *Interviews; Conversations With Filmmakers Series*, ed. R. Elder, University Press of Mississippi, 2005
M. Wood. *Cine East: Hong Kong Cinema Through the Looking Glass*, F.A.B. Press, 1998
R. Wood. *Hollywood From Vietnam To Reagan... and Beyond*, Columbia University Press, New York, NY, 2003
T. Woods. *Beginning Postmodernism,* Manchester University Press, Manchester, 1999
J. Wyatt. *High Concept: Movies and Marketing In Hollywood*, University of Texas Press, Austin, TX, 1994
J. Yang et al. *Eastern Standard Time: A Guide To Asian Influence On American Culture*, Houghton Mifflin, Boston, MA, 1997
—. *Once Upon a Time In China*, Atria Books, New York, NY, 2003
E.C.M. Yau, ed. *At Full Speed: Hong Kong Cinema In a Borderless World,* University of Minnesota Press, Minneapolis, MN, 1998
Z. Yimou. *Zhang Yimou: Interviews, Conversations With Filmmakers Series*, ed. F. Gateward, University Press of Mississippi, 2001
Judith T. Zeitlin. *Historian of the Strange: Pu Songling and the Chinese Classical Tale*, Stanford University Press, Stanford, CA, 1993
Y. Zhang & X. Zhiwei, eds. *Encyclopedia of Chinese Film*, Routledge, 1998
J. Zipes. *The Enchanted Screen: The Unknown History of Fairy-tale Films*, Routledge, New York, NY, 2011
S. Zizek. *Enjoy Your Symptom Jacques Lacan In Hollywood and Out*, Routledge, New York, NY, 1992
—. *The Fright of Real Tears: The Uses and Misuses of Lacan In Film Theory*, British Film Institute, London, 1999

JEREMY ROBINSON has published poetry, fiction, and studies of J.R.R. Tolkien, Samuel Beckett, Thomas Hardy, André Gide and D.H. Lawrence. Robinson has edited poetry books by Novalis, Ursula Le Guin, Friedrich Hölderlin, Francesco Petrarch, Dante Alighieri, Arseny Tarkovsky, and Rainer Maria Rilke.

Books on film and animation include: *The Akira Book* • *The Art of Katsuhiro Otomo* • *The Art of Masamune Shirow* • *The Ghost In the Shell Book* • *Fullmetal Alchemist* • *Cowboy Bebop: The Anime and Movie* • *The Cinema of Hayao Miyazaki* • *Hayao Miyazaki: Pocket Guide* • *Princess Mononoke: Pocket Movie Guide* • *Spirited Away: Pocket Movie Guide* • *Blade Runner and the Cinema of Philip K. Dick* • *Blade Runner: Pocket Movie Guide* • *The Cinema of Donald Cammell* • *Performance: Donald Cammell: Nic Roeg: Pocket Movie Guide* • *Pasolini: Il Cinema di Poesia/ The Cinema of Poetry* • *Salo: Pocket Movie Guide* • *The Trilogy of Life Movies: Pocket Movie Guide* • *The Gospel According To Matthew: Pocket Movie Guide* • *The Ecstatic Cinema of Tony Ching Siu-tung* • *Tsui Hark: The Dragon Master of Chinese Cinema* • *The Swordsman: Pocket Movie Guide* • *A Chinese Ghost Story: Pocket Movie Guide* • *Ken Russell: England's Great Visionary Film Director and Music Lover* • *Tommy: Ken Russell: The Who: Pocket Movie Guide* • *Women In Love: Ken Russell: D.H. Lawrence: Pocket Movie Guide* • *The Devils: Ken Russell: Pocket Movie Guide* • *Walerian Borowczyk: Cinema of Erotic Dreams* • *The Beast: Pocket Movie Guide* • *The Lord of the Rings Movies* • *The Fellowship of the Ring: Pocket Movie Guide* • *The Two Towers: Pocket Movie Guide* • *The Return of the King: Pocket Movie Guide* • *Jean-Luc Godard: The Passion of Cinema* • *The Sacred Cinema of Andrei Tarkovsky* • *Andrei Tarkovsky: Pocket Guide*.

'It's amazing for me to see my work treated with such passion and respect. There is nothing resembling it in the U.S. in relation to my work.'
(Andrea Dworkin)

'This model monograph – it is an exemplary job, and I'm very proud that he has accorded me a couple of mentions… The subject matter of his book is beautifully organised and dead on beam.'
(Lawrence Durrell, on *The Light Eternal: A Study of J.M.W. Turner*)

'Jeremy Robinson's poetry is certainly jammed with ideas, and I find it very interesting for that reason. It's certainly a strong imprint of his personality.'
(Colin Wilson)

'*Sex-Magic-Poetry-Cornwall* is a very rich essay... It is a very good piece… vastly stimulating and insightful.'
(Peter Redgrove)

CRESCENT MOON PUBLISHING

web: www.crmoon.com e-mail: cresmopub@yahoo.co.uk

ARTS, PAINTING, SCULPTURE

The Art of Andy Goldsworthy
Andy Goldsworthy: Touching Nature
Andy Goldsworthy in Close-Up
Andy Goldsworthy: Pocket Guide
Andy Goldsworthy In America
Land Art: A Complete Guide
The Art of Richard Long
Richard Long: Pocket Guide
Land Art In the UK
Land Art in Close-Up
Land Art In the U.S.A.
Land Art: Pocket Guide
Installation Art in Close-Up
Minimal Art and Artists In the 1960s and After
Colourfield Painting
Land Art DVD, TV documentary
Andy Goldsworthy DVD, TV documentary
The Erotic Object: Sexuality in Sculpture From Prehistory to the Present Day
Sex in Art: Pornography and Pleasure in Painting and Sculpture
Postwar Art
Sacred Gardens: The Garden in Myth, Religion and Art
Glorification: Religious Abstraction in Renaissance and 20th Century Art
Early Netherlandish Painting
Leonardo da Vinci
Piero della Francesca
Giovanni Bellini
Fra Angelico: Art and Religion in the Renaissance
Mark Rothko: The Art of Transcendence
Frank Stella: American Abstract Artist
Jasper Johns
Brice Marden
Alison Wilding: The Embrace of Sculpture
Vincent van Gogh: Visionary Landscapes
Eric Gill: Nuptials of God
Constantin Brancusi: Sculpting the Essence of Things
Max Beckmann
Caravaggio
Gustave Moreau
Egon Schiele: Sex and Death In Purple Stockings
Delizioso Fotografico Fervore: Works In Process 1
Sacro Cuore: Works In Process 2
The Light Eternal: J.M.W. Turner
The Madonna Glorified: Karen Arthurs

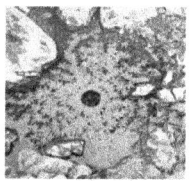

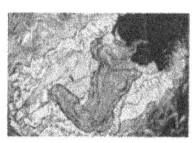

LITERATURE

J.R.R. Tolkien: The Books, The Films, The Whole Cultural Phenomenon
J.R.R. Tolkien: Pocket Guide
Tolkien's Heroic Quest
The *Earthsea* Books of Ursula Le Guin
Beauties, Beasts and Enchantment: Classic French Fairy Tales
German Popular Stories by the Brothers Grimm
Philip Pullman and *His Dark Materials*
Sexing Hardy: Thomas Hardy and Feminism
Thomas Hardy's *Tess of the d'Urbervilles*
Thomas Hardy's *Jude the Obscure*
Thomas Hardy: The Tragic Novels
Love and Tragedy: Thomas Hardy
The Poetry of Landscape in Hardy
Wessex Revisited: Thomas Hardy and John Cowper Powys
Wolfgang Iser: Essays and Interviews
Petrarch, Dante and the Troubadours
Maurice Sendak and the Art of Children's Book Illustration
Andrea Dworkin
Cixous, Irigaray, Kristeva: The *Jouissance* of French Feminism
Julia Kristeva: Art, Love, Melancholy, Philosophy, Semiotics and Psychoanalysis
Hélène Cixous I Love You: The *Jouissance* of Writing
Luce Irigaray: Lips, Kissing, and the Politics of Sexual Difference
Peter Redgrove: Here Comes the Flood
Peter Redgrove: Sex-Magic-Poetry-Cornwall
Lawrence Durrell: Between Love and Death, East and West
Love, Culture & Poetry: Lawrence Durrell
Cavafy: Anatomy of a Soul
German Romantic Poetry: Goethe, Novalis, Heine, Hölderlin
Feminism and Shakespeare
Shakespeare: Love, Poetry & Magic
The Passion of D.H. Lawrence
D.H. Lawrence: Symbolic Landscapes
D.H. Lawrence: Infinite Sensual Violence
Rimbaud: Arthur Rimbaud and the Magic of Poetry
The Ecstasies of John Cowper Powys
Sensualism and Mythology: The Wessex Novels of John Cowper Powys
Amorous Life: John Cowper Powys and the Manifestation of Affectivity (H.W. Fawkner)
Postmodern Powys: New Essays on John Cowper Powys (Joe Boulter)
Rethinking Powys: Critical Essays on John Cowper Powys
Paul Bowles & Bernardo Bertolucci
Rainer Maria Rilke
Joseph Conrad: *Heart of Darkness*
In the Dim Void: Samuel Beckett
Samuel Beckett Goes into the Silence
André Gide: Fiction and Fervour
Jackie Collins and the Blockbuster Novel
Blinded By Her Light: The Love-Poetry of Robert Graves
The Passion of Colours: Travels In Mediterranean Lands
Poetic Forms

POETRY

Ursula Le Guin: Walking In Cornwall
Peter Redgrove: Here Comes The Flood
Peter Redgrove: Sex-Magic-Poetry-Cornwall
Dante: Selections From the Vita Nuova
Petrarch, Dante and the Troubadours
William Shakespeare: Sonnets
William Shakespeare: Complete Poems
Blinded By Her Light: The Love-Poetry of Robert Graves
Emily Dickinson: Selected Poems
Emily Brontë: Poems
Thomas Hardy: Selected Poems
Percy Bysshe Shelley: Poems
John Keats: Selected Poems
Joh n Keats: Poems of 1820
D.H. Lawrence: Selected Poems
Edmund Spenser: Poems
Edmund Spenser: Amoretti
John Donne: Poems
Henry Vaughan: Poems
Sir Thomas Wyatt: Poems
Robert Herrick: Selected Poems
Rilke: Space, Essence and Angels in the Poetry of Rainer Maria Rilke
Rainer Maria Rilke: Selected Poems
Friedrich Hölderlin: Selected Poems
Arseny Tarkovsky: Selected Poems
Arthur Rimbaud: Selected Poems
Arthur Rimbaud: A Season in Hell
Arthur Rimbaud and the Magic of Poetry
Novalis: Hymns To the Night
German Romantic Poetry
Paul Verlaine: Selected Poems
Elizaethan Sonnet Cycles
D.J. Enright: By-Blows
Jeremy Reed: Brigitte's Blue Heart
Jeremy Reed: Claudia Schiffer's Red Shoes
Gorgeous Little Orpheus
Radiance: New Poems
Crescent Moon Book of Nature Poetry
Crescent Moon Book of Love Poetry
Crescent Moon Book of Mystical Poetry
Crescent Moon Book of Elizabethan Love Poetry
Crescent Moon Book of Metaphysical Poetry
Crescent Moon Book of Romantic Poetry
Pagan America: New American Poetry

MEDIA, CINEMA, FEMINISM and CULTURAL STUDIES

J.R.R. Tolkien: The Books, The Films, The Whole Cultural Phenomenon
J.R.R. Tolkien: Pocket Guide
The *Lord of the Rings* Movies: Pocket Guide
The Cinema of Hayao Miyazaki
Hayao Miyazaki: *Princess Mononoke*: Pocket Movie Guide
Hayao Miyazaki: *Spirited Away*: Pocket Movie Guide
Tim Burton : Hallowe'en For Hollywood
Ken Russell
Ken Russell: *Tommy*: Pocket Movie Guide
The Ghost Dance: The Origins of Religion
The Peyote Cult
Cixous, Irigaray, Kristeva: The *Jouissance* of French Feminism
Julia Kristeva: Art, Love, Melancholy, Philosophy, Semiotics and Psychoanalysis
Luce Irigaray: Lips, Kissing, and the Politics of Sexual Difference
Hélene Cixous I Love You: The *Jouissance* of Writing
Andrea Dworkin
'Cosmo Woman': The World of Women's Magazines
Women in Pop Music
HomeGround: The Kate Bush Anthology
Discovering the Goddess (Geoffrey Ashe)
The Poetry of Cinema
The Sacred Cinema of Andrei Tarkovsky
Andrei Tarkovsky: Pocket Guide
Andrei Tarkovsky: *Mirror*: Pocket Movie Guide
Andrei Tarkovsky: *The Sacrifice*: Pocket Movie Guide
Walerian Borowczyk: Cinema of Erotic Dreams
Jean-Luc Godard: The Passion of Cinema
Jean-Luc Godard: *Hail Mary*: Pocket Movie Guide
Jean-Luc Godard: *Contempt*: Pocket Movie Guide
Jean-Luc Godard: *Pierrot le Fou*: Pocket Movie Guide
John Hughes and Eighties Cinema
Ferris Bueller's Day Off: Pocket Movie Guide
Jean-Luc Godard: Pocket Guide
The Cinema of Richard Linklater
Liv Tyler: Star In Ascendance
Blade Runner and the Films of Philip K. Dick
Paul Bowles and Bernardo Bertolucci
Media Hell: Radio, TV and the Press
An Open Letter to the BBC
Detonation Britain: Nuclear War in the UK
Feminism and Shakespeare
Wild Zones: Pornography, Art and Feminism
Sex in Art: Pornography and Pleasure in Painting and Sculpture
Sexing Hardy: Thomas Hardy and Feminism

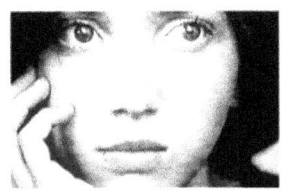

The Light Eternal is a model monograph, an exemplary job. The subject matter of the book is beautifully organised and dead on beam. (Lawrence Durrell)

It is amazing for me to see my work treated with such passion and respect. (Andrea Dworkin)

CRESCENT MOON PUBLISHING
P.O. Box 1312, Maidstone, Kent, ME14 5XU, Great Britain. www.crmoon.com

cresmopub@yahoo.co.uk   www.crescentmoon.org.uk

www.ingramcontent.com/pod-product-compliance
Lightning Source LLC
Chambersburg PA
CBHW062213080426
42734CB00010B/1873